HAVE A NICE APOCALYPSE

SOUTHLA

I II III

GRAPHITTI DESIGNS • VIEW ASKEW

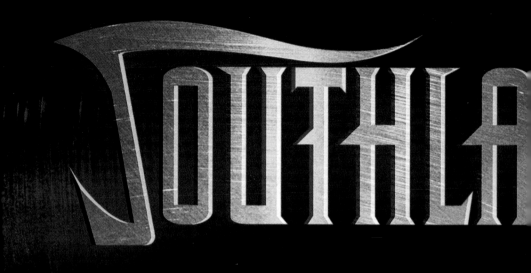

ND TALES™

IV V VI

BY

RICHARD KELLY

ILLUSTRATIONS BY

BRETT WELDELE

RICHARD STARKINGS
AND JOHN ROSHELL
OF COMICRAFT
LETTERING & DESIGN

ALEXANDER HAMMOND
ZACHARY FANNIN
PRISCILLA ELLIOTT
CONCEPTUAL ARTISTS

DALE ROBINETTE
PRODUCTION STILLS

BOB CHAPMAN
EDITOR

FOR GRAPHITTI DESIGNS
BOB CHAPMAN - PUBLISHER
GAYLE BLUME - STAFF
GINA CHAPMAN
DAVID SOTO
TAYLOR JARRETT

FOR VIEW ASKEW
KEVIN SMITH - PUBLISHER
GAIL STANLEY - STAFF
MING CHEN
CAROL HAMMOND
MIKE CECCONI

FOR DARKO ENTERTAINMENT
RICHARD KELLY
SEAN MCKITTRICK
JEFF CULOTTA
JAY KELLY
LANE KELLY

 DARKO

PUBLISHED BY GRAPHITTI DESIGNS, INC. AND VIEW ASKEW PRODUCTIONS, INC..
8045 EAST CRYSTAL DRIVE, ANAHEIM, CA 92807-2523. SOUTHLAND TALES TM & © 2006 DARKO
ENTERTAINMENT. ALL RIGHTS RESERVED. GRAPHITTI DESIGNS LOGO AND ICON TM & © 2006
GRAPHITTI DESIGNS, INC. VIEW ASKEW TM & © 2006 VIEW ASKEW PRODUCTIONS, INC.
ALL RIGHTS RESERVED.

PRINTED IN CANADA · ISBN 0-936211-77-6

SOUTHLANDTALES.COM

III

THE MECHANICALS

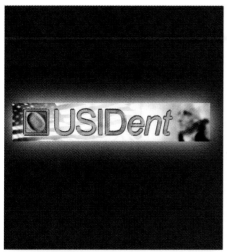

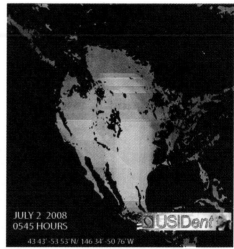

USIDent
JULY 2 2008
0545 HOURS
43 43'-53 53'N/ 146 34'-50 76'W
USIDent
34 30'-18 21'N/ 116 16'-12 05'W
USIDent
The Senator and his wife slept peacefully as their jet began its descent into the Southland.

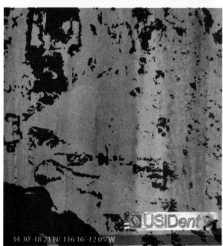

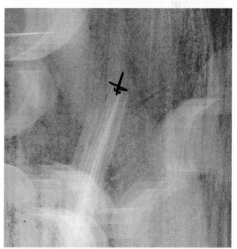

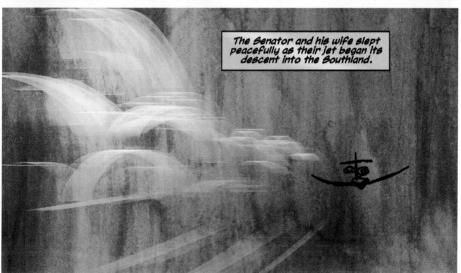

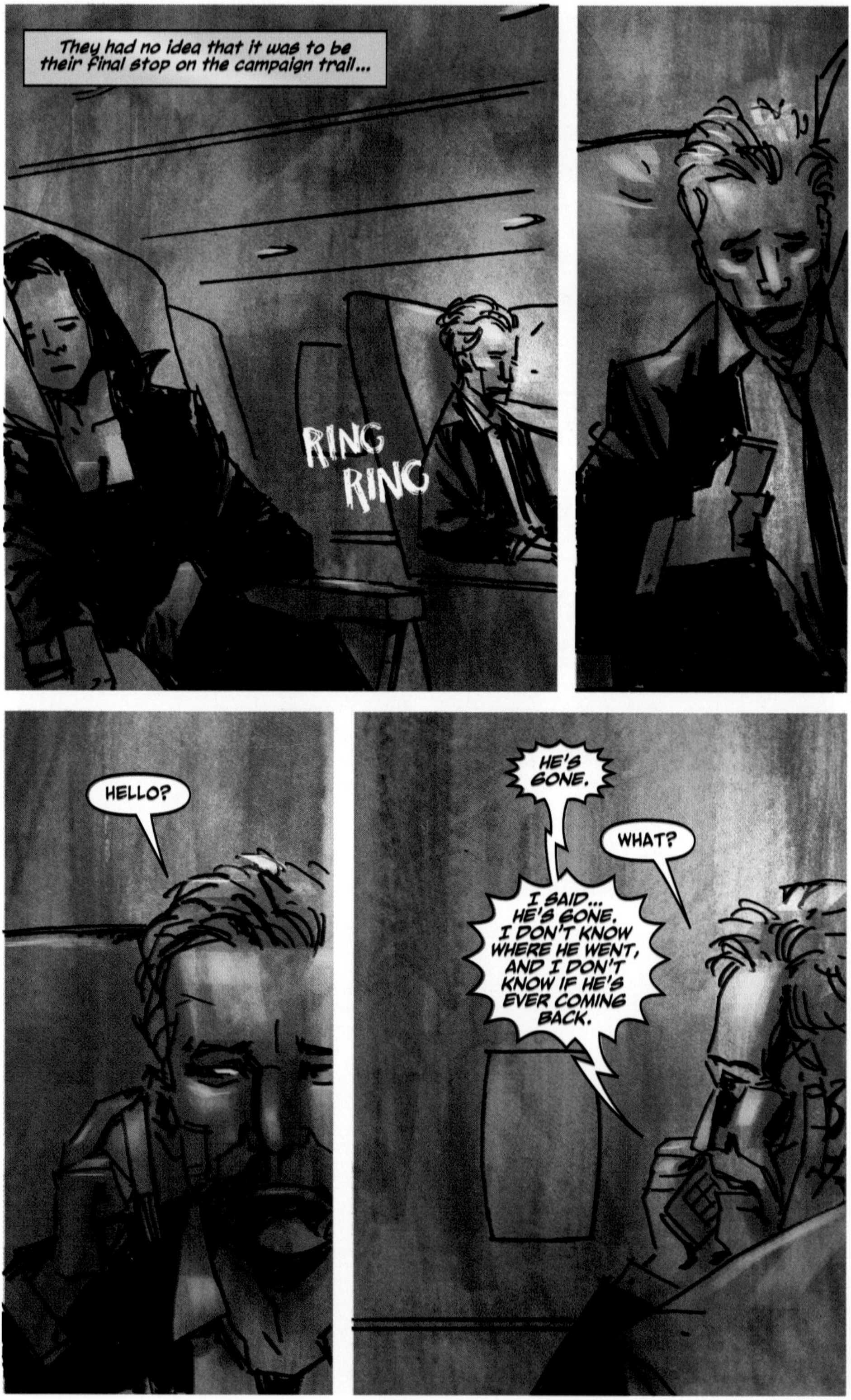
They had no idea that it was to be their final stop on the campaign trail...
RING RING
HELLO?
WHAT?
HE'S GONE.
I SAID... HE'S GONE. I DON'T KNOW WHERE HE WENT, AND I DON'T KNOW IF HE'S EVER COMING BACK.

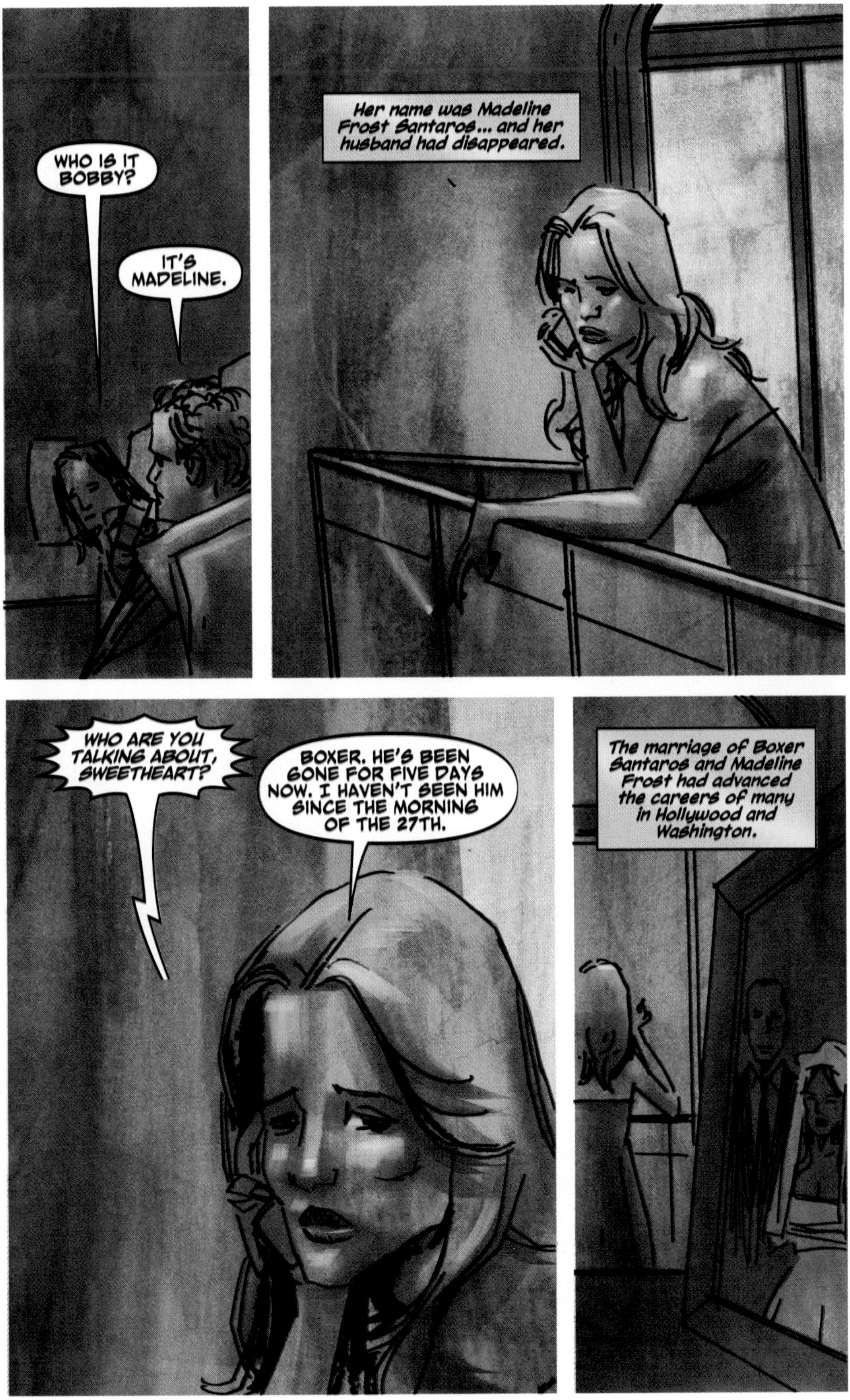
WHO IS IT BOBBY?
IT'S MADELINE.
Her name was Madeline Frost Santaros... and her husband had disappeared.
WHO ARE YOU TALKING ABOUT, SWEETHEART?
BOXER. HE'S BEEN GONE FOR FIVE DAYS NOW. I HAVEN'T SEEN HIM SINCE THE MORNING OF THE 27TH.
The marriage of Boxer Santaros and Madeline Frost had advanced the careers of many in Hollywood and Washington.

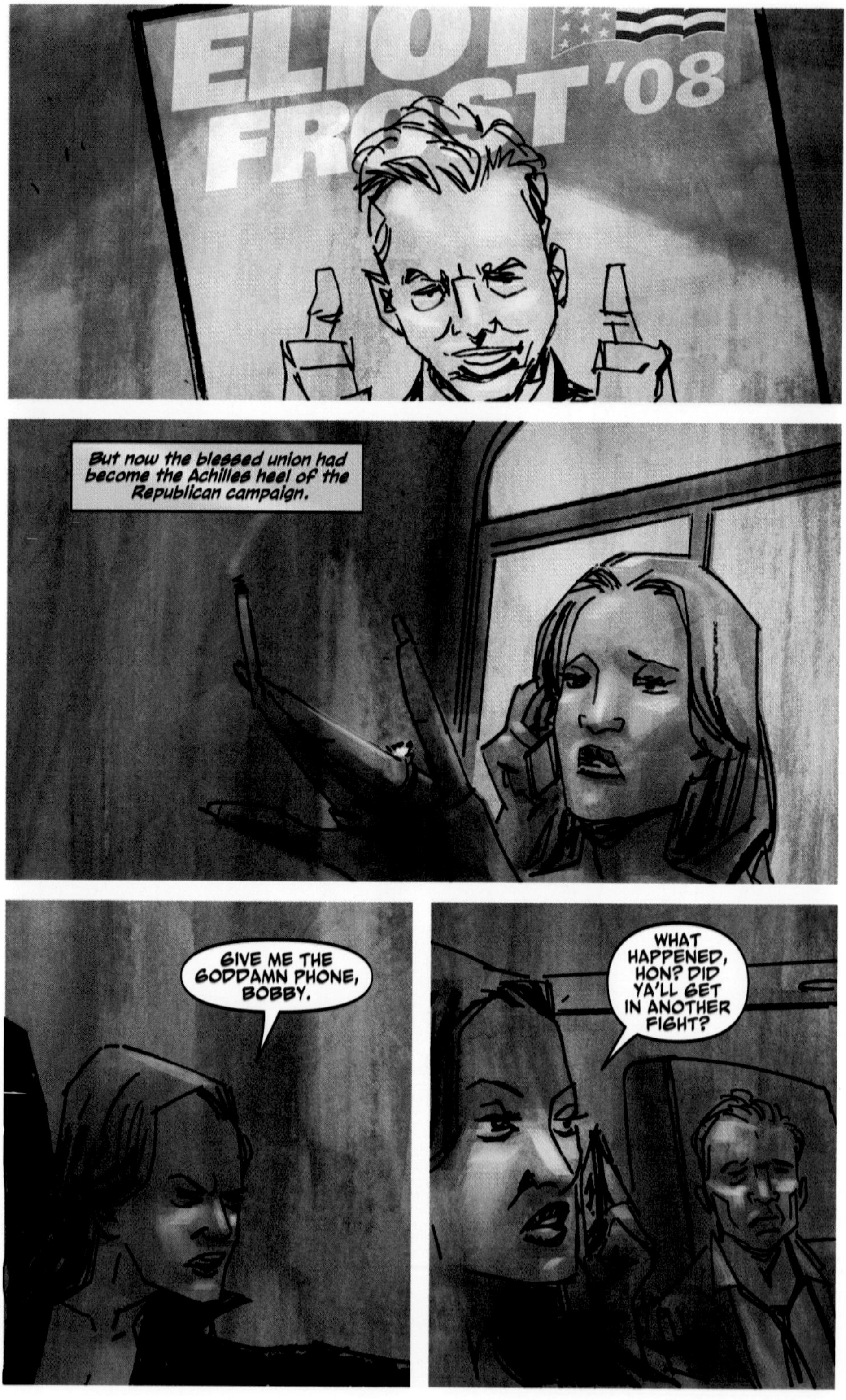
ELIOT FROST '08
But now the blessed union had become the Achilles heel of the Republican campaign.
GIVE ME THE GODDAMN PHONE, BOBBY.
WHAT HAPPENED, HON? DID YA'LL GET IN ANOTHER FIGHT?

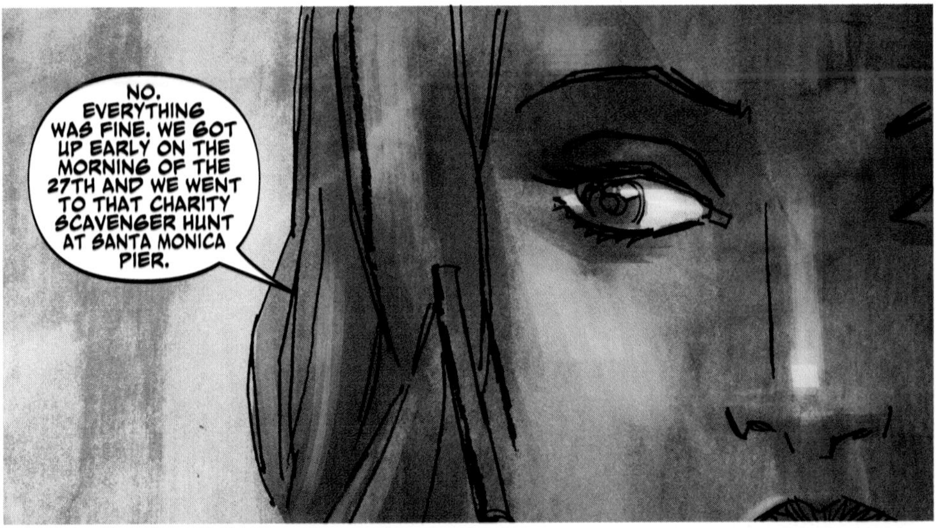
NO. EVERYTHING WAS FINE. WE GOT UP EARLY ON THE MORNING OF THE 27TH AND WE WENT TO THAT CHARITY SCAVENGER HUNT AT SANTA MONICA PIER.

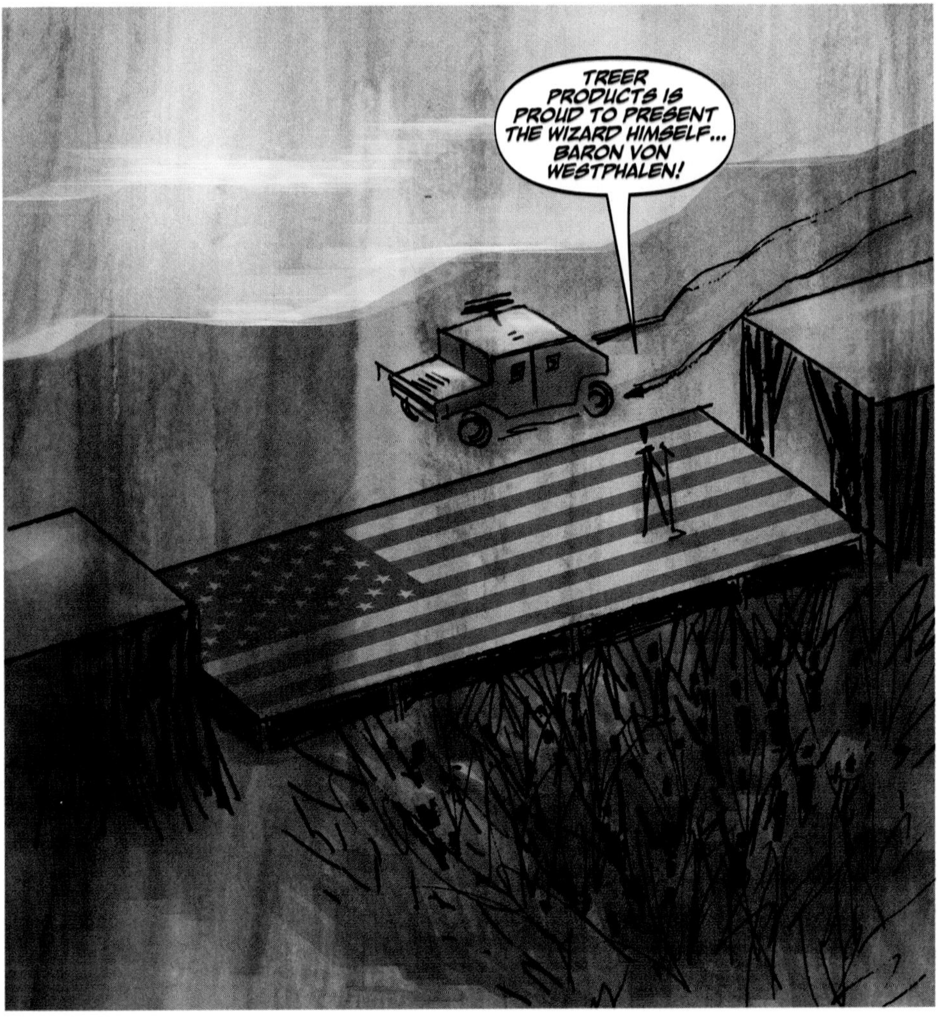
TREER PRODUCTS IS PROUD TO PRESENT THE WIZARD HIMSELF... BARON VON WESTPHALEN!

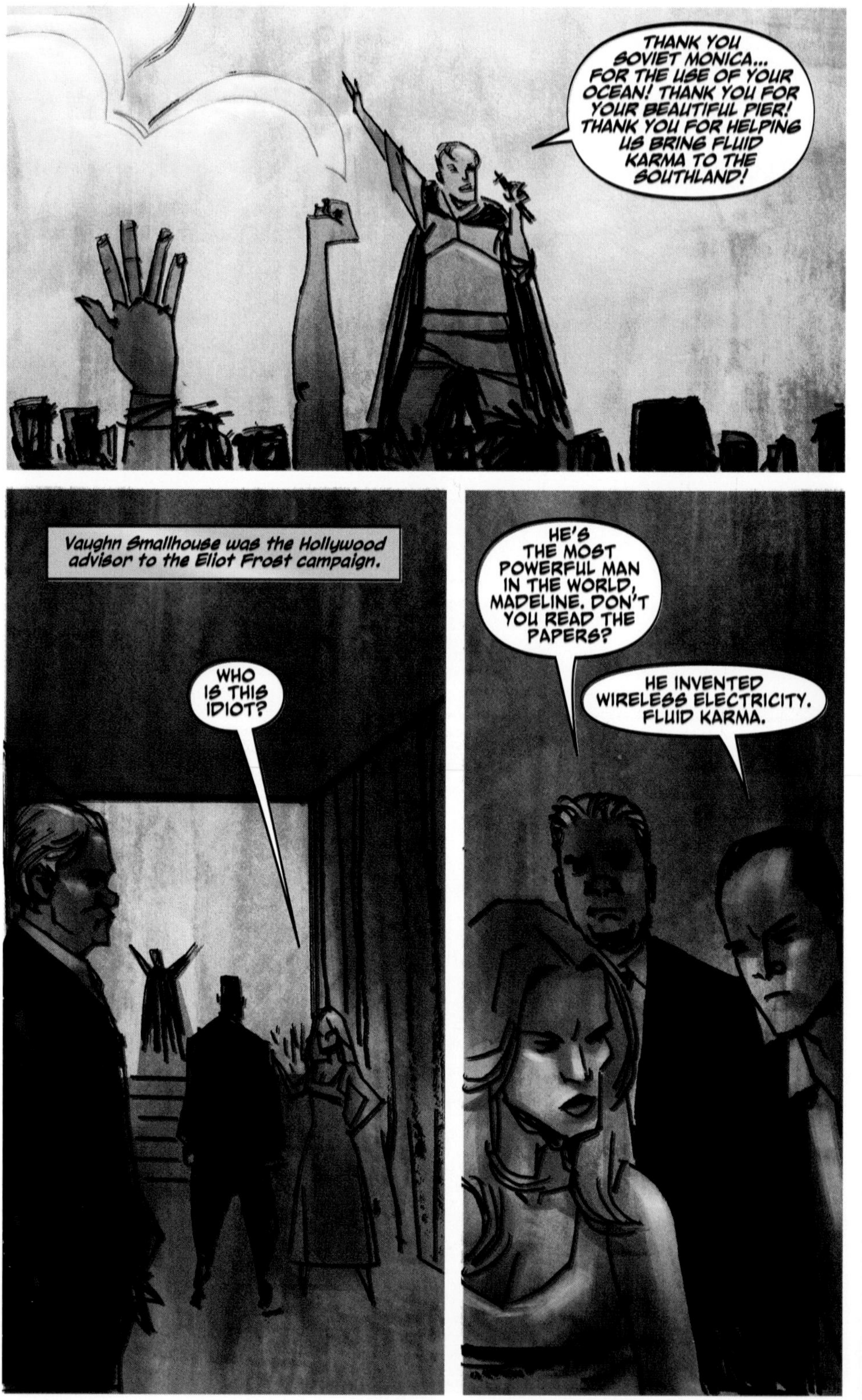
THANK YOU SOVIET MONICA... FOR THE USE OF YOUR OCEAN! THANK YOU FOR YOUR BEAUTIFUL PIER! THANK YOU FOR HELPING US BRING FLUID KARMA TO THE SOUTHLAND!
Vaughn Smallhouse was the Hollywood advisor to the Eliot Frost campaign.
WHO IS THIS IDIOT?
HE'S THE MOST POWERFUL MAN IN THE WORLD, MADELINE. DON'T YOU READ THE PAPERS?
HE INVENTED WIRELESS ELECTRICITY. FLUID KARMA.

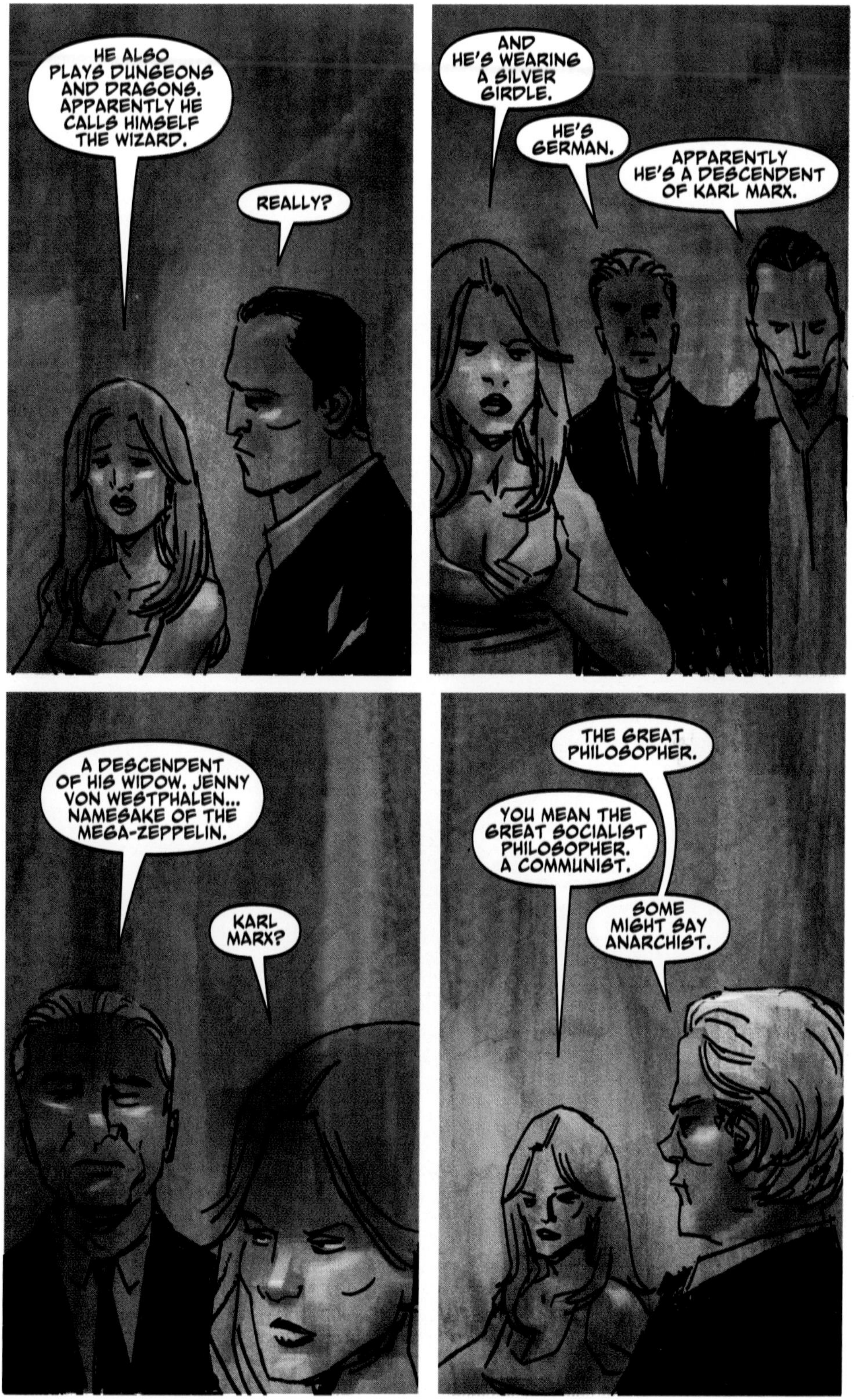
HE ALSO PLAYS DUNGEONS AND DRAGONS. APPARENTLY HE CALLS HIMSELF THE WIZARD.
REALLY?
AND HE'S WEARING A SILVER GIRDLE.
HE'S GERMAN.
APPARENTLY HE'S A DESCENDENT OF KARL MARX.
A DESCENDENT OF HIS WIDOW. JENNY VON WESTPHALEN... NAMESAKE OF THE MEGA-ZEPPELIN.
KARL MARX?
THE GREAT PHILOSOPHER.
YOU MEAN THE GREAT SOCIALIST PHILOSOPHER. A COMMUNIST.
SOME MIGHT SAY ANARCHIST.

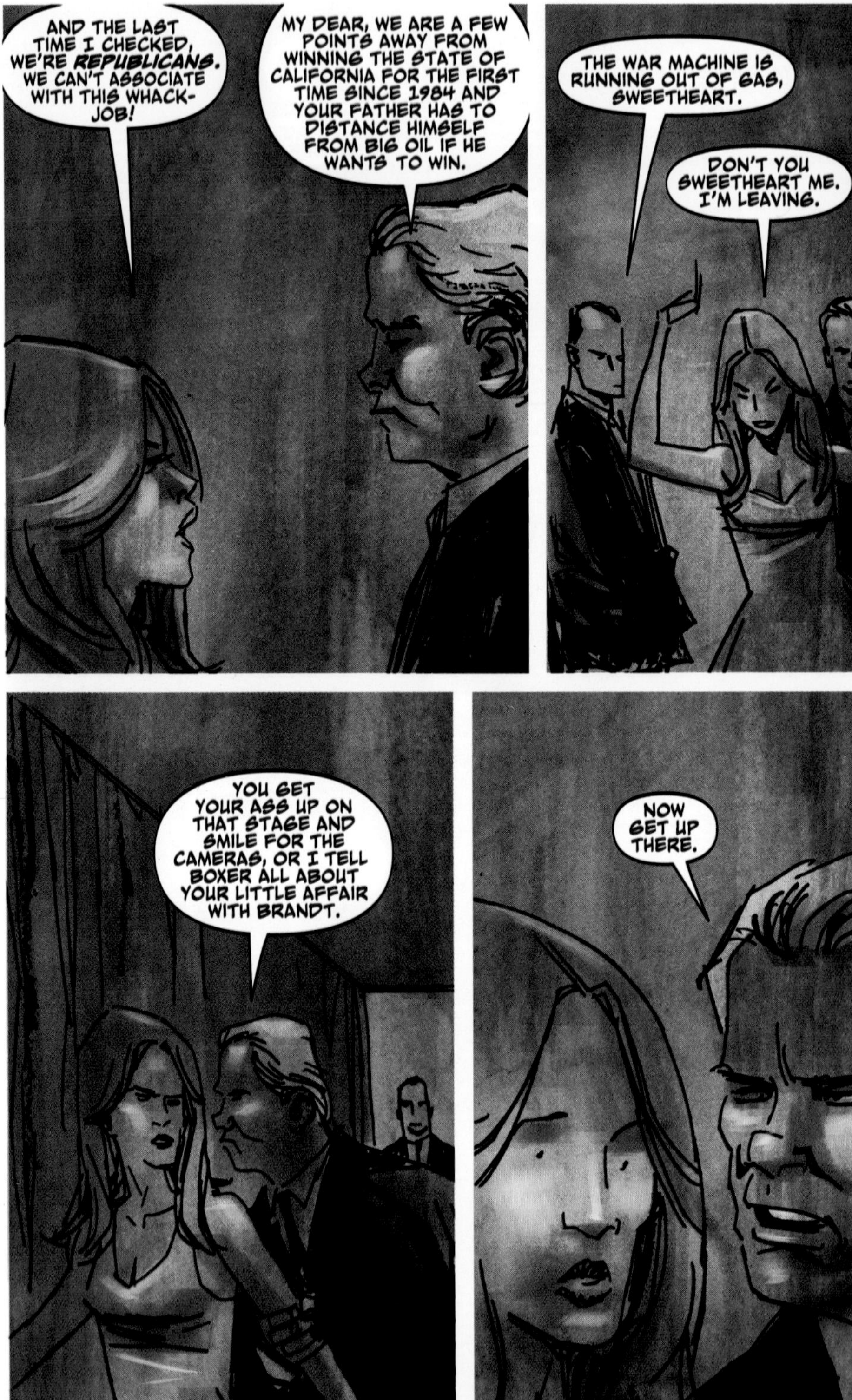
AND THE LAST TIME I CHECKED, WE'RE *REPUBLICANS*. WE CAN'T ASSOCIATE WITH THIS WHACK-JOB!
MY DEAR, WE ARE A FEW POINTS AWAY FROM WINNING THE STATE OF CALIFORNIA FOR THE FIRST TIME SINCE 1984 AND YOUR FATHER HAS TO DISTANCE HIMSELF FROM BIG OIL IF HE WANTS TO WIN.
THE WAR MACHINE IS RUNNING OUT OF GAS, SWEETHEART.
DON'T YOU SWEETHEART ME. I'M LEAVING.
YOU GET YOUR ASS UP ON THAT STAGE AND SMILE FOR THE CAMERAS, OR I TELL BOXER ALL ABOUT YOUR LITTLE AFFAIR WITH BRANDT.
NOW GET UP THERE.

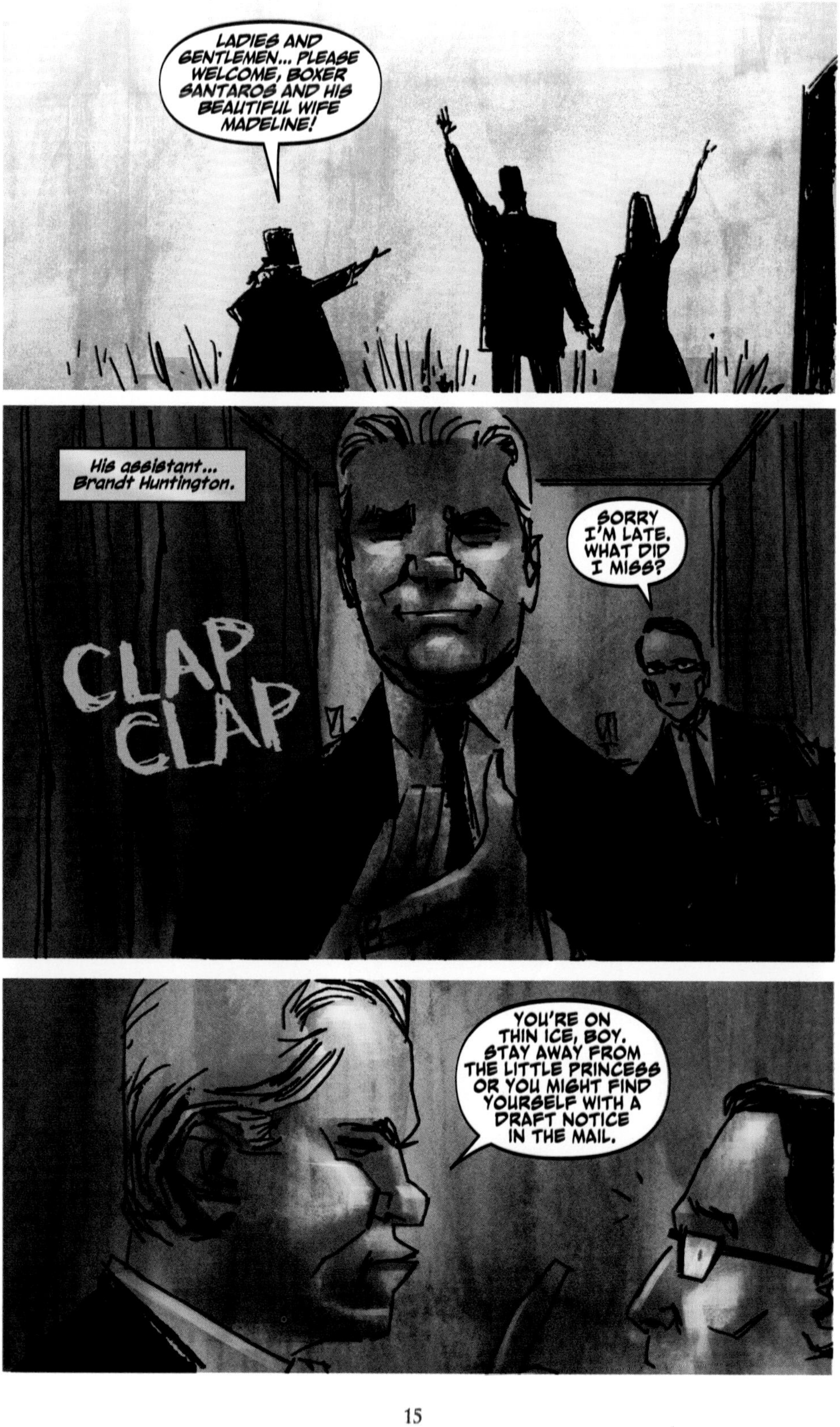
LADIES AND GENTLEMEN... PLEASE WELCOME, BOXER SANTAROS AND HIS BEAUTIFUL WIFE MADELINE!
His assistant... Brandt Huntington.
SORRY I'M LATE. WHAT DID I MISS?
CLAP CLAP
YOU'RE ON THIN ICE, BOY. STAY AWAY FROM THE LITTLE PRINCESS OR YOU MIGHT FIND YOURSELF WITH A DRAFT NOTICE IN THE MAIL.

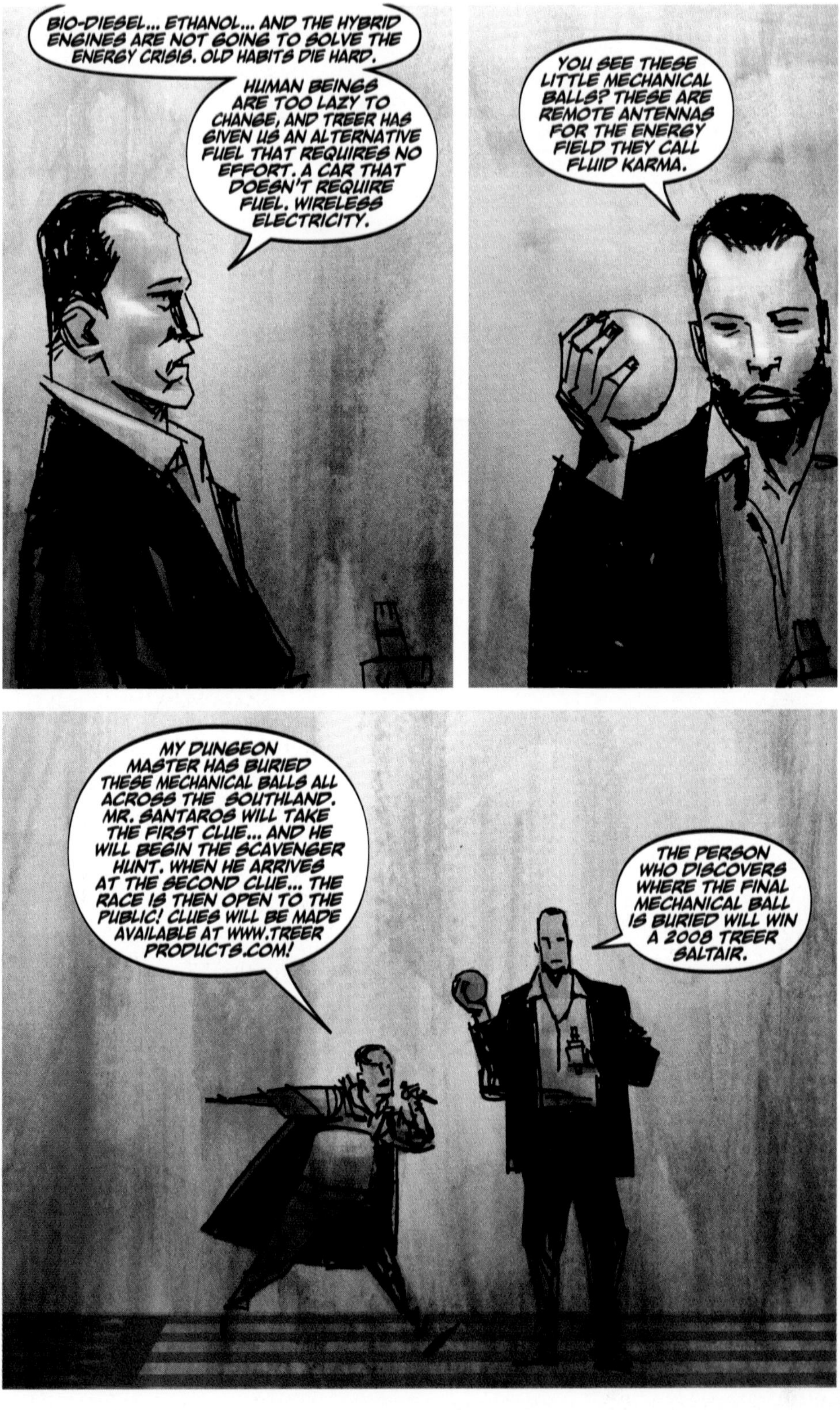
BIO-DIESEL... ETHANOL... AND THE HYBRID ENGINES ARE NOT GOING TO SOLVE THE ENERGY CRISIS. OLD HABITS DIE HARD.
HUMAN BEINGS ARE TOO LAZY TO CHANGE, AND TREER HAS GIVEN US AN ALTERNATIVE FUEL THAT REQUIRES NO EFFORT. A CAR THAT DOESN'T REQUIRE FUEL. WIRELESS ELECTRICITY.
YOU SEE THESE LITTLE MECHANICAL BALLS? THESE ARE REMOTE ANTENNAS FOR THE ENERGY FIELD THEY CALL FLUID KARMA.
MY DUNGEON MASTER HAS BURIED THESE MECHANICAL BALLS ALL ACROSS THE SOUTHLAND. MR. SANTAROS WILL TAKE THE FIRST CLUE... AND HE WILL BEGIN THE SCAVENGER HUNT. WHEN HE ARRIVES AT THE SECOND CLUE... THE RACE IS THEN OPEN TO THE PUBLIC! CLUES WILL BE MADE AVAILABLE AT WWW.TREER PRODUCTS.COM!
THE PERSON WHO DISCOVERS WHERE THE FINAL MECHANICAL BALL IS BURIED WILL WIN A 2008 TREER SALTAIR.

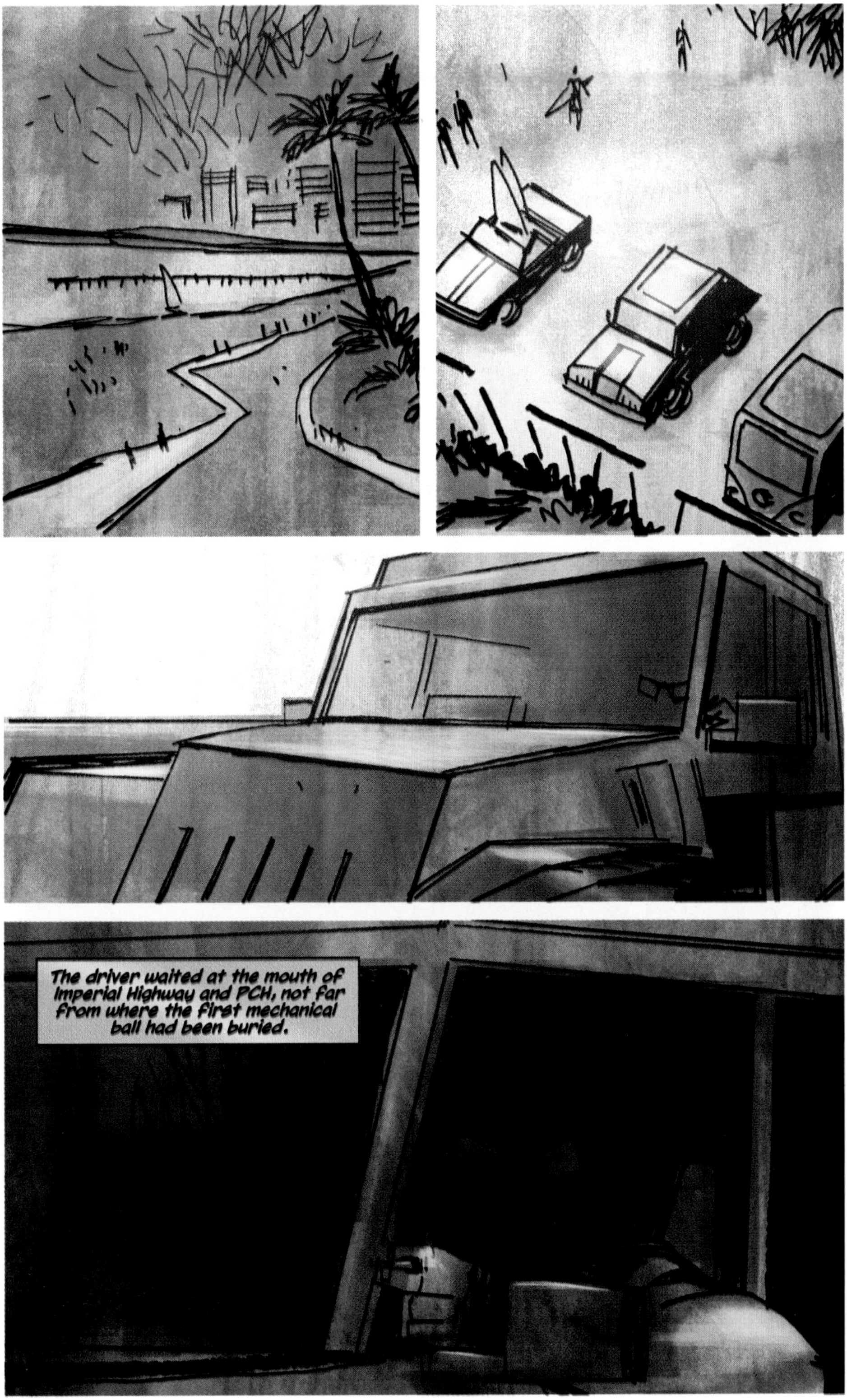
The driver waited at the mouth of Imperial Highway and PCH, not far from where the first mechanical ball had been buried.

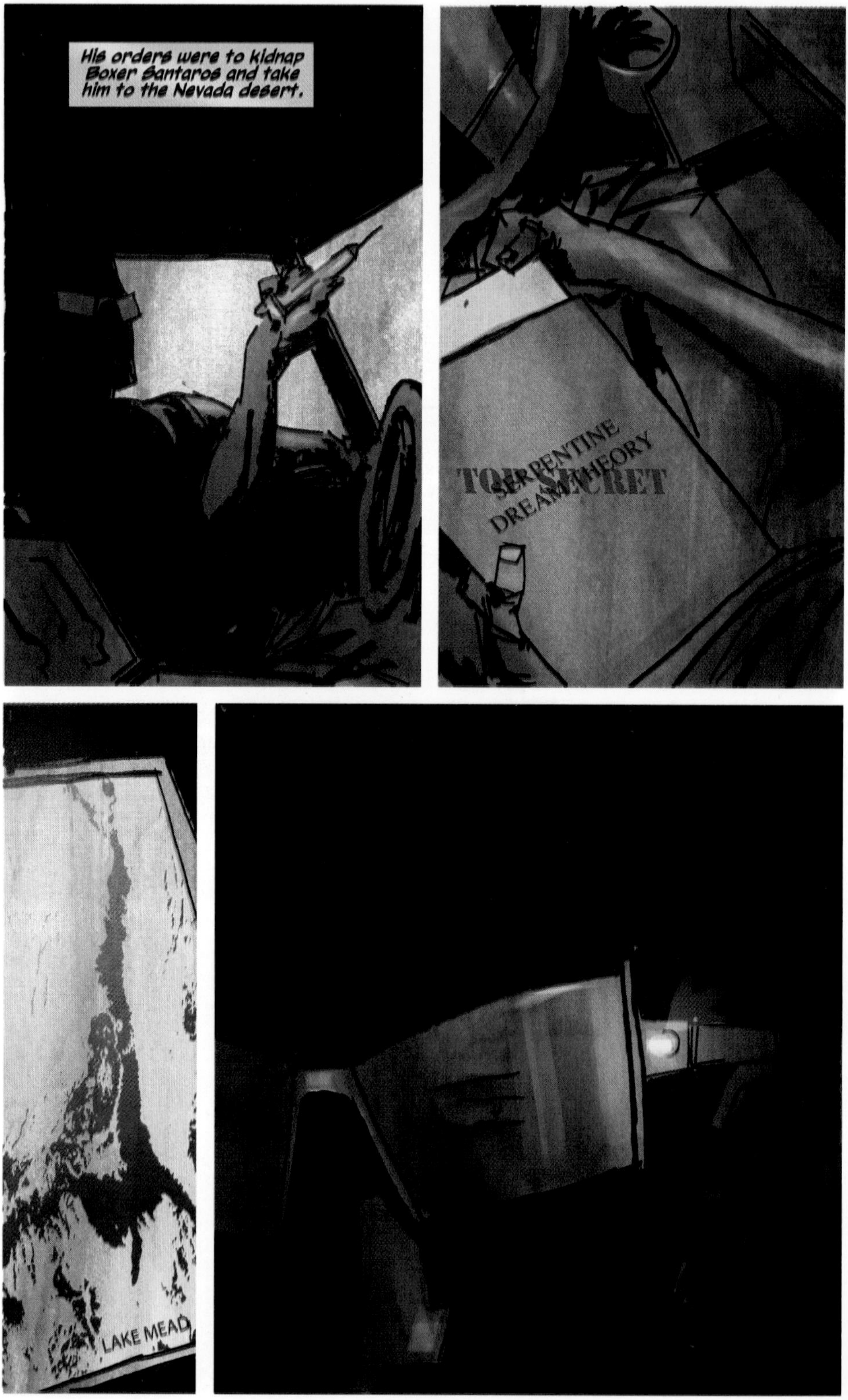
His orders were to kidnap Boxer Santaros and take him to the Nevada desert.
SERPENTINE DREAM THEORY
LAKE MEAD

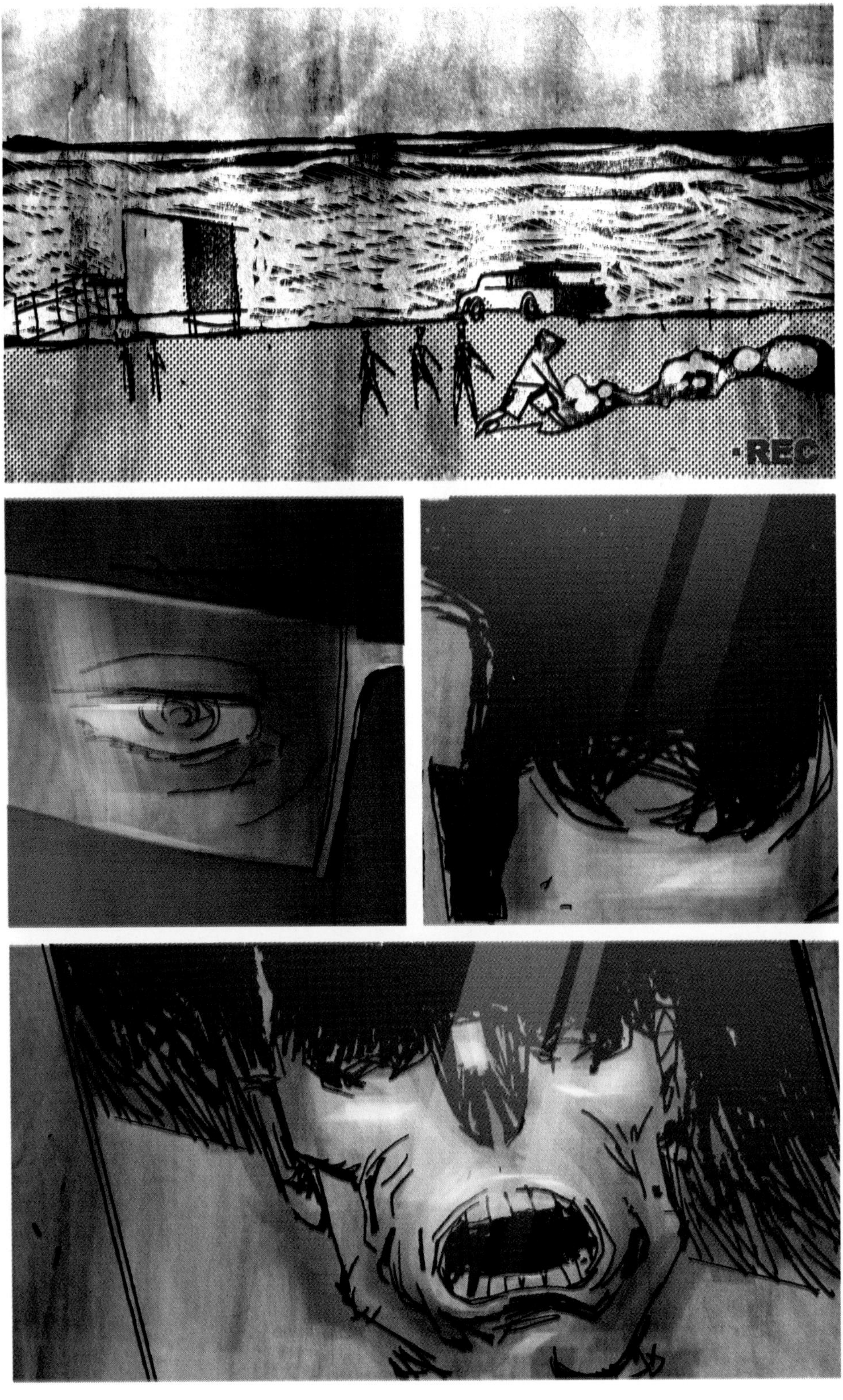
•REC

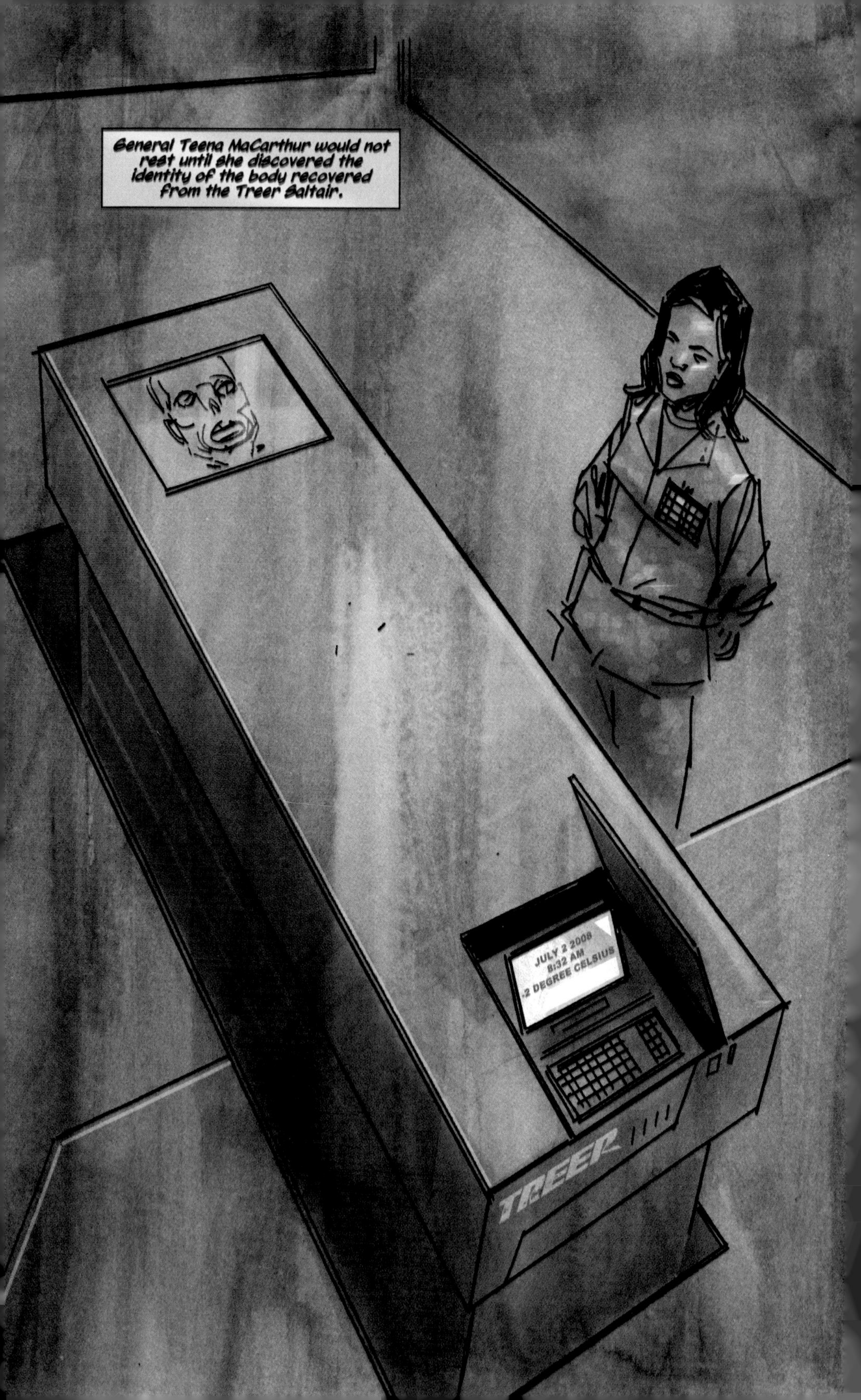
General Teena MaCarthur would not rest until she discovered the identity of the body recovered from the Treer Saltair.
JULY 2 2008
8:32 AM
-2 DEGREE CELSIUS
TREER
TREER

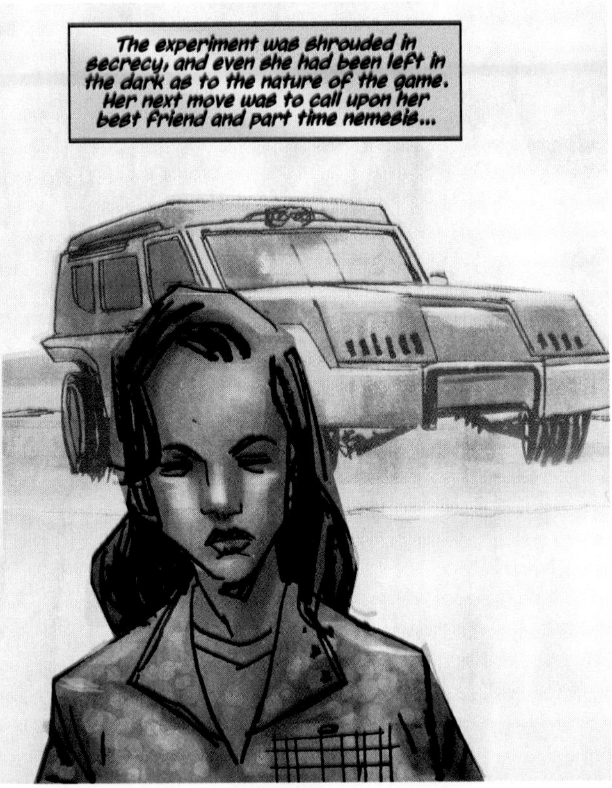
The experiment was shrouded in secrecy, and even she had been left in the dark as to the nature of the game. Her next move was to call upon her best friend and part time nemesis...

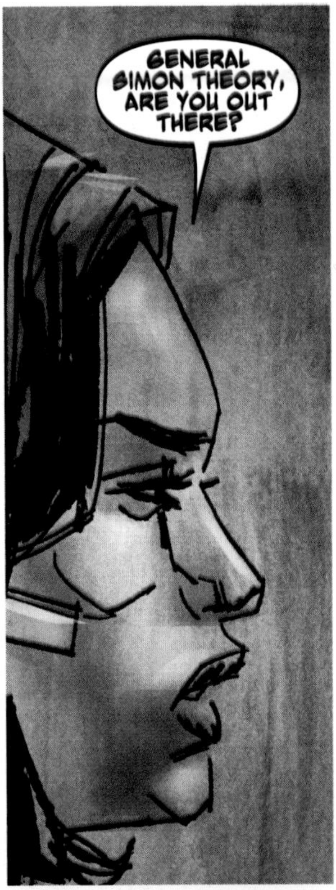
GENERAL SIMON THEORY, ARE YOU OUT THERE?

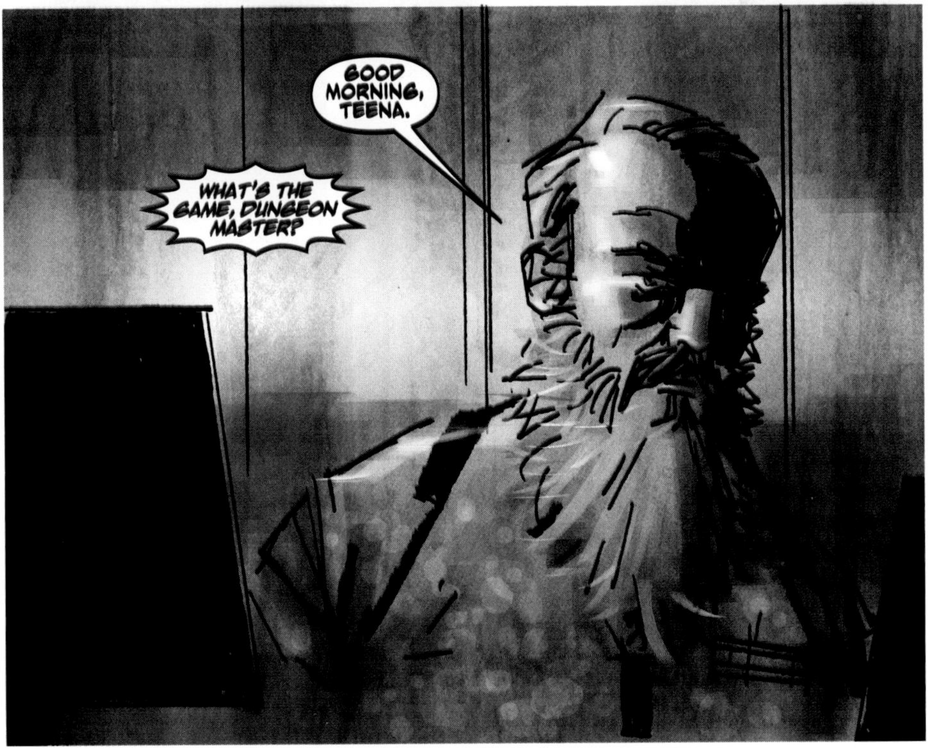
GOOD MORNING, TEENA.
WHAT'S THE GAME, DUNGEON MASTER?

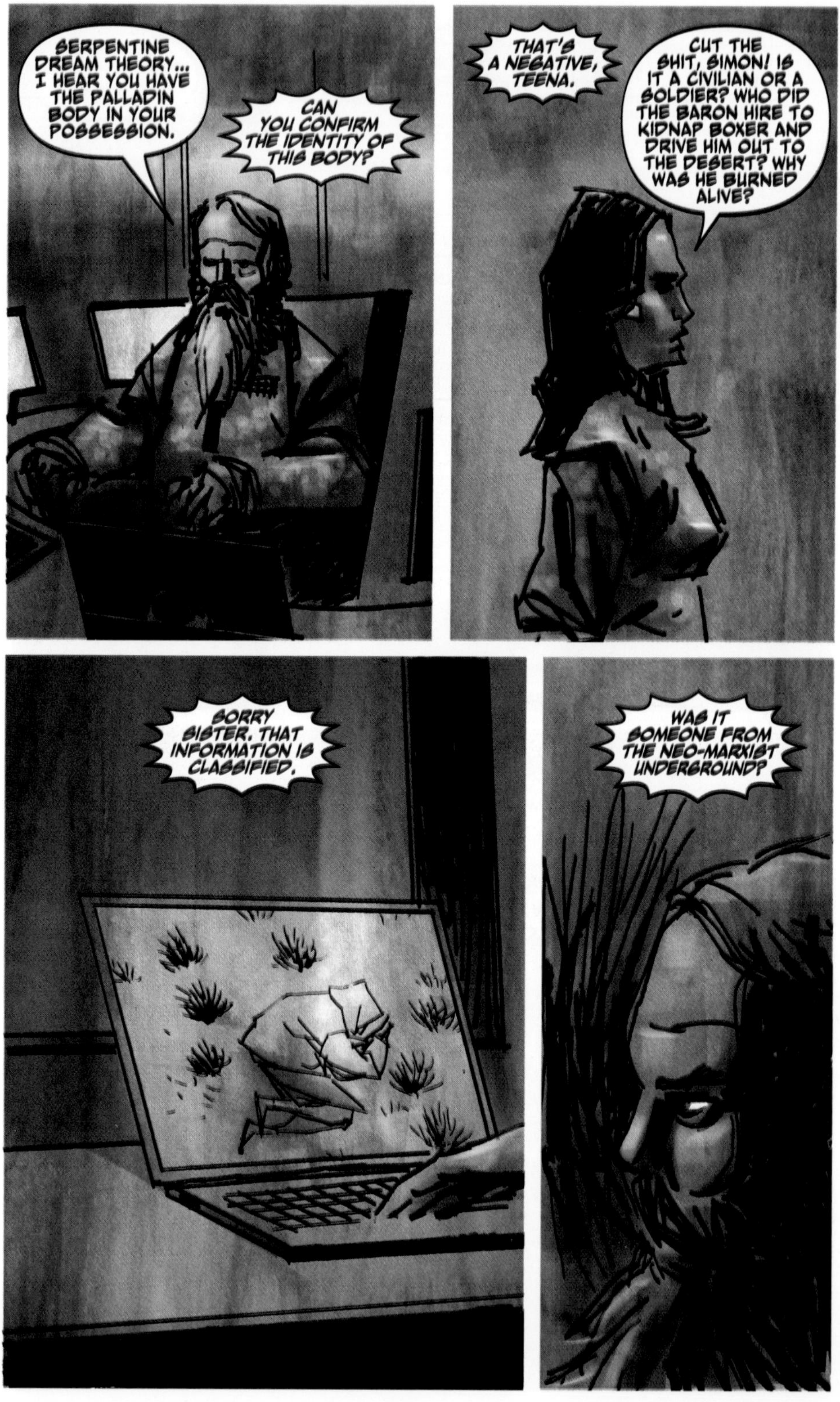
SERPENTINE DREAM THEORY... I HEAR YOU HAVE THE PALLADIN BODY IN YOUR POSSESSION.
CAN YOU CONFIRM THE IDENTITY OF THIS BODY?
THAT'S A NEGATIVE, TEENA.
CUT THE SHIT, SIMON! IS IT A CIVILIAN OR A SOLDIER? WHO DID THE BARON HIRE TO KIDNAP BOXER AND DRIVE HIM OUT TO THE DESERT? WHY WAS HE BURNED ALIVE?
SORRY SISTER. THAT INFORMATION IS CLASSIFIED.
WAS IT SOMEONE FROM THE NEO-MARXIST UNDERGROUND?

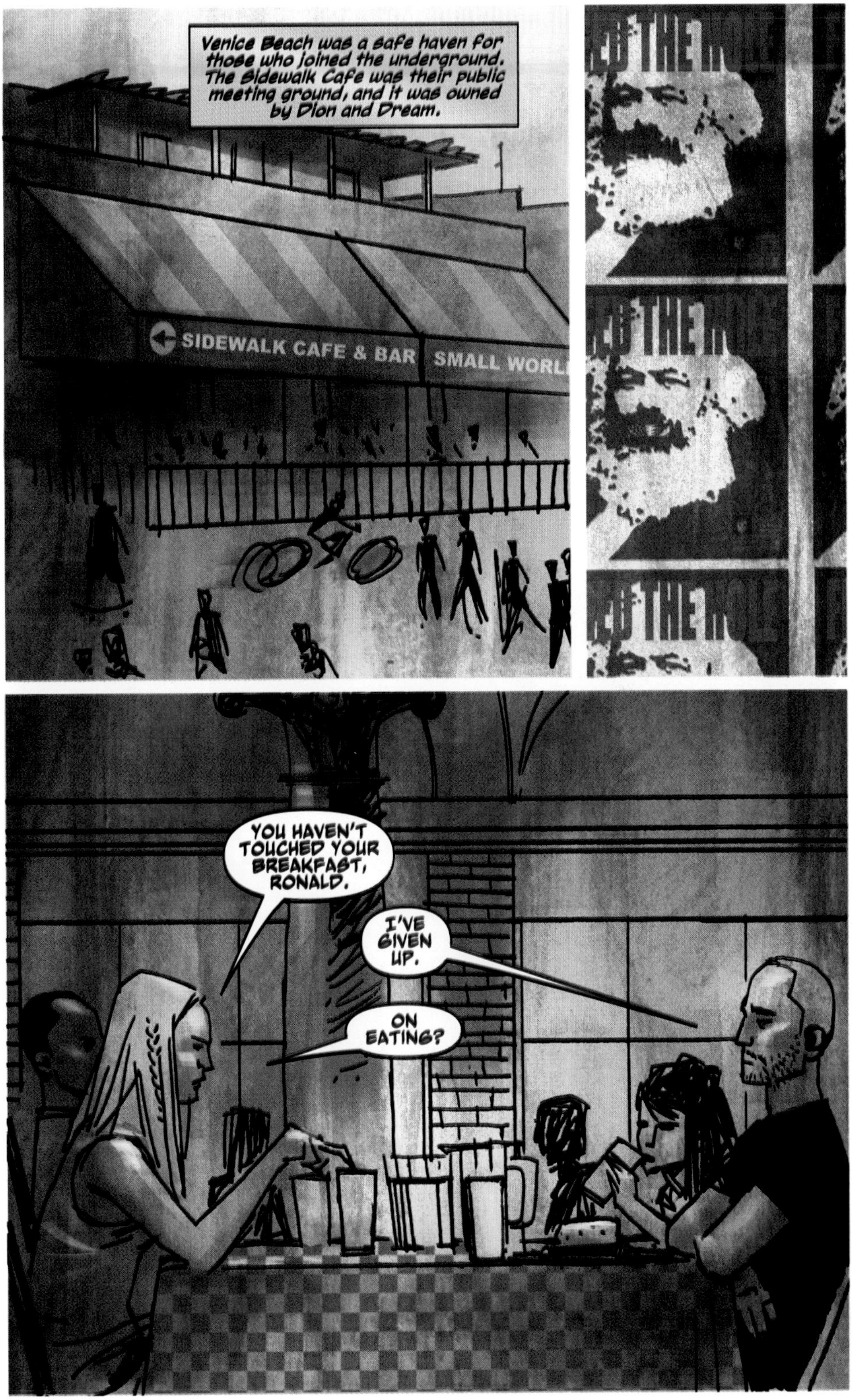

Venice Beach was a safe haven for those who joined the underground. The Sidewalk Cafe was their public meeting ground, and it was owned by Dion and Dream.
SIDEWALK CAFE & BAR
YOU HAVEN'T TOUCHED YOUR BREAKFAST, RONALD.
I'VE GIVEN UP.
ON EATING?

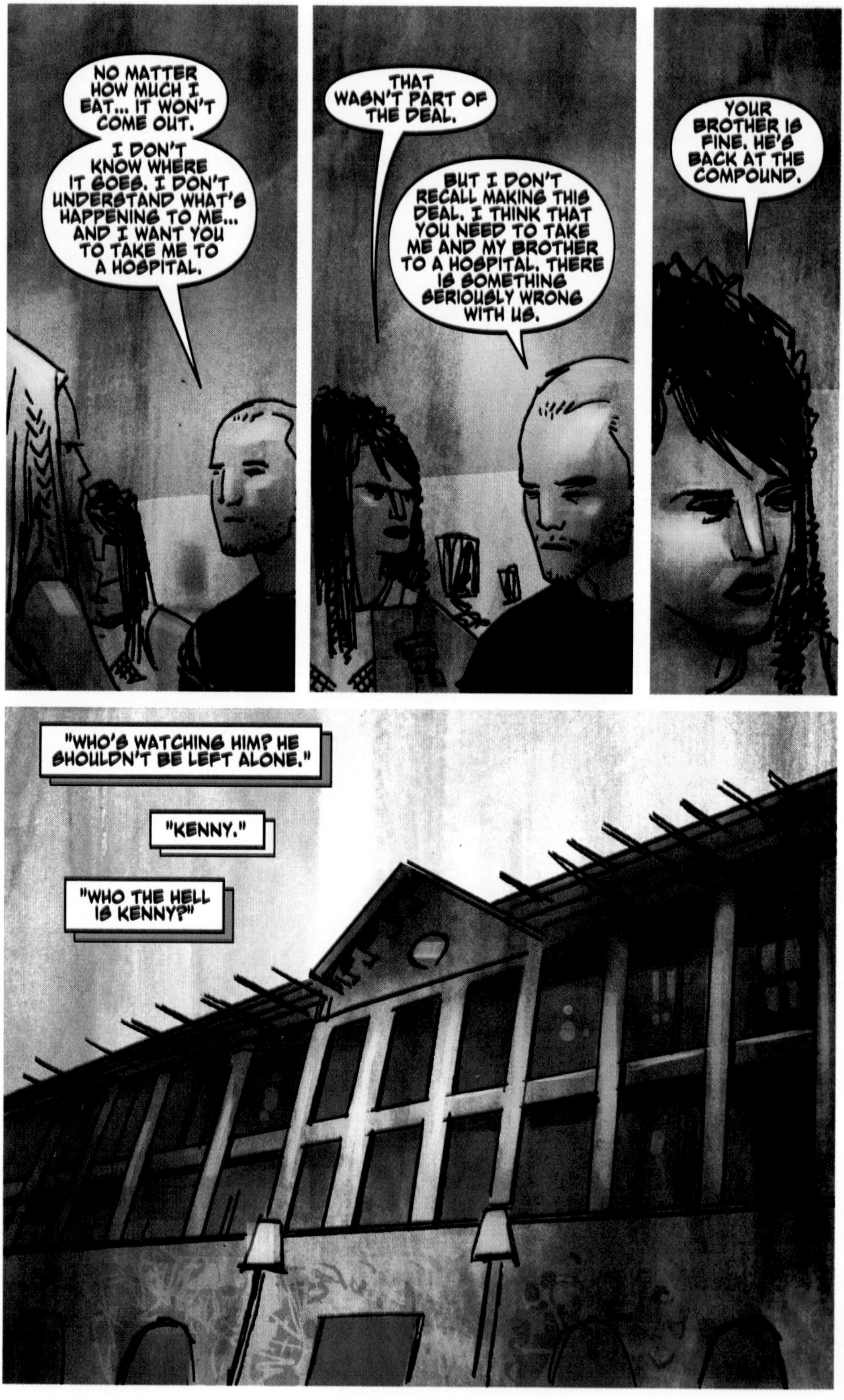
NO MATTER HOW MUCH I EAT... IT WON'T COME OUT.
I DON'T KNOW WHERE IT GOES. I DON'T UNDERSTAND WHAT'S HAPPENING TO ME... AND I WANT YOU TO TAKE ME TO A HOSPITAL.
THAT WASN'T PART OF THE DEAL.
BUT I DON'T RECALL MAKING THIS DEAL. I THINK THAT YOU NEED TO TAKE ME AND MY BROTHER TO A HOSPITAL. THERE IS SOMETHING SERIOUSLY WRONG WITH US.
YOUR BROTHER IS FINE. HE'S BACK AT THE COMPOUND.
"WHO'S WATCHING HIM? HE SHOULDN'T BE LEFT ALONE."
"KENNY."
"WHO THE HELL IS KENNY?"

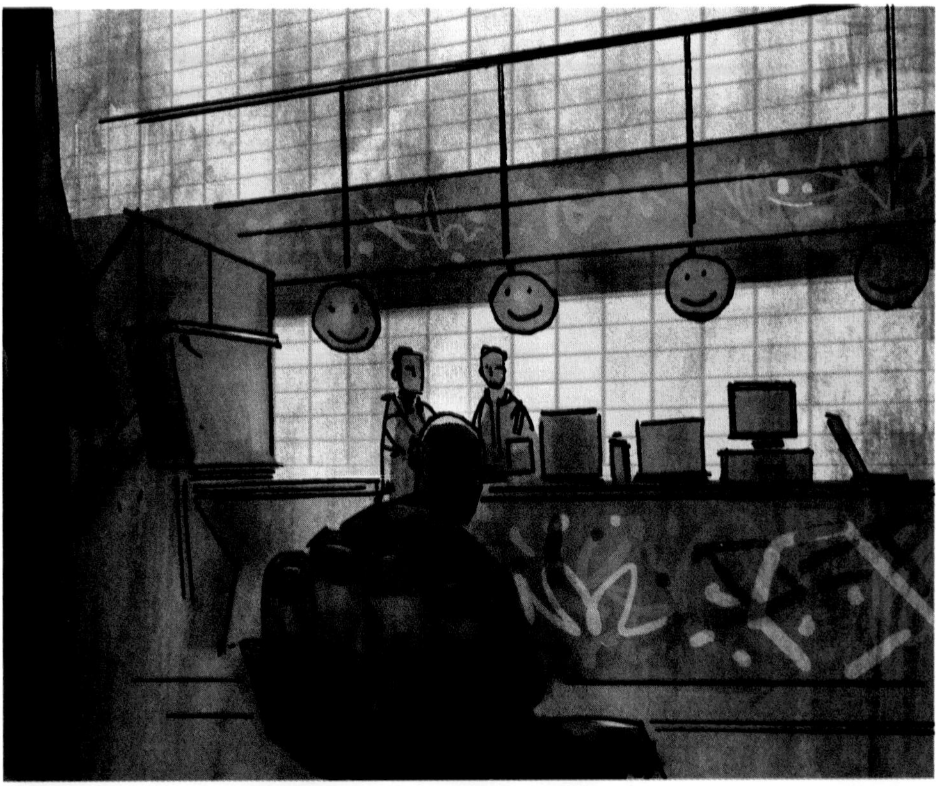

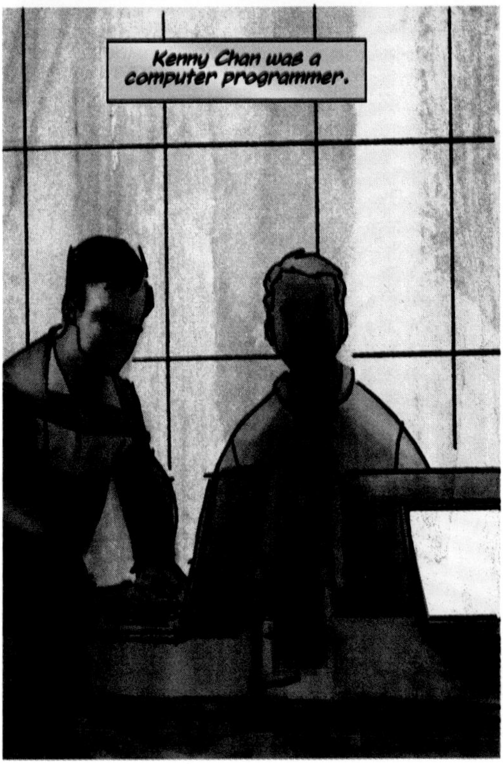
Kenny Chan was a computer programmer.

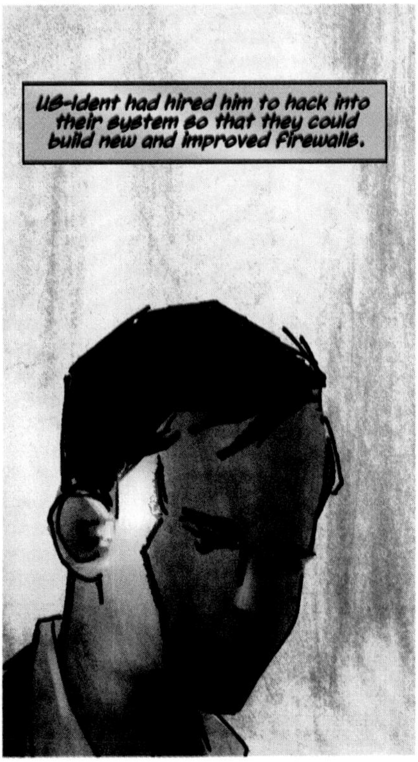
US-Ident had hired him to hack into their system so that they could build new and improved firewalls.

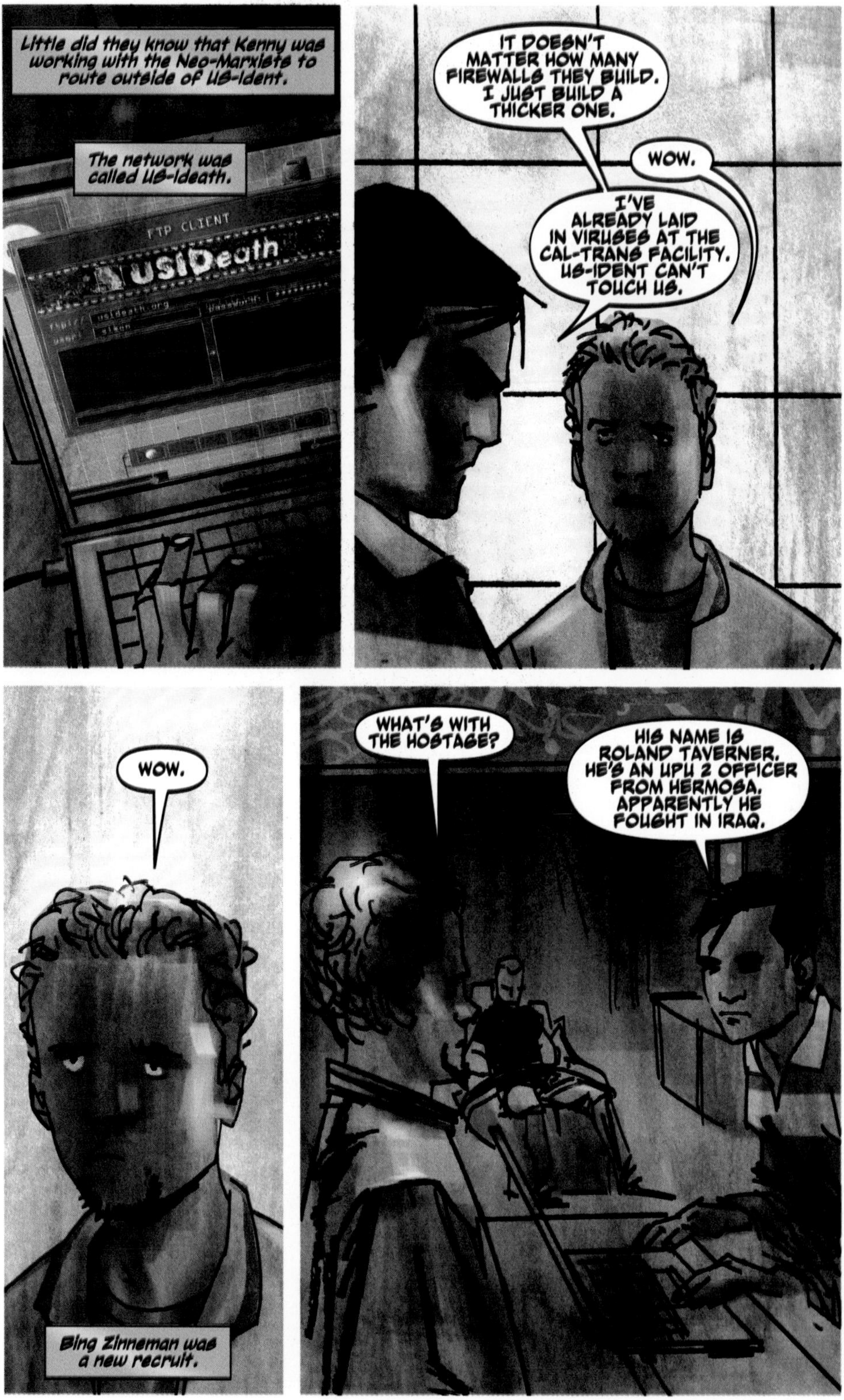
Little did they know that Kenny was working with the Neo-Marxists to route outside of US-Ident.
The network was called US-Ideath.
FTP CLIENT
usIDeath
IT DOESN'T MATTER HOW MANY FIREWALLS THEY BUILD. I JUST BUILD A THICKER ONE.
WOW.
I'VE ALREADY LAID IN VIRUSES AT THE CAL-TRANS FACILITY. US-IDENT CAN'T TOUCH US.
WOW.
Bing Zinneman was a new recruit.
WHAT'S WITH THE HOSTAGE?
HIS NAME IS ROLAND TAVERNER. HE'S AN UPU 2 OFFICER FROM HERMOSA. APPARENTLY HE FOUGHT IN IRAQ.

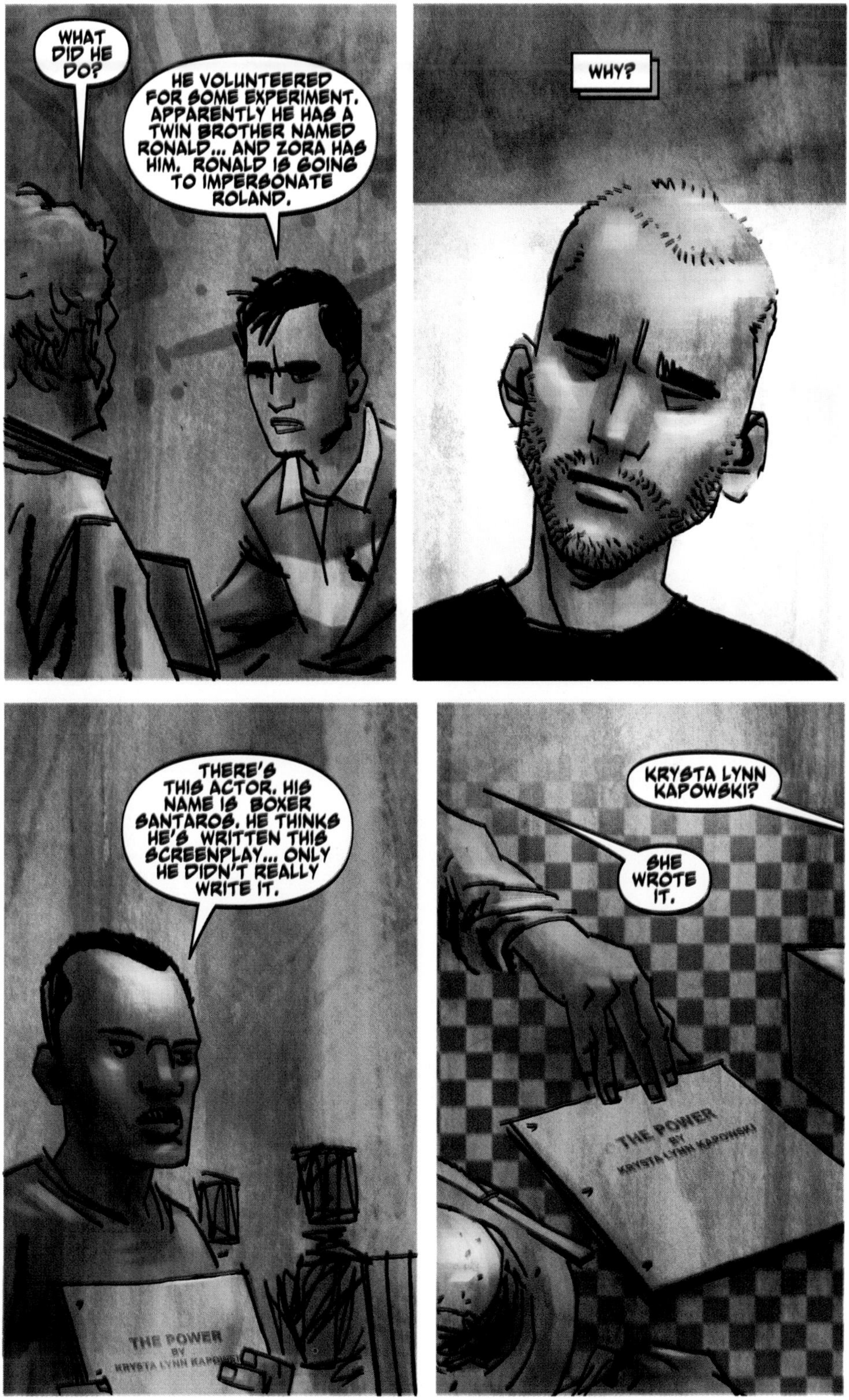
WHAT DID HE DO?
HE VOLUNTEERED FOR SOME EXPERIMENT. APPARENTLY HE HAS A TWIN BROTHER NAMED RONALD... AND ZORA HAS HIM. RONALD IS GOING TO IMPERSONATE ROLAND.
WHY?
THERE'S THIS ACTOR. HIS NAME IS BOXER SANTAROS. HE THINKS HE'S WRITTEN THIS SCREENPLAY... ONLY HE DIDN'T REALLY WRITE IT.
THE POWER
BY
KRYSTA LYNN KAPOWSKI?
SHE WROTE IT.
THE POWER
BY
KRYSTA LYNN KAPOWSKI

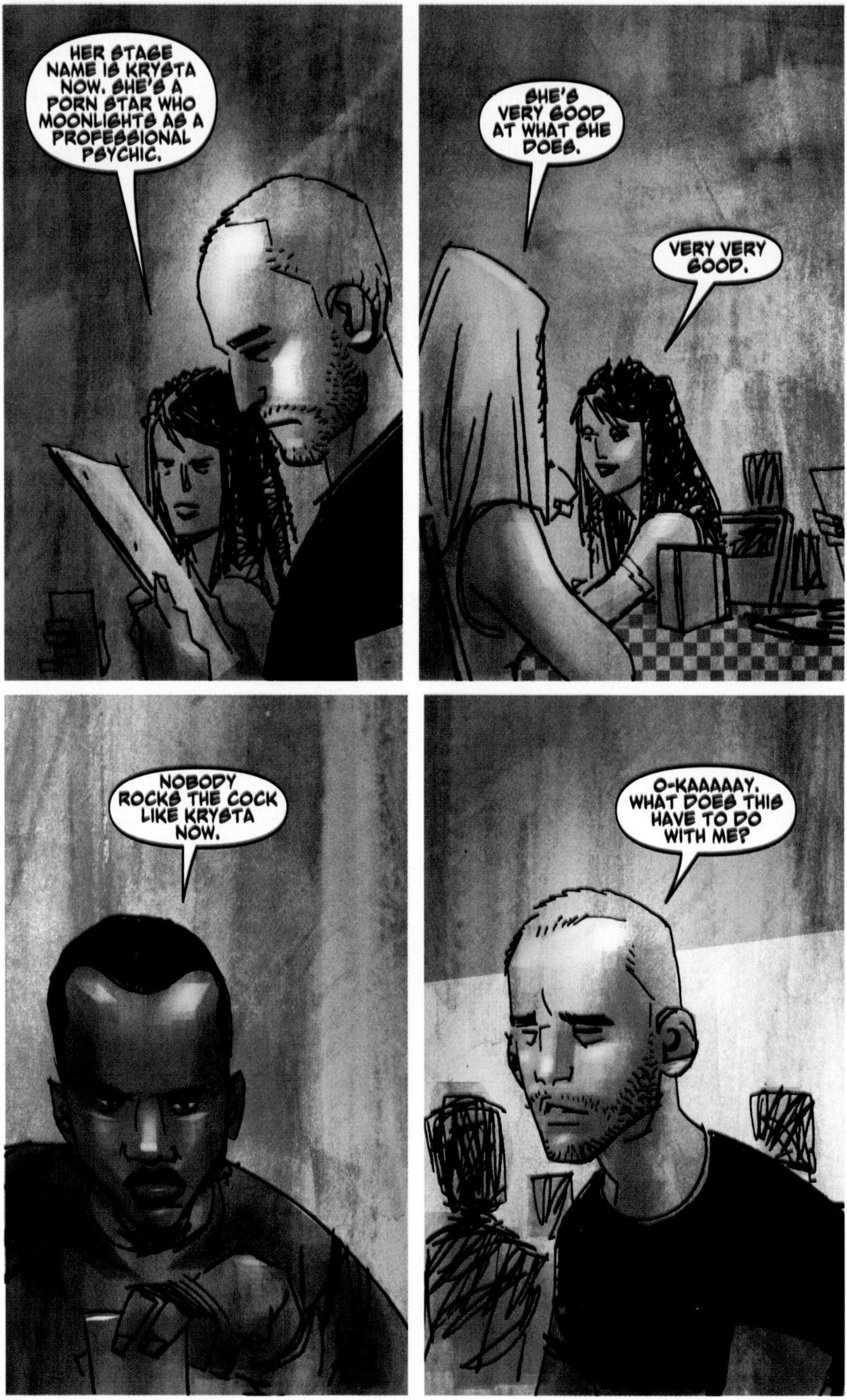
HER STAGE NAME IS KRYSTA NOW. SHE'S A PORN STAR WHO MOONLIGHTS AS A PROFESSIONAL PSYCHIC.
SHE'S VERY GOOD AT WHAT SHE DOES.
VERY VERY GOOD.
NOBODY ROCKS THE COCK LIKE KRYSTA NOW.
O-KAAAAAY. WHAT DOES THIS HAVE TO DO WITH ME?

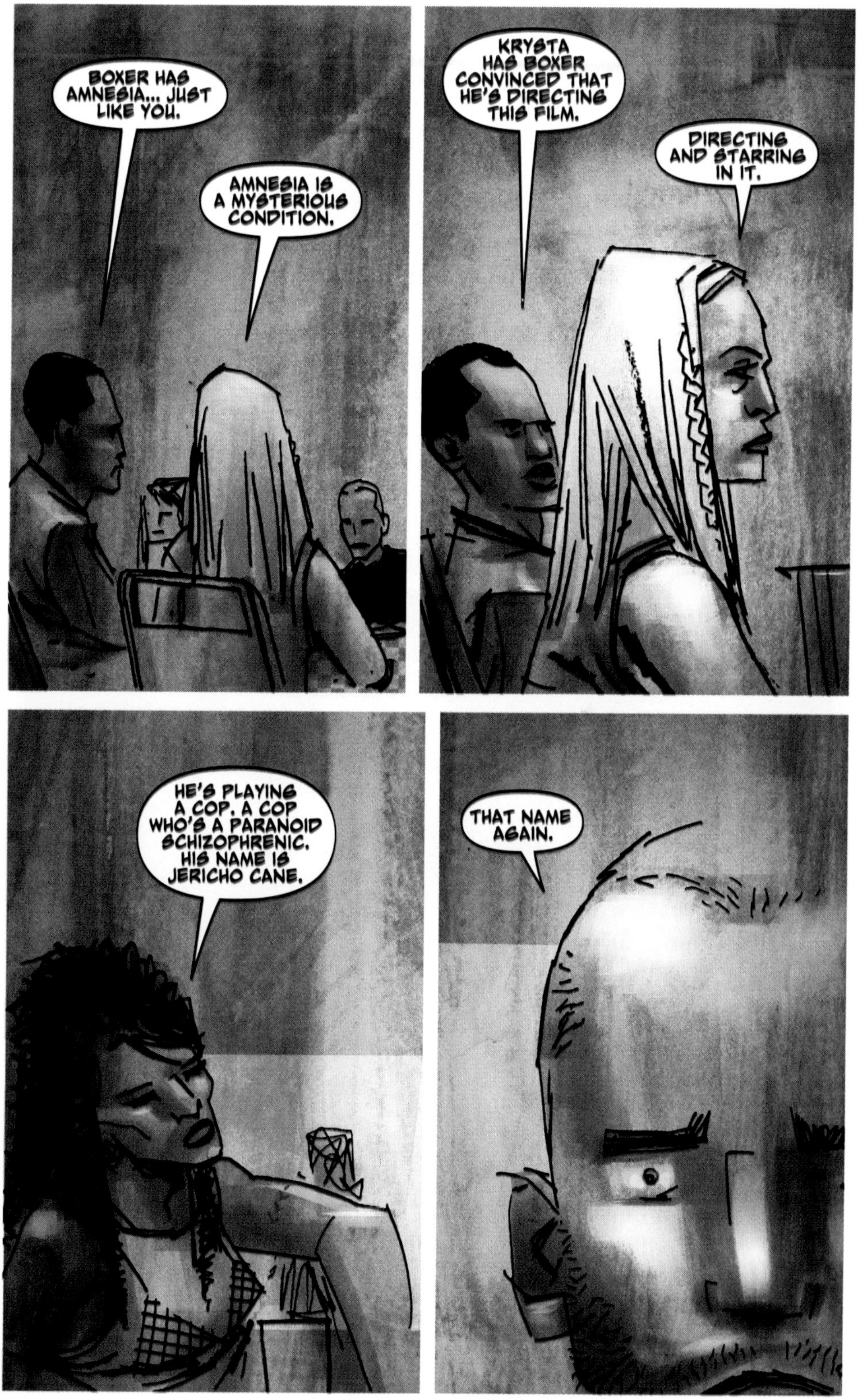
BOXER HAS AMNESIA... JUST LIKE YOU.
AMNESIA IS A MYSTERIOUS CONDITION.
KRYSTA HAS BOXER CONVINCED THAT HE'S DIRECTING THIS FILM.
DIRECTING AND STARRING IN IT.
HE'S PLAYING A COP. A COP WHO'S A PARANOID SCHIZOPHRENIC. HIS NAME IS JERICHO CANE.
THAT NAME AGAIN.

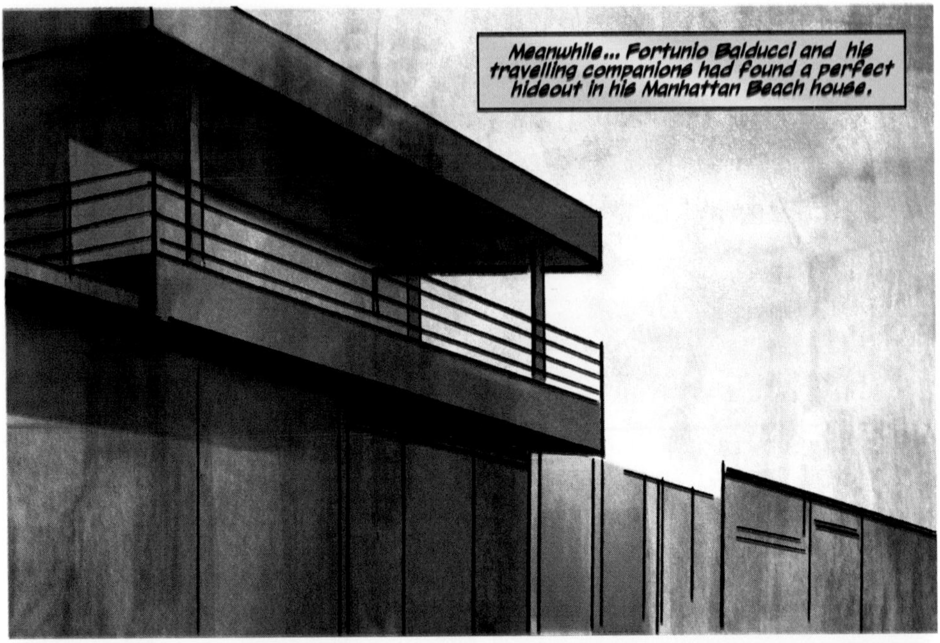
Meanwhile... Fortunio Balducci and his travelling companions had found a perfect hideout in his Manhattan Beach house.

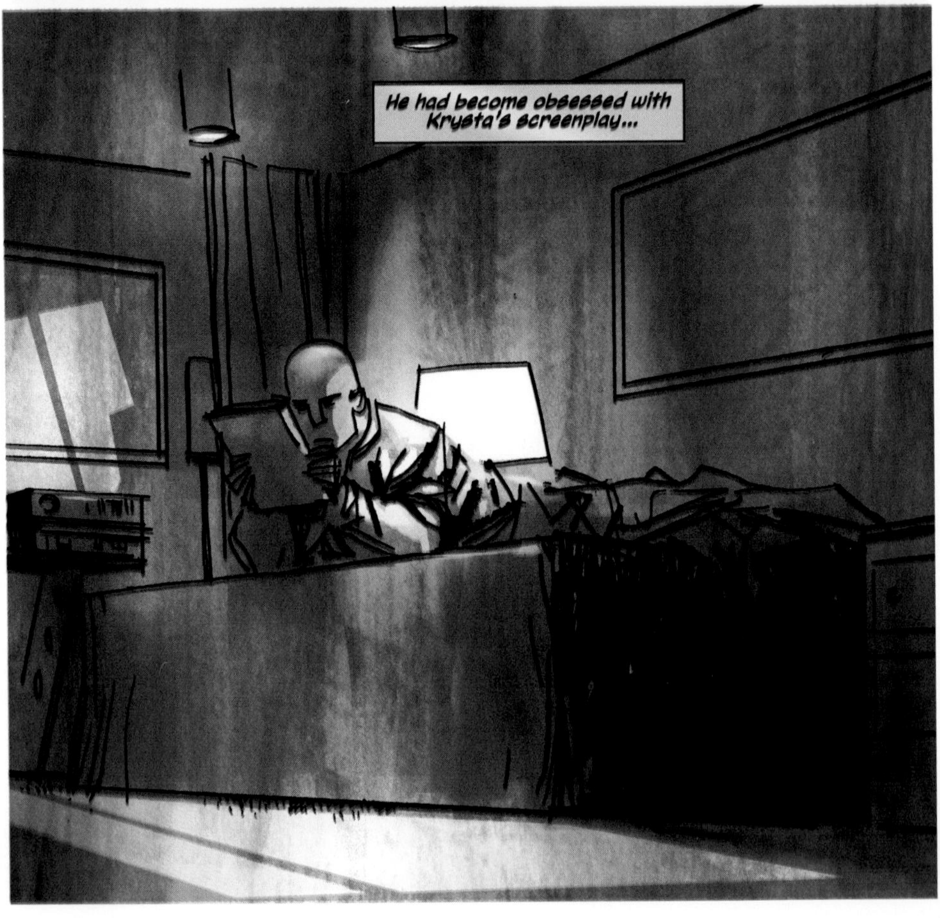
He had become obsessed with Krysta's screenplay...

INT. BLACK HOUSE -- DAWN

The tattoo procedure has taken all night to complete. Jericho
now stands before a LARGE MIRROR on the parlor wall. His
upper body is covered in tattoos. A JEWISH STAR OF DAVID
surrounds his navel.

Muriel approaches him from behind... admiring the tattoos.
She hands him a button-down SHIRT.

> MURIEL
> Get dressed. We've got places to
> go.

Muriel grabs a cold BUD LIGHT from the cooler and hands it to
him. Jericho cracks it open and takes a long chug.

> JERICHO
> Thanks.

*He smiles at her. The sexual tension between the two of them
is building.*

EXT. BLACK HOUSE -- DAWN

MacPherson and Jericho are now inside the cruiser. Muriel
sits in the back seat. Caleb is strapped into a BABY CAR SEAT
next to her. MacPherson starts the engine.

Jericho glances out the passenger-side window. Serpentine
stands on the porch, flanked by Mohawked Man and the other
goons. A BOA CONSTRICTOR is draped over her shoulders.

> SERPENTINE
> *Do not forget to feed da Messiah.
> You must feed him every hour... or
> he will loose his strength, and
> grow irritable. You do not want to
> see what happen when da Messiah get
> cranky.*

> JERICHO
> Point taken.

> SERPENTINE
> *Good luck... Mista Cane...*

Serpentine takes a drag from her cigarette and blows smoke in
their direction as MacPherson puts the car into drive and
speeds off.

EXT. DESERT HIGHWAY -- MORNING

The POLICE CRUISER drives east... approaching the STATE LINE.
Traffic is grid-locked at the MILITARY CHECKPOINT up ahead.

INT. POLICE CRUISER -- NEXT

Caleb is asleep in the back seat. He has clearly grown to an
age that resembles TWO-YEARS OLD since we last saw him.

Muriel looks at her watch.

                    MURIEL
          It's been more than an hour. We
          should feed baby Caleb.

Muriel spies a pair of GOLDEN ARCHES through the windshield.

                    MURIEL
          McDonald's. We have to pull over
          and go to that McDonald's.

MacPherson hits the turn signal and begins to merge into the
exit lane.

                    MACPHERSON
          Whatever you say, princess.

EXT. MCDONALD'S -- PARKING LOT -- MOMENTS LATER

Jericho, Muriel and MacPherson walk with baby Caleb across
the parking lot. Caleb is now walking like a toddler.

                    MACPHERSON
          Jesus... he can walk now?

Caleb looks around the parking lot... pointing up at the
McDonald's sign.

                    CALEB
          McDonald's.

Jericho takes off his glasses.

                    JERICHO
          Who taught him to read?

They move toward the entrance.

ACROSS THE PARKING LOT... a BLACK LIMOUSINE is idling.

The REAR WINDOW rolls down and BARON VON WESTPHALEN (50s) appears. He watches the group enter the restaurant.

> BARON
> The specimen is growing faster than
> I expected.

INT. LIMOUSINE -- NEXT

Seated next to him is DR. SOBERIN EXX (40s).

Dr. Exx points a LONG LENS CAMERA out the window and begins to snap photos of the group just before they disappear inside the restaurant.

> DR. EXX
> You hired Muriel Fox?

> BARON
> Why yes. She is the most prominent
> psychic in North America.

> DR. EXX
> Is it true that she was on board
> United Flight 23?

> BARON
> Yes. She was the only passenger to
> emerge with her mind intact. It was
> the incident on Flight 23 that gave
> Ms. Fox her clairvoyant powers.

Dr. Exx rubs his chin... fascinated by this new revelation.

> DR. EXX
> Now that they have the specimen,
> shouldn't we take them all into
> custody?

> BARON
> No. Not yet. The specimen must
> spend time with Jericho. They have
> something in common. Let them
> follow the path together.

Dr. Exx smiles.

> DR. EXX
> The road not taken.

EXT. MCDONALD'S -- PARKING LOT -- NEXT

The window rolls up and the limousine drives off.

INT. MCDONALD'S -- NEXT

The McDonald's is filled with several dozen MORBIDLY OBESE
PALMDALE RESIDENTS and their CHILDREN. Jericho eyes them all.

                    JERICHO
          I've never seen so many fat people.

Muriel leads the group to the counter. She makes eye contact
with the CASHIER. She looks very familiar. That's because her
name is SHAWNA MCBRIDE (27)... *twin sister of the late Tawna
McBride.*

Muriel looks down at her name tag. It reads: SHAWNA

                    SHAWNA
          Welcome to McDonald's. Can I take
          your order?

                    MURIEL
          Shawna McBride?

Shawna furrows her brow.

                    SHAWNA
          Yeah? Do I know you?

                    MURIEL
          Are you the twin sister of Tawna
          McBride?

                    SHAWNA
          Yeah... why?

                    MURIEL
          I'm sorry Shawna... but your sister
          is dead.

Shawna's upper lip begins to quiver as she realizes that
Muriel is not kidding.

INT. MCDONALD'S -- BOOTH -- MOMENTS LATER

Shawna now sits across from Muriel in one of the booths,
sobbing quietly.

                    SHAWNA
          Ever since he came back from Iraq,
          Rick was never the same. At first
          she thought it was because he got
          exposed to radiation in El Paso.
          But it was something in Iraq. Some
          drug test. Tawna said people would
          show up at their house in the
          middle of the night and take him
          away.

                    MURIEL
          Where would they take him?

                    SHAWNA
          Edwards Air Force base. Apparently
          they were holding a bunch of
          civilians there. Something about a
          plane.

                    MURIEL
          Are you referring to the incident
          on United flight 23?

                    SHAWNA
          Yeah. How'd you know?

                    MURIEL
          I was on that flight. I'm the only
          one who remembers what happened.

EXT. EDWARDS AIR FORCE BASE -- SUNSET [FLASHBACK]

A LARGE 767 is parked on the desert air strip of EDWARDS AIR
FORCE BASE near Palmdale. EMERGENCY VEHICLES are parked
everywhere.

Muriel emerges from the ENTRANCE PORTAL and looks down at a
LARGE INFLATABLE EMERGENCY SLIDE. Wind blows through her hair
as she stares across the desert tarmac.

                    DR. MURIEL FOX (V.O.)
          From that day on... I was never the
          same.

A STEWARDESS helps Muriel down the slide.

INT. EDWARDS AIR FORCE BASE -- WAREHOUSE -- LATER ON

Muriel is now sitting on a COT in a LARGE WAREHOUSE on the base. Each PASSENGER is being treated inside the building as there are more than a hundred COTS assembled in rows.

US ARMY GENERAL SIMON THEORY (50s), a wheelchair-bound man with missing legs... sits across from her with a CLIP BOARD. He has a long silver beard.

> SIMON
> When did you notice that something
> was wrong?

> MURIEL
> We were cruising along... no
> turbulence or anything. I had a
> window seat... and I happened to be
> looking outside when I saw the
> light.

INT. UNITED FLIGHT 23 -- DAY [FLASHBACK]

Muriel sits in a WINDOW SEAT on the flight... thumbing through a magazine. Something catches her eye... and she glances out the window.

WHITE LIGHT begins to shine through... illuminating the entire cabin. She looks forward into the front section of the plane and sees that the light is streaming in from both sides... *bathing the entire cabin in an ethereal glow.*

Moments later... the low-end roar of the JET ENGINE disappears.

> MURIEL (V.O.)
> *Then... all of a sudden... the*
> *engine cut off.*

> SIMON (V.O.)
> *Did the plane start to drop into a*
> *free fall?*

> MURIEL (V.O.)
> *No. It just kept going. Smooth as*
> *could be. There was no turbulence*
> *at all.*

Muriel looks over and sees that the WOMAN next to her has fallen unconscious.

Muriel unlatches her seat belt and slides into the aisle...
looking at the faces of the passengers.

All of them are unconscious.

She moves down the aisle... her body silhouetted in the
glowing light from outside.

>   MURIEL
>   Hello?

No one responds. The plane is silent. You could hear a pin
drop.

>   MURIEL
>   *HELLO? IS ANYONE AWAKE?!!*

Muriel approaches the closed door to the COCKPIT. There are
two STEWARDESSES collapsed on the floor... unconscious.

Muriel hears a LOUD THUMPING SOUND coming from behind her.

She turns to see that it is coming from the MAIN ENTRANCE
DOOR to the plane on her left.

THUMP... THUMP...

*The sound of something very large knocking itself into the
outer hull of the jet.*

>   VOICE (O.S.)
>   *Murrrriiieeellllll...*

Muriel stares at the door... frozen with terror.

>   VOICE (O.S.)
>   *Murriieeellll... open the
>   dooorrr...*

The voice is low and menacing... like some demon.

>   MURIEL
>   Who are you?

>   VOICE (O.S.)
>   *Someone you can trusssst. Open the
>   door and you'll ssseeeee...*

Muriel reaches out to turn the LARGE METAL DOOR HANDLE. The
vacuum seal is broken and she pushes the door open... but
there is no wind or rush of air... just a calm stillness and
a blinding white light.

Muriel's body begins to float out into the light.

She notices a sea of CLOUDS billowing beneath her... when
something flies up through them into view.

It is a WINGED SERPENT WITH SEVEN HEADS. The heads swim up
and down in unison through the cloud layer... examining
her... whispering to one another in some ancient LATIN
TONGUE.

Finally... one of the CENTRAL HEADS slithers forward...
staring her in the face as she floats helplessly.

                    WINGED SERPENT
          We've brought someone to ssseeeee
          you...

The six other heads pivot back toward their tail section...
as the rest of the creature's massive girth emerges from the
clouds.

There is a beautiful YOUNG WOMAN (20s) sitting on a SILVER
PLATED SADDLE strapped to the serpent's back.

She appears to be Muriel's IDENTICAL TWIN... except she has
BLONDE HAIR... whereas Muriel's hair is DARK BROWN. The two
women stare deep into each others eyes.

                  DR. MURIEL FOX (V.O.)
          Revelation 17. The Apostle John
          writes of the appearance of a
          great whore. She rides a seven-
          headed beast.

Muriel's blonde doppelganger is wearing tiny cut-off jeans
and a PINK TANK TOP with a logo sewn onto it that reads:
KRYSTA NOW.

                  DR. MURIEL FOX (V.O.)
          She is the drunken whore who has
          committed adultery with all the
          kings of the earth.

Tears begin to well in Muriel's eyes. She notices that Krysta
has a bottle of PINK CHAMPAGNE in her right hand. She takes a
long drink from it.

                  MURIEL
        Tell me your name...

                  KRYSTA
        I'm Krysta. Krysta... Now.

> MURIEL
> You're the great whore. The whore
> that ruined my life.

> KRYSTA
> We all make decisions in our youth.
> Decisions that we must learn to
> live with.

Krysta is clearly drunk. Her speech is slurring.

> MURIEL
> I'm leaving you behind. Your past
> is coming back to haunt me.

> KRYSTA
> Judge not... lest you be judged and
> cast the first stone. Teen
> horniness is not a crime.

> MURIEL
> I've met someone. He's the one...
> the one I've been waiting for. His
> name is Cane. Jericho Cane.

> KRYSTA
> He is the pawn. You are the broker.
> And together you must bring the
> messiah to the great city that
> rules over the kings of the earth.

> MURIEL
> Los Angeles. The seven hills of the
> Southland.

> KRYSTA
> Soon to be re-built as the new
> Jerusalem.

> MURIEL
> Time is running out. The messiah is
> growing... soon he will be a man.

> KRYSTA
> When the messiah reaches
> maturity... Jericho Cane will be
> sacrificed. He will die in your
> arms... within a great Tower of
> Fire.

Muriel is transfixed by her twin... horrified at the thought
of Jericho's death.

                         MURIEL
          For the great whore will meet a
          catastrophic end as God destroys
          the city in judgement.

                         KRYSTA
          For the path to salvation will be
          drenched in the blood of those who
          have sinned.

                         KRYSTA
          And you shall be reborn in the new
          Jerusalem, where you will reign
          forever and ever.

Muriel nods her head... the wind blows through her beautiful
brown tresses. She wipes the tears from her eyes.

                         MURIEL
          Fuck yeah.

Krysta grabs the reigns as the Winged Serpent arcs down and
disappears into the clouds. Muriel waves good-bye.

INT. UNITED FLIGHT 23 -- DAY

Muriel's eyes snap open from the dream. She is back in her
window seat. The white glow is gone... and the plane cruises
along smoothly.

She begins to hear commotion in the forward part of the
cabin. PASSENGERS have started to freak out... some of them
getting up from their seats.

Muriel turns to the woman next to her. Her face is white. She
grabs a BARF BAG and hurls her lunch into it.

INT. EDWARDS AIR FORCE BASE -- WAREHOUSE -- DAY

Muriel sits on her cot across from Simon. He continues to
take notes as she tells her story from the flight.

                         MURIEL
          And then they all started to freak
          out.

                         SIMON
          Except for you.

                    MURIEL
          That's right. I remember
          everything.

INT. EDWARDS AIR FORCE BASE -- LABORATORY -- LATER ON

Muriel now sits at a LABORATORY TABLE wearing a HOSPITAL
GOWN. She has ELECTRODES attached to her forehead and arms.
Wires run to a device that resembles a POLYGRAPH MACHINE.

Simon sits across from her. He is joined by another US ARMY
GENERAL named TEENA MACARTHUR (40). *She is
uncharacteristically glamorous for an army general.*

Simon withdraws a 14-SIDED DIE used in DUNGEONS AND DRAGONS.
He rolls the die and it lands with the highest number facing
up: 14.

                    SIMON
          I am going to write out fourteen
          letters on fourteen separate note-
          cards.

Simon grabs a BLACK MARKER and begins to write out a series
of LETTERS on each card:

          E A T R M A U R V E I N F K

                    SIMON
          I'm going to hold up the cards with
          the letters facing me... and I want
          you to tell me which one you think
          I'm holding up.

He then begins to hold up the cards individually. The first
one is R.

                    MURIEL
          R.

Simon checks it off. He then holds up a second card that
reads V.

                    MURIEL
          V.

Simon checks it off. He continues through each letter... and
Muriel guesses each one correctly.

                         TEENA
               Very impressive. Do you know what
               an anagram is?

                         MURIEL
               Of course.

                         TEENA
               Can you re-arrange these letters in
               your head and give me an anagram
               for them?

Muriel thinks for a moment.

                         MURIEL
               Freak... man... virtue.

Simon writes the words out.

               F R E A K   M A N   V I R T U E

The CAMERA moves in slowly toward Muriel's face.

                         MURIEL
               Martin Kefauver.

Simon writes out the name.

               M A R T I N   K E F A U V E R

Teena grabs a phone from the desk and dials a number.

                         TEENA
               Can you run a search on a Martin
               Kefauver please?

She hangs up the phone and turns back to Muriel.

                         TEENA
               Ms. Fox... we're going to need to
               run some more tests. You'll have to
               remain in quarantine for several
               more days.

INT. EDWARDS AIR FORCE BASE -- LABORATORY -- DAY

Simon and Teena watch Muriel sleep from a closed-circuit surveillance camera in the lab. She appears on a monitor.

>   TEENA
>   There's a Martin Kefauver in
>   Beverly Hills. He attends USC...
>   lives with his parents. He was on
>   the Lake Mead houseboat with the
>   kid who got shot trying to cross
>   the border on the jet ski.
>
>   SIMON
>   The signs are emerging.
>
>   TEENA
>   Dr. Kuntzler has an idea. She would
>   like to place Ms. Fox under
>   hypnosis.
>
>   SIMON
>   What for?

Teena hands Simon a copy of *The New Testament*.

>   TEENA
>   Revelation. She wants to try and
>   decode it.

Simon sighs out loud.

>   SIMON
>   Heavens to Betsy. This is getting
>   complicated.

INT. EDWARDS AIR FORCE BASE -- HOSPITAL ROOM -- DAY

Muriel is asleep in a hospital bed.

>   DR. MURIEL FOX (V.O.)
>   *Heavens to Betsy indeed. I could*
>   *hear their entire conversation...*
>   *word for word.*
>   (beat)
>   *Days turned into weeks.*

The CAMERA drifts closer to her petite frame... curled up under the hospital sheets.

INT. MCDONALD'S -- BOOTH -- DAY

Muriel stares deep into Shawna's eyes... having recounted the whole story to her. Muriel then glances around the restaurant... studying the faces of the various patrons...

>   MURIEL
>   This restaurant... is a point of
>   convergence. Something
>   extraordinary is about to happen.

ACROSS THE RESTAURANT... Jericho and MacPherson are seated at a table with baby Caleb. There is a huge pile of BURGERS and FRIES stacked in front of him.

Caleb is shoving a QUARTER POUNDER down his throat.

>   JERICHO
>   What the hell are we doing here at
>   McDonald's, MacPherson?

>   MACPHERSON
>   I don't know... but pass me a
>   McNapkin.

Jericho passes him a napkin. Caleb inhales another cheeseburger.

>   JERICHO
>   I think I'm gonna McVomit. That's
>   his tenth cheeseburger. Where does
>   it go?

>   MACPHERSON
>   Kid must have some kind of super
>   liver. Goddamn I'd kill for one of
>   those.

Jericho tries to get the child's attention.

>   JERICHO
>   Caleb... do you understand what I'm
>   saying right now?

Caleb swallows his mouthful of food.

>   CALEB
>   Yes.

>   JERICHO
>   How did you learn to talk so
>   quickly?

                         CALEB
               Listening to you.

                         JERICHO
               Do you understand... who you are?
               Do you know why you have these
               special powers?

                         CALEB
               No.

Caleb rips open a BIG MAC and shoves it in his mouth.

ACROSS THE RESTAURANT... Muriel's eyes widen. *She senses
something.*

                         SHAWNA
               What is it?

                         MURIEL
               Someone is coming.

                         SHAWNA
               Who?

Muriel rubs the pink crystal against her palm.

                         MURIEL
               He drives a black Hummer.

EXT. MCDONALD'S -- PARKING LOT -- MOMENTS LATER

A BLACK HUMMER pulls into the parking lot. HIP-HOP MUSIC
blasts from inside. The engine shuts off.

The Hummer door opens and a teenager named MARTIN KEFAUVER
(19) steps out. He wears baggy jeans and an oversize white t-
shirt and SILVER BLING DOG TAGS... CELL PHONE placed against
his ear.

                         KEFAUVER
               Yo dawg... I just pulled over to
               get some chow.

Kefauver moves toward the entrance to the restaurant.

INT. MCDONALD'S -- BOOTH -- NEXT

Muriel watches Kefauver enter the restaurant and approach the
counter. He begins to place his order.

                        MURIEL
          Him.
                    (points in his direction)
          That kid... he's the one. He is the
          one that will pull the trigger.

Shawna stares Kefauver down. He wears a TIGHT BLACK NYLON
SKULL CAP over his head.

                        MURIEL
          He is the executioner.

Kefauver takes his tray of FOOD and walks over to a table
next to where Jericho and MacPherson are sitting.

Caleb begins to stare at Kefauver as he shoves french fries
in his mouth. Caleb then burps out loud... turning heads
throughout the eatery.

                        KEFAUVER
          Yo dawg... your baby has got some
          skank breath! Get that kid some
          breath mints, dawg! That shit is
          nasty!

                        MACPHERSON
          Take your jive to somewhere else,
          Poindexter. Some people are trying
          to eat here.

                        KEFAUVER
          You need to take that baby to a
          hospital, dawg!

Muriel approaches their dining area... transfixed.

                        MURIEL
          What is your name?

                        KEFAUVER
          Beg pardon?

                        MURIEL
          Tell me your name.

                        KEFAUVER
          Kefauver. Martin Kefauver.

Caleb's eyes widen when he hears this name.

                        CALEB
          Mar-tin Ke-fau-ver.

Caleb then lets out a fierce hissing sound... as a cloud of WHITE SMOKE erupts from his mouth.

Kefauver begins to cough as the smoke engulfs him. Diners in the surrounding booths begin to notice this... as the restaurant quickly fills with NOXIOUS WHITE GAS.

>   MACPHERSON
>   Christ almighty!

A FAT WOMAN seated at an adjacent table VOMITS all over the floor. Other patrons begin to follow suit.

Kefauver seems paralyzed by the smoke... his eyes do not blink.

EXT. MCDONALD'S -- PARKING LOT -- NEXT

The BLACK SUBURBANS pull into the parking lot. The tinted windows roll down and the MASKED MEN emerge with their AK-47's once again... aiming toward the restaurant.

The earth begins to shake...

INT. MCDONALD'S -- NEXT

The restaurant begins to tremble from the earthquake.

>   MURIEL
>   HIT THE FLOOR!

Jericho and MacPherson dive to the floor.

The front windows SHATTER as gunfire begins to rip through the restaurant. *Shawna McBride takes a bullet to the chest... falling to the floor.*

Other PATRONS are hit by stray bullets... BLOOD sprays through the smoke across table tops and onto the white tile floor.

Baby Caleb walks toward the front of the restaurant... oblivious to the torrent of bullets that tear through the smoke.

He opens his RIGHT PALM and a FIREBALL begins to form several inches above it. *He then launches the fireball out the window...*

EXT. MCDONALD'S -- PARKING LOT -- NEXT

The FIREBALL streaks across the parking lot and hits one of
the black suburbans... detonating a huge EXPLOSION.

Seconds later... another FIREBALL is launched and engulfs the
second truck... exploding it in a MAELSTROM OF FIRE.

INT. MCDONALD'S -- BOOTH -- MOMENTS LATER

Caleb turns back toward the inside of the restaurant. *His
mouth contorts into the demented grin of a toddler.*

The earthquake continues to rock the foundation upon which
the restaurant is built.

Within moments... the entire BUILDING appears to detach from
the concrete foundation.

EXT. MCDONALD'S -- PARKING LOT -- NEXT

The entire restaurant RIPS APART FROM THE CEMENT and begins
to levitate up into the air.

As the suburbans continue to burn in the parking lot... the
restaurant rises even higher up into the sky... rotating
slowly in a clock-wise direction.

INT. MCDONALD'S -- NEXT

Muriel crawls across the floor toward Shawna. Blood gushes
from her stomach and mouth.

                    MURIEL
          Shawna!

                    SHAWNA
          Muriel...

Muriel takes her hand. Life drains from her eyes as she joins
her twin sister in the hereafter.

*Muriel turns and locks eyes with Jericho as the restaurant
continues its ascent into the desert sky.*

His eyes drift closed... as he falls unconscious.

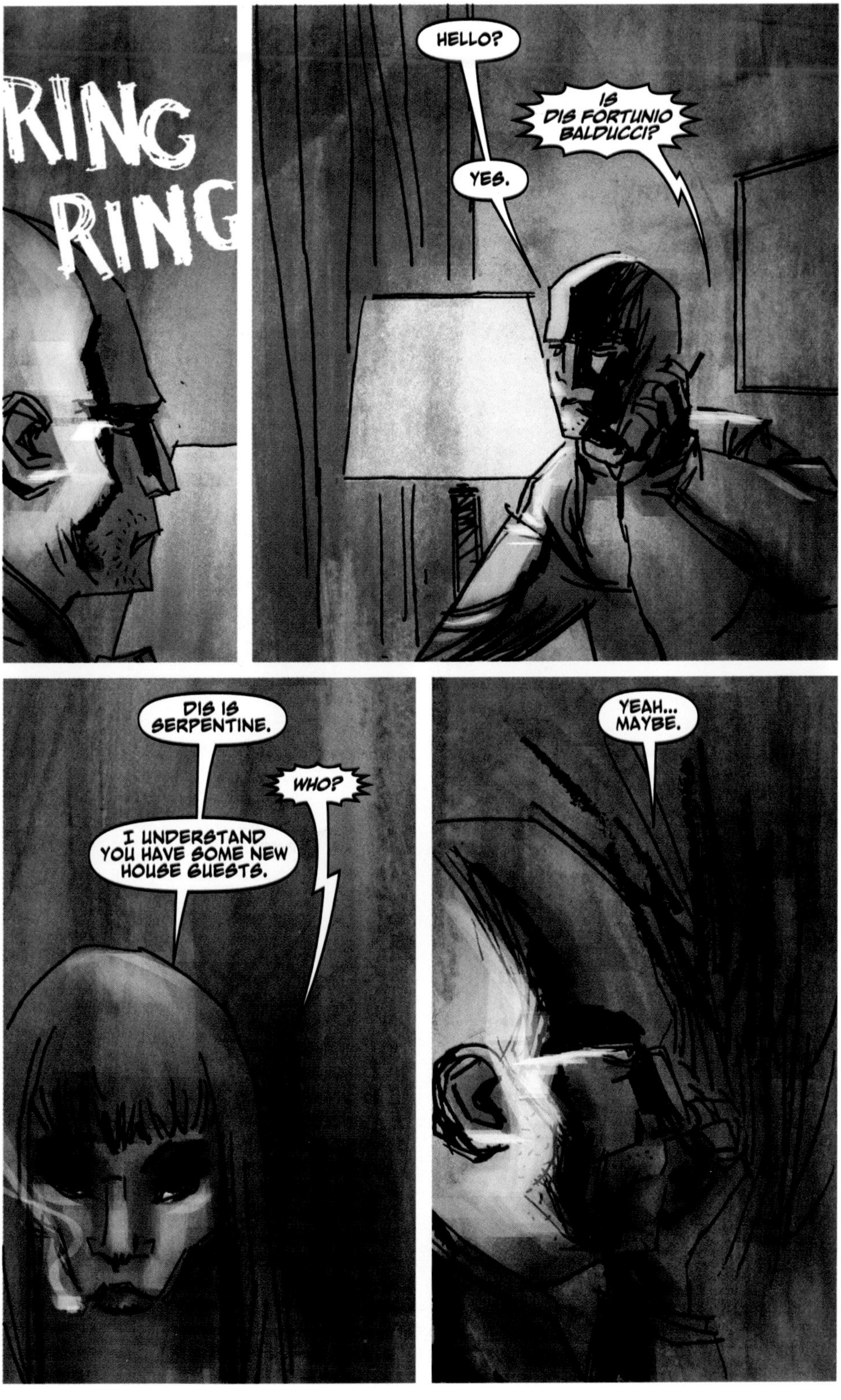
RING
RING
HELLO?
IS DIS FORTUNIO BALDUCCI?
YES.
DIS IS SERPENTINE.
WHO?
I UNDERSTAND YOU HAVE SOME NEW HOUSE GUESTS.
YEAH... MAYBE.

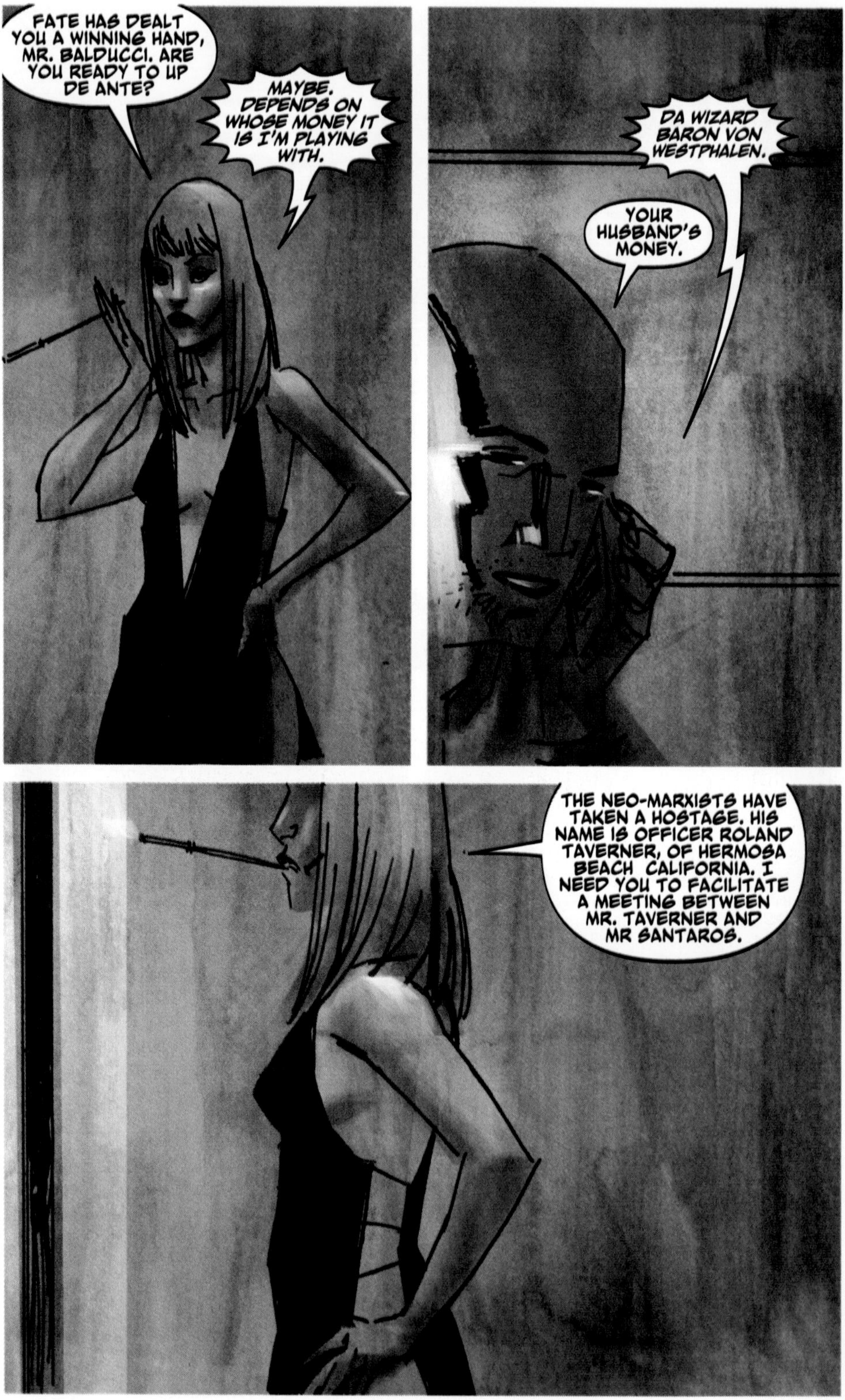
FATE HAS DEALT YOU A WINNING HAND, MR. BALDUCCI. ARE YOU READY TO UP DE ANTE?
MAYBE. DEPENDS ON WHOSE MONEY IT IS I'M PLAYING WITH.
YOUR HUSBAND'S MONEY.
DA WIZARD BARON VON WESTPHALEN.
THE NEO-MARXISTS HAVE TAKEN A HOSTAGE. HIS NAME IS OFFICER ROLAND TAVERNER, OF HERMOSA BEACH CALIFORNIA. I NEED YOU TO FACILITATE A MEETING BETWEEN MR. TAVERNER AND MR SANTAROS.

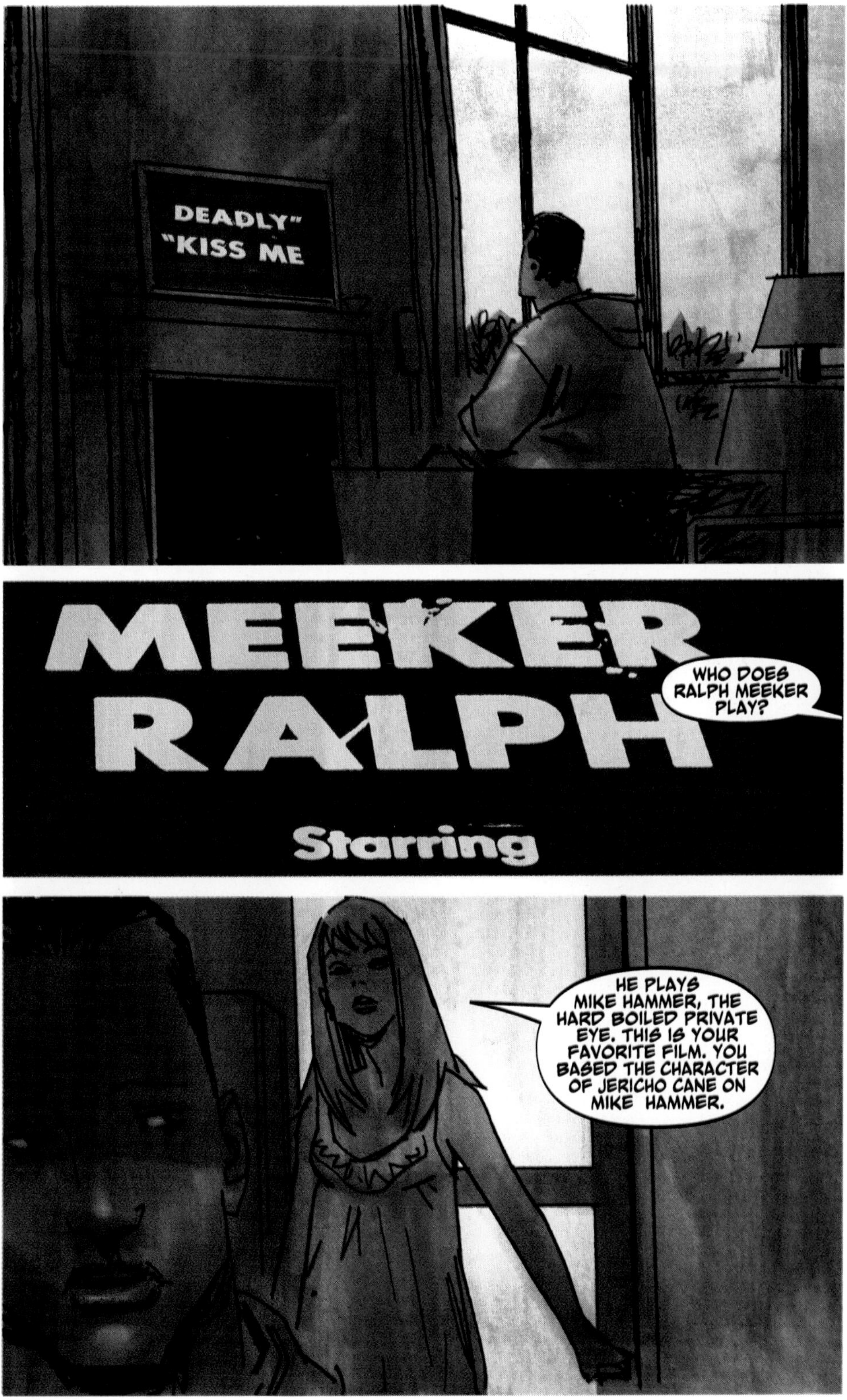
DEADLY"
"KISS ME
MEEKER
RALPH
Starring
WHO DOES RALPH MEEKER PLAY?
HE PLAYS MIKE HAMMER, THE HARD BOILED PRIVATE EYE. THIS IS YOUR FAVORITE FILM. YOU BASED THE CHARACTER OF JERICHO CANE ON MIKE HAMMER.

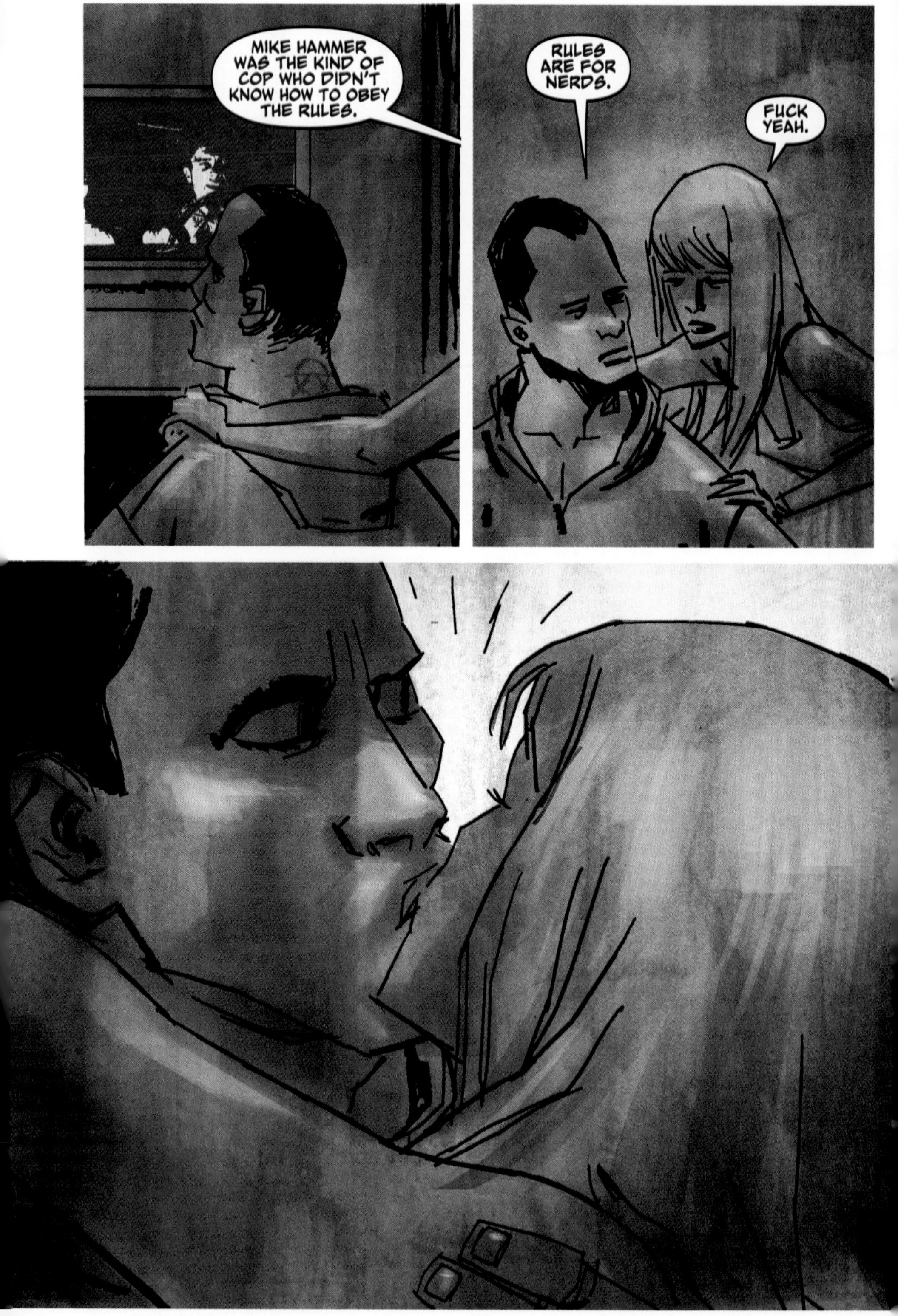
MIKE HAMMER WAS THE KIND OF COP WHO DIDN'T KNOW HOW TO OBEY THE RULES.
RULES ARE FOR NERDS.
FUCK YEAH.

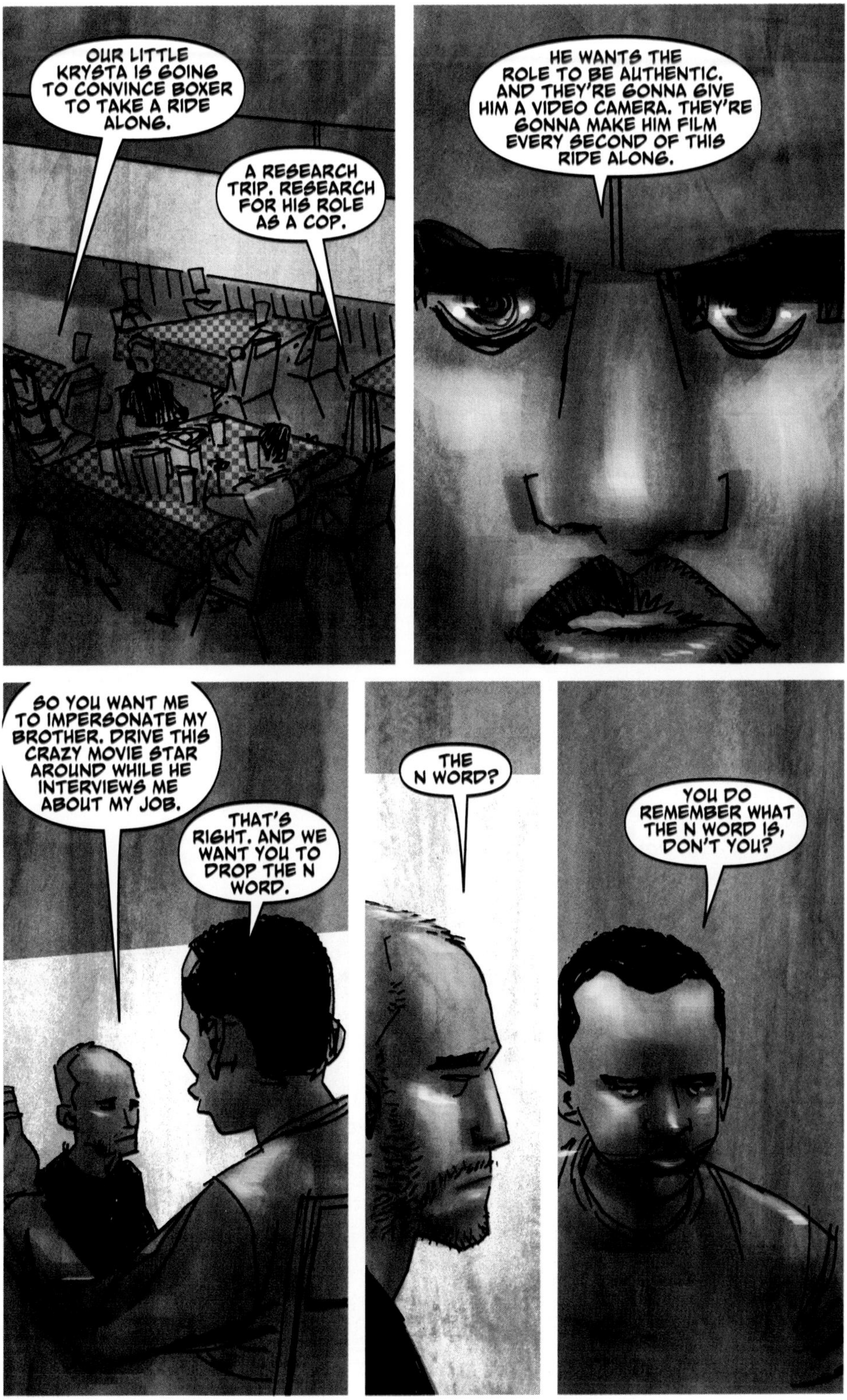
OUR LITTLE KRYSTA IS GOING TO CONVINCE BOXER TO TAKE A RIDE ALONG.
A RESEARCH TRIP. RESEARCH FOR HIS ROLE AS A COP.
HE WANTS THE ROLE TO BE AUTHENTIC. AND THEY'RE GONNA GIVE HIM A VIDEO CAMERA. THEY'RE GONNA MAKE HIM FILM EVERY SECOND OF THIS RIDE ALONG.
SO YOU WANT ME TO IMPERSONATE MY BROTHER. DRIVE THIS CRAZY MOVIE STAR AROUND WHILE HE INTERVIEWS ME ABOUT MY JOB.
THAT'S RIGHT. AND WE WANT YOU TO DROP THE N WORD.
THE N WORD?
YOU DO REMEMBER WHAT THE N WORD IS, DON'T YOU?

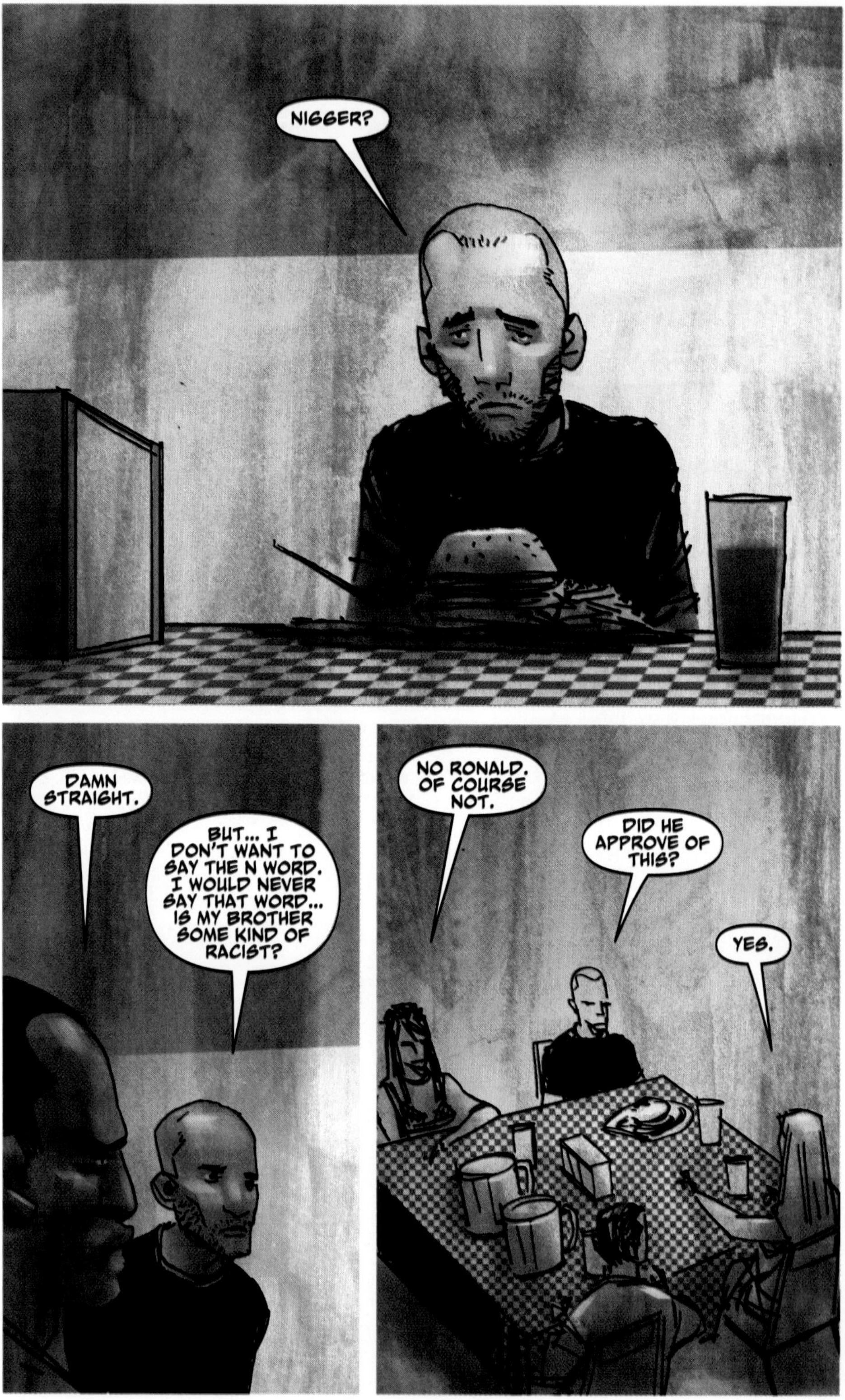
NIGGER?
DAMN STRAIGHT.
BUT... I DON'T WANT TO SAY THE N WORD. I WOULD NEVER SAY THAT WORD... IS MY BROTHER SOME KIND OF RACIST?
NO RONALD. OF COURSE NOT.
DID HE APPROVE OF THIS?
YES.

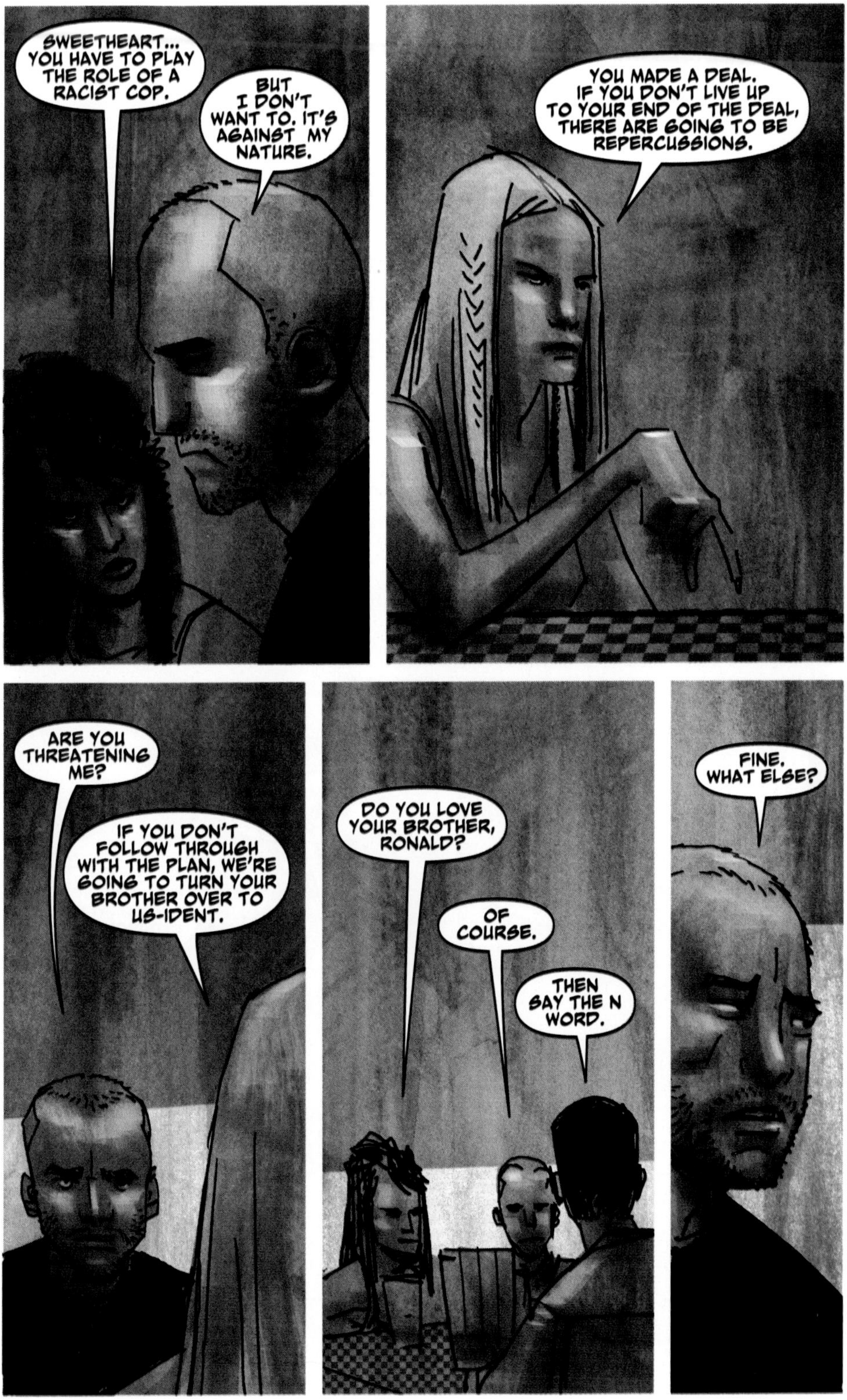
SWEETHEART... YOU HAVE TO PLAY THE ROLE OF A RACIST COP.
BUT I DON'T WANT TO. IT'S AGAINST MY NATURE.
YOU MADE A DEAL. IF YOU DON'T LIVE UP TO YOUR END OF THE DEAL, THERE ARE GOING TO BE REPERCUSSIONS.
ARE YOU THREATENING ME?
IF YOU DON'T FOLLOW THROUGH WITH THE PLAN, WE'RE GOING TO TURN YOUR BROTHER OVER TO US-IDENT.
DO YOU LOVE YOUR BROTHER, RONALD?
OF COURSE.
THEN SAY THE N WORD.
FINE. WHAT ELSE?

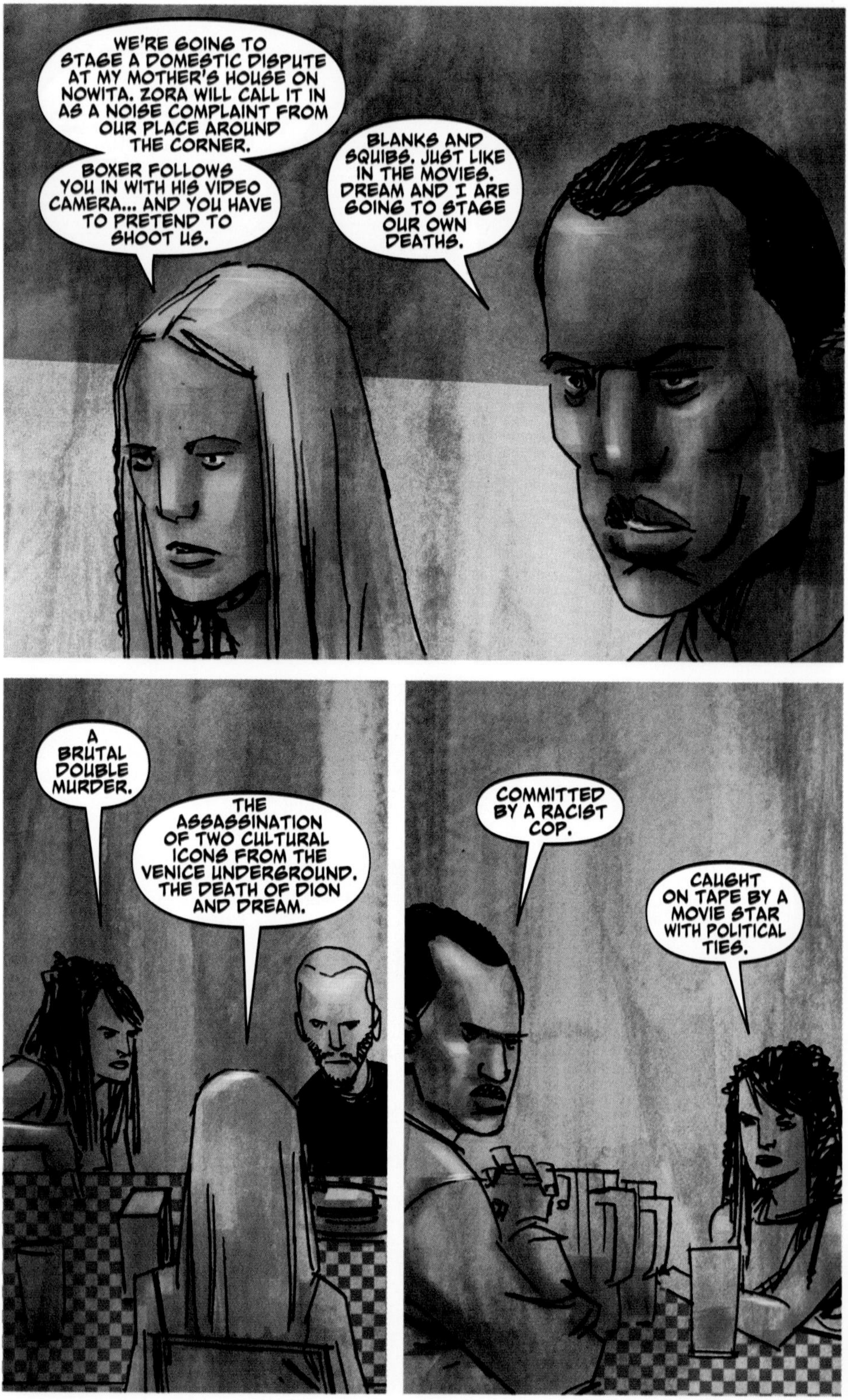
WE'RE GOING TO STAGE A DOMESTIC DISPUTE AT MY MOTHER'S HOUSE ON NOWITA. ZORA WILL CALL IT IN AS A NOISE COMPLAINT FROM OUR PLACE AROUND THE CORNER.
BOXER FOLLOWS YOU IN WITH HIS VIDEO CAMERA... AND YOU HAVE TO PRETEND TO SHOOT US.
BLANKS AND SQUIBS. JUST LIKE IN THE MOVIES. DREAM AND I ARE GOING TO STAGE OUR OWN DEATHS.
A BRUTAL DOUBLE MURDER.
THE ASSASSINATION OF TWO CULTURAL ICONS FROM THE VENICE UNDERGROUND. THE DEATH OF DION AND DREAM.
COMMITTED BY A RACIST COP.
CAUGHT ON TAPE BY A MOVIE STAR WITH POLITICAL TIES.

TIES TO THE GREAT SENATOR FROM TEXAS AND THE FASCIST QUEEN OF US-IDENT... NANA MAE FROST.

JESUS CHRIST. THIS IS INSANE.

WE LIVE IN AN INSANE WORLD, RONALD.

SOMETIMES THE ONLY WAY TO DEAL WITH INSANITY... IS TO GIVE IT A DOSE OF ITS OWN MEDICINE.

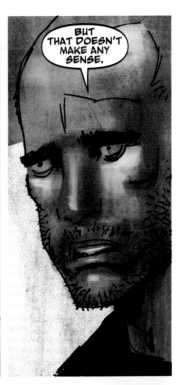

BUT THAT DOESN'T MAKE ANY SENSE.

NEITHER DOES THIS WORLD. REVOLUTIONS ARE THE LOCOMOTIVES OF HISTORY. BREATHE... TRANSFORM... DREAM.

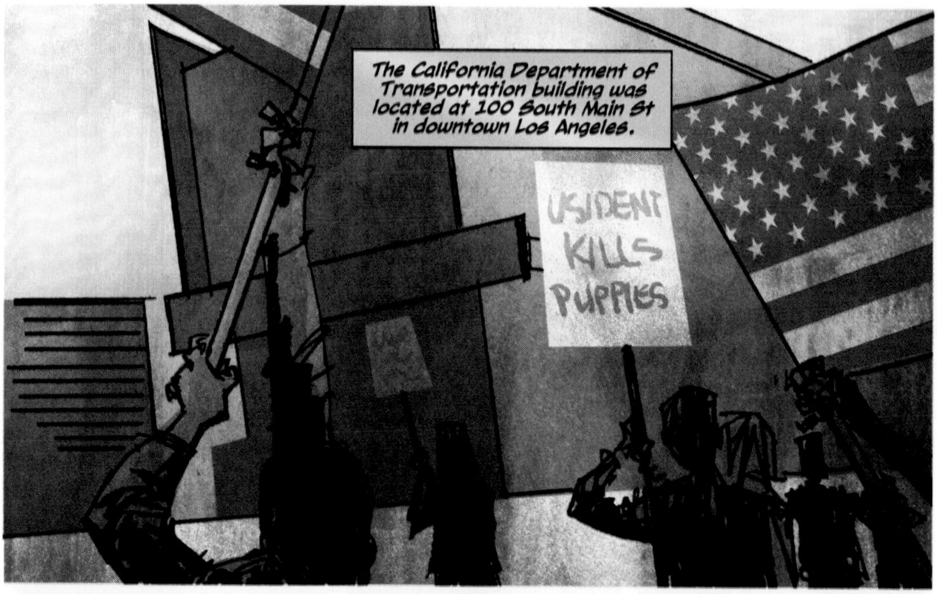
The California Department of Transportation building was located at 100 South Main St in downtown Los Angeles.
USIDENT KILLS PUPPIES

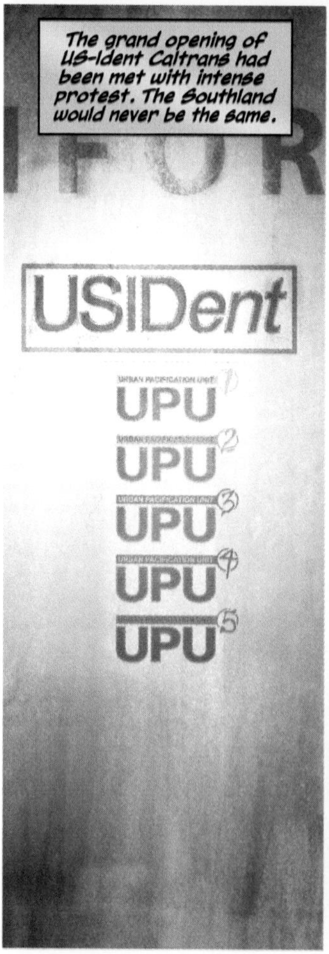
The grand opening of US-Ident Caltrans had been met with intense protest. The Southland would never be the same.
USIDent
UPU
UPU
UPU
UPU
UPU

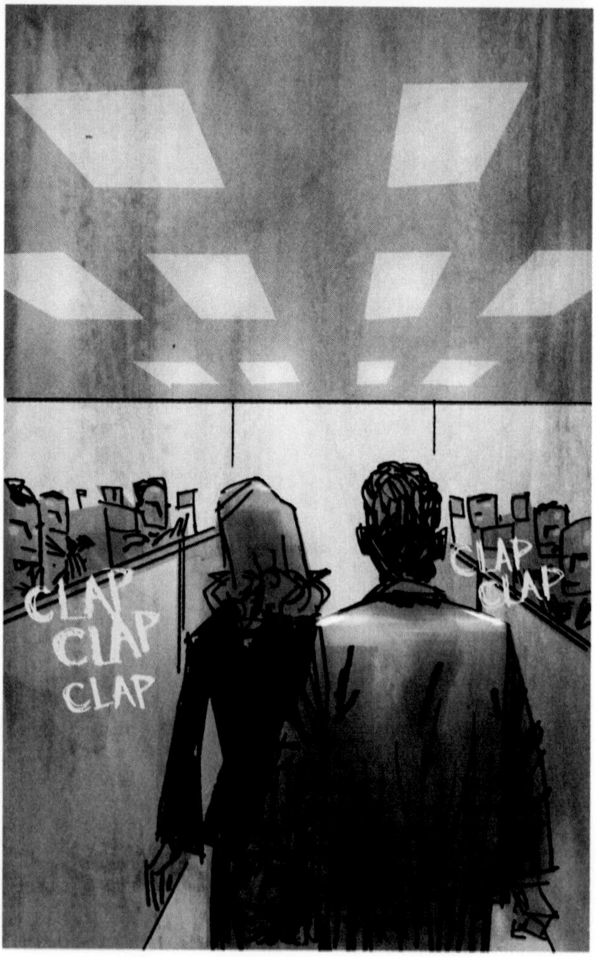
CLAP CLAP CLAP
CLAP CLAP

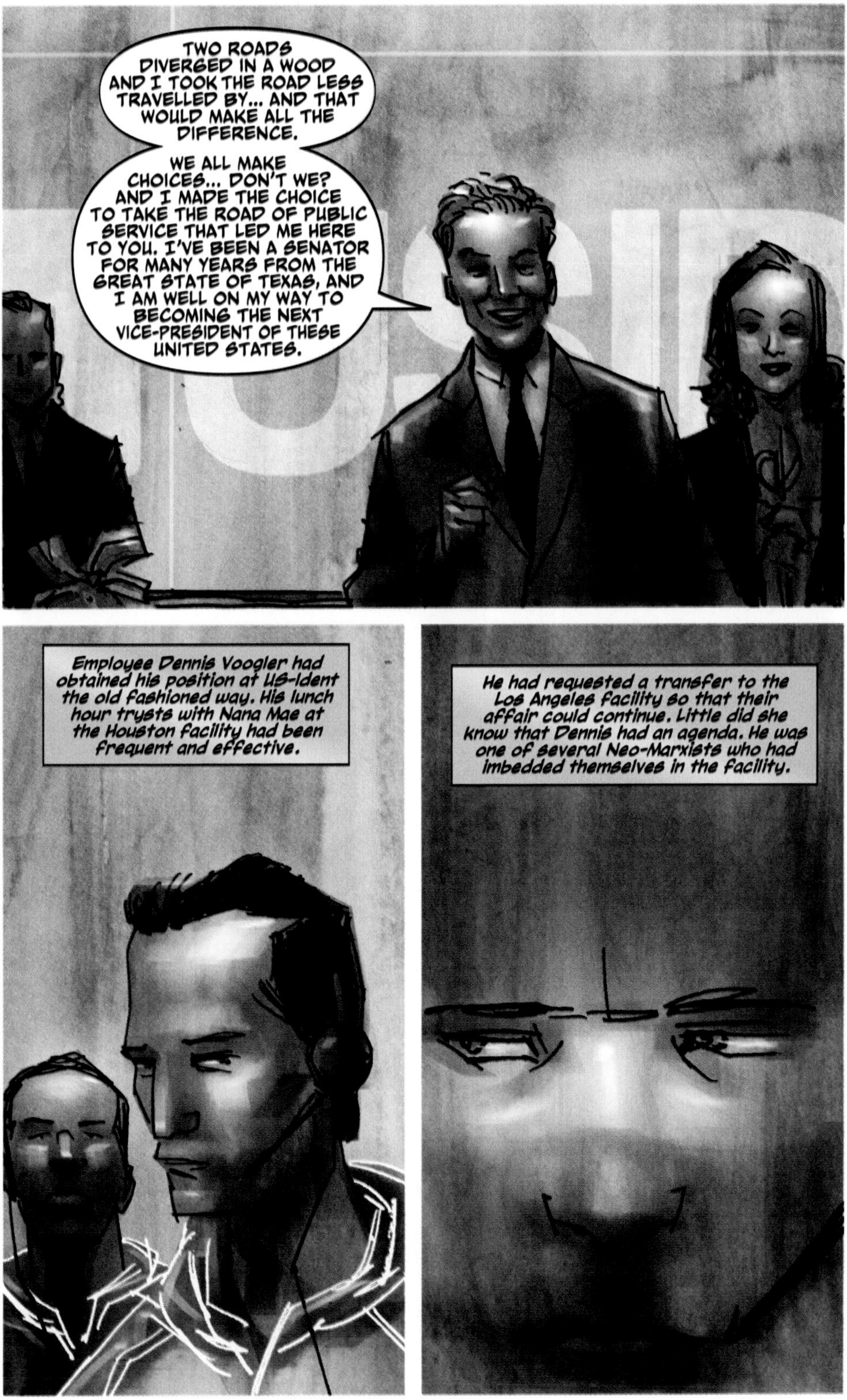
TWO ROADS DIVERGED IN A WOOD AND I TOOK THE ROAD LESS TRAVELLED BY... AND THAT WOULD MAKE ALL THE DIFFERENCE.
WE ALL MAKE CHOICES... DON'T WE? AND I MADE THE CHOICE TO TAKE THE ROAD OF PUBLIC SERVICE THAT LED ME HERE TO YOU. I'VE BEEN A SENATOR FOR MANY YEARS FROM THE GREAT STATE OF TEXAS, AND I AM WELL ON MY WAY TO BECOMING THE NEXT VICE-PRESIDENT OF THESE UNITED STATES.
Employee Dennis Voogler had obtained his position at US-Ident the old fashioned way. His lunch hour trysts with Nana Mae at the Houston facility had been frequent and effective.
He had requested a transfer to the Los Angeles facility so that their affair could continue. Little did she know that Dennis had an agenda. He was one of several Neo-Marxists who had imbedded themselves in the facility.

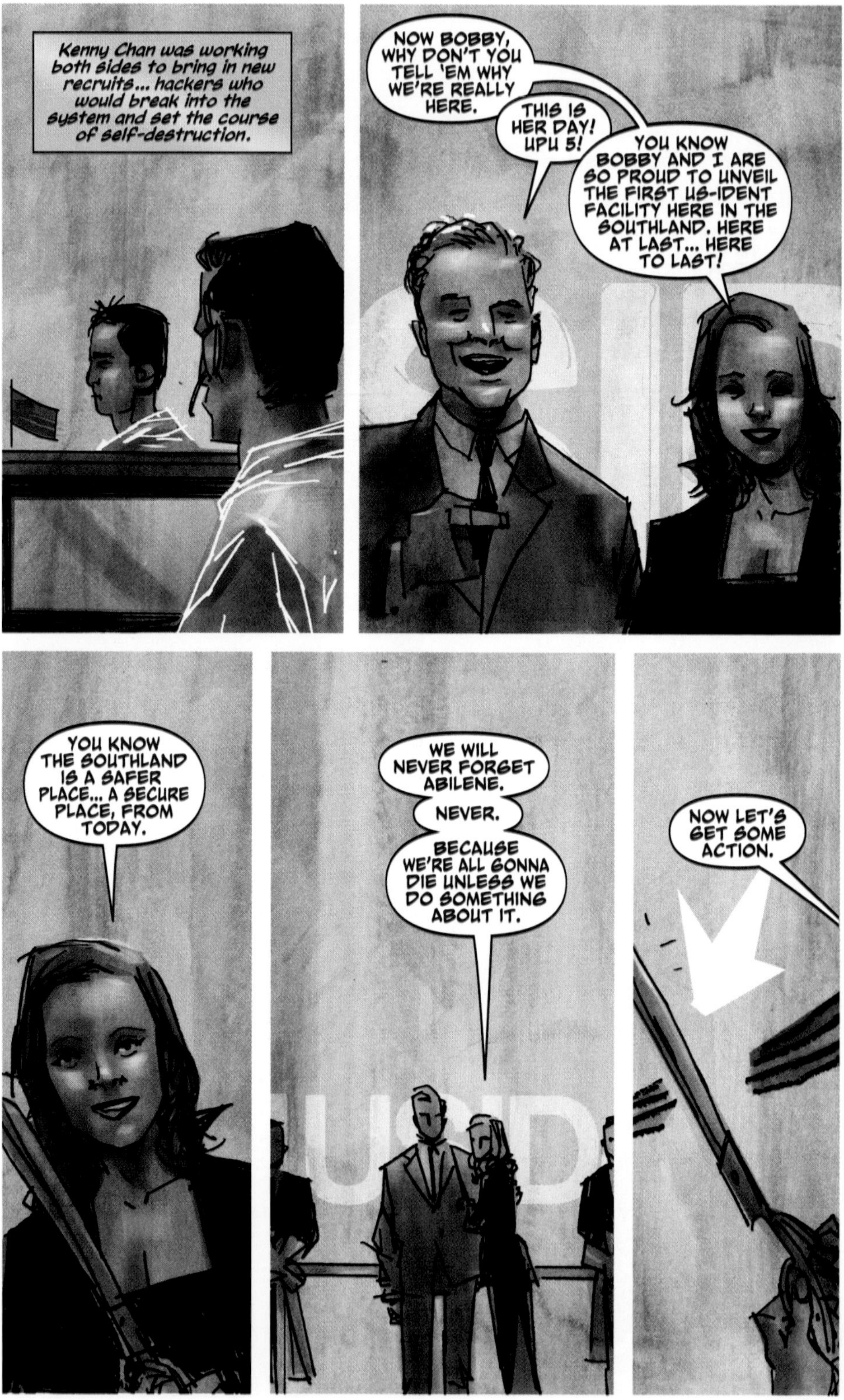
Kenny Chan was working both sides to bring in new recruits... hackers who would break into the system and set the course of self-destruction.
NOW BOBBY, WHY DON'T YOU TELL 'EM WHY WE'RE REALLY HERE.
THIS IS HER DAY! UPU 5!
YOU KNOW BOBBY AND I ARE SO PROUD TO UNVEIL THE FIRST US-IDENT FACILITY HERE IN THE SOUTHLAND. HERE AT LAST... HERE TO LAST!
YOU KNOW THE SOUTHLAND IS A SAFER PLACE... A SECURE PLACE, FROM TODAY.
WE WILL NEVER FORGET ABILENE.
NEVER.
BECAUSE WE'RE ALL GONNA DIE UNLESS WE DO SOMETHING ABOUT IT.
NOW LET'S GET SOME ACTION.

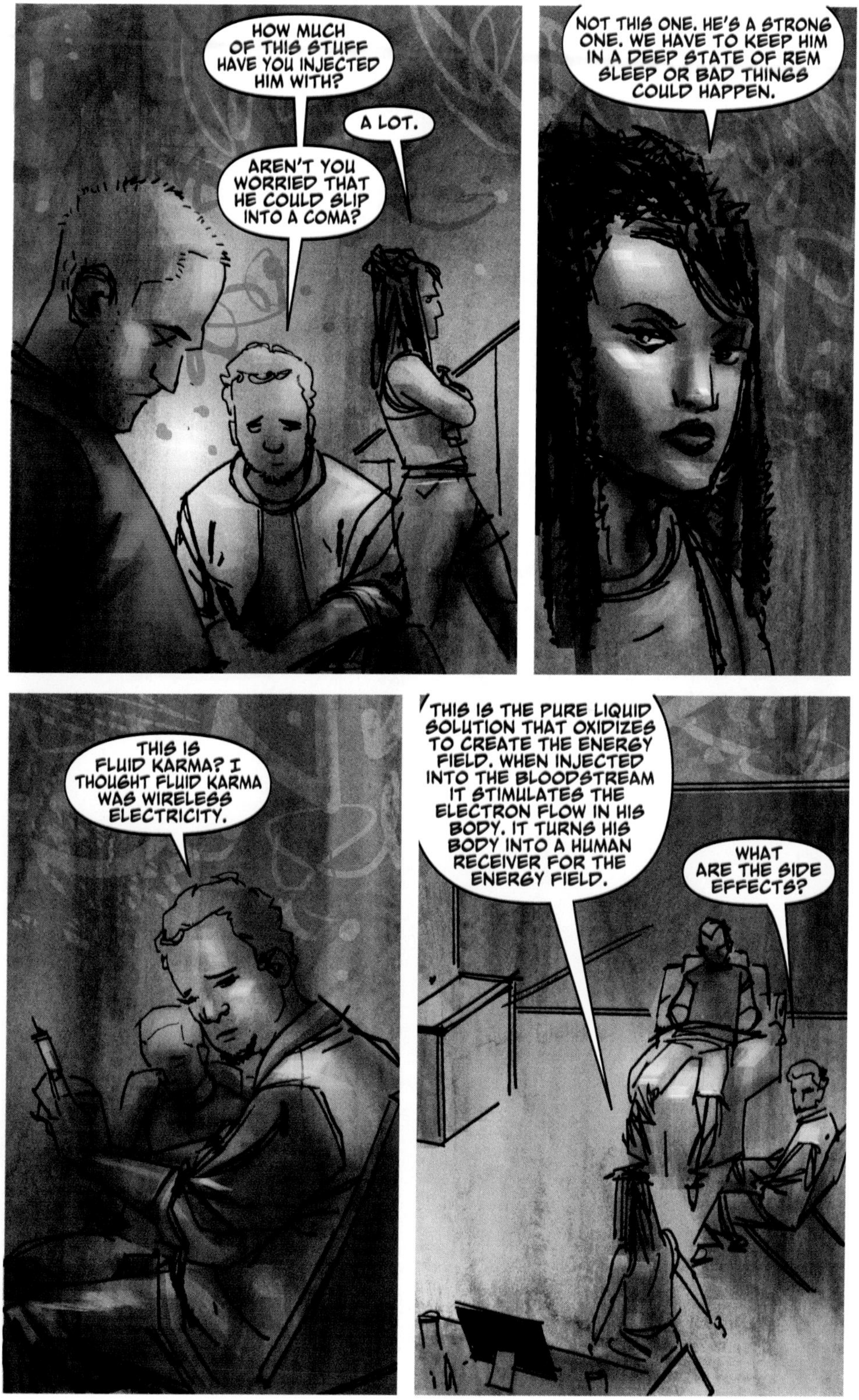
HOW MUCH OF THIS STUFF HAVE YOU INJECTED HIM WITH?
A LOT.
AREN'T YOU WORRIED THAT HE COULD SLIP INTO A COMA?
NOT THIS ONE. HE'S A STRONG ONE. WE HAVE TO KEEP HIM IN A DEEP STATE OF REM SLEEP OR BAD THINGS COULD HAPPEN.
THIS IS FLUID KARMA? I THOUGHT FLUID KARMA WAS WIRELESS ELECTRICITY.
THIS IS THE PURE LIQUID SOLUTION THAT OXIDIZES TO CREATE THE ENERGY FIELD. WHEN INJECTED INTO THE BLOODSTREAM IT STIMULATES THE ELECTRON FLOW IN HIS BODY. IT TURNS HIS BODY INTO A HUMAN RECEIVER FOR THE ENERGY FIELD.
WHAT ARE THE SIDE EFFECTS?

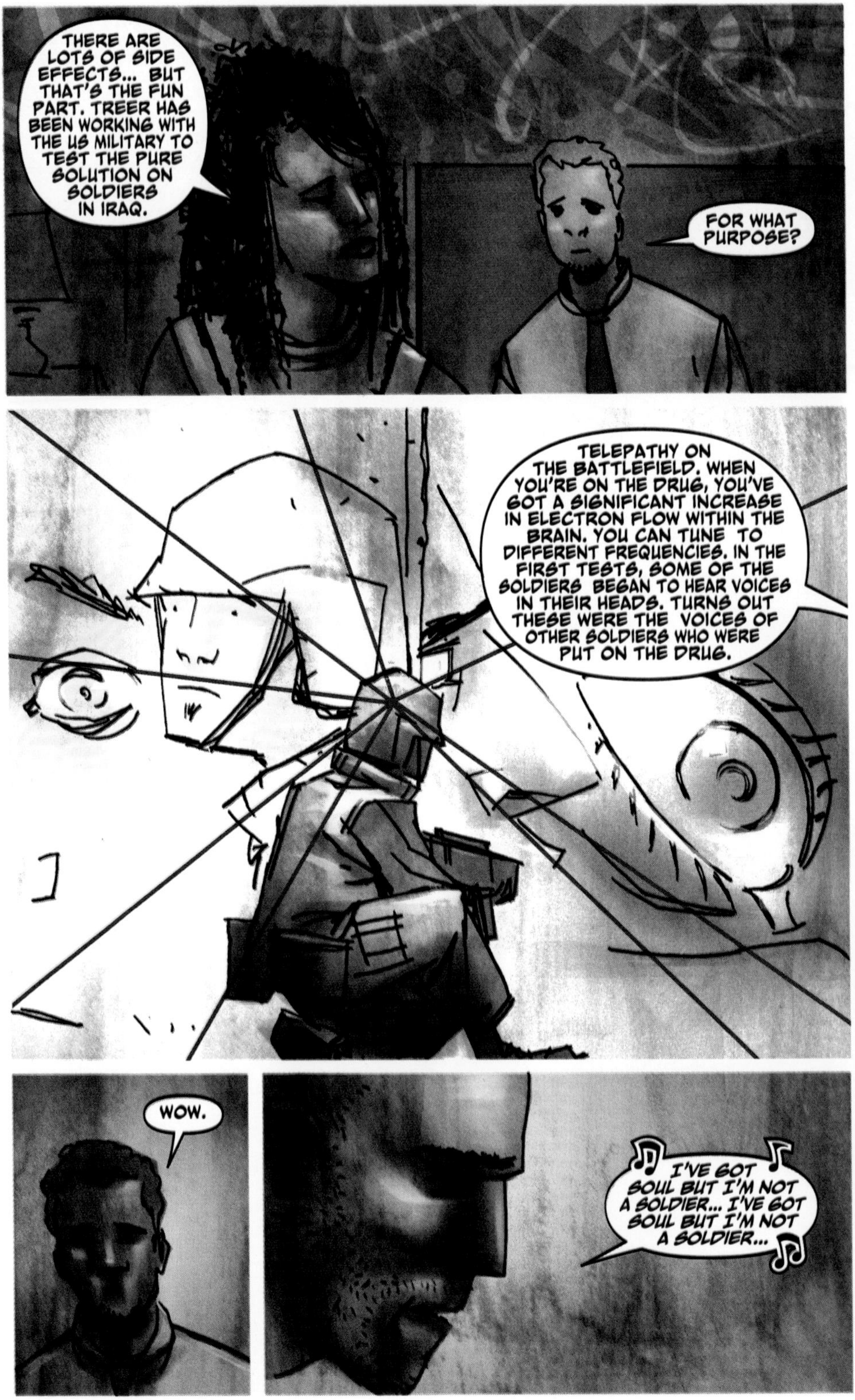
THERE ARE LOTS OF SIDE EFFECTS... BUT THAT'S THE FUN PART. TREER HAS BEEN WORKING WITH THE US MILITARY TO TEST THE PURE SOLUTION ON SOLDIERS IN IRAQ.
FOR WHAT PURPOSE?
TELEPATHY ON THE BATTLEFIELD. WHEN YOU'RE ON THE DRUG, YOU'VE GOT A SIGNIFICANT INCREASE IN ELECTRON FLOW WITHIN THE BRAIN. YOU CAN TUNE TO DIFFERENT FREQUENCIES. IN THE FIRST TESTS, SOME OF THE SOLDIERS BEGAN TO HEAR VOICES IN THEIR HEADS. TURNS OUT THESE WERE THE VOICES OF OTHER SOLDIERS WHO WERE PUT ON THE DRUG.
WOW.
I'VE GOT SOUL BUT I'M NOT A SOLDIER... I'VE GOT SOUL BUT I'M NOT A SOLDIER...

IS HE SINGING?
TIME FOR ANOTHER INJECTION...
OVER AND OUT... LAST CALL FOR SIN... WHILE EVERYONE'S LOST, THE BATTLE IS WON... WITH ALL THESE THINGS THAT I'VE DONE.
ALL THESE THINGS THAT I'VE DONE... IF YOU CAN HOLD ON... IF YOU CAN HOLD ON...

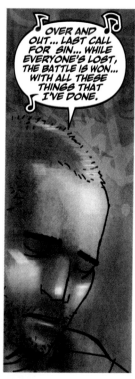

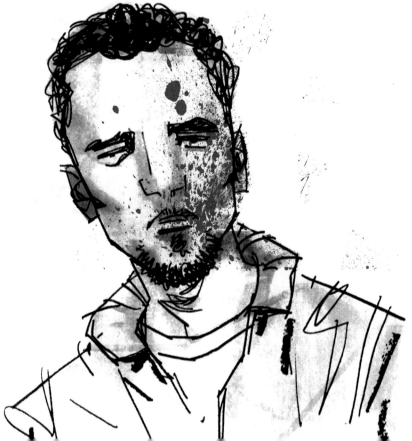

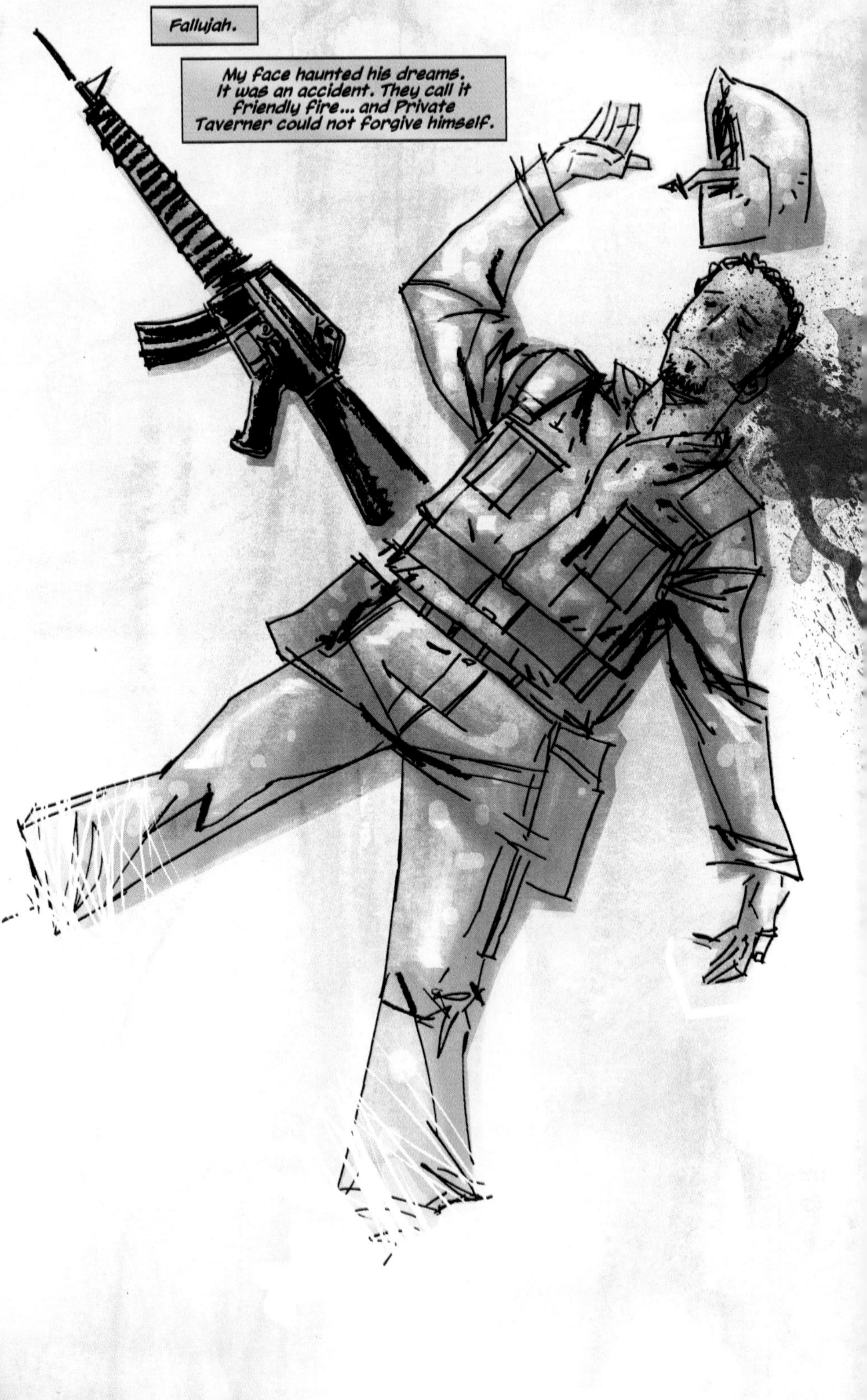
Fallujah.
My face haunted his dreams. It was an accident. They call it friendly fire... and Private Taverner could not forgive himself.

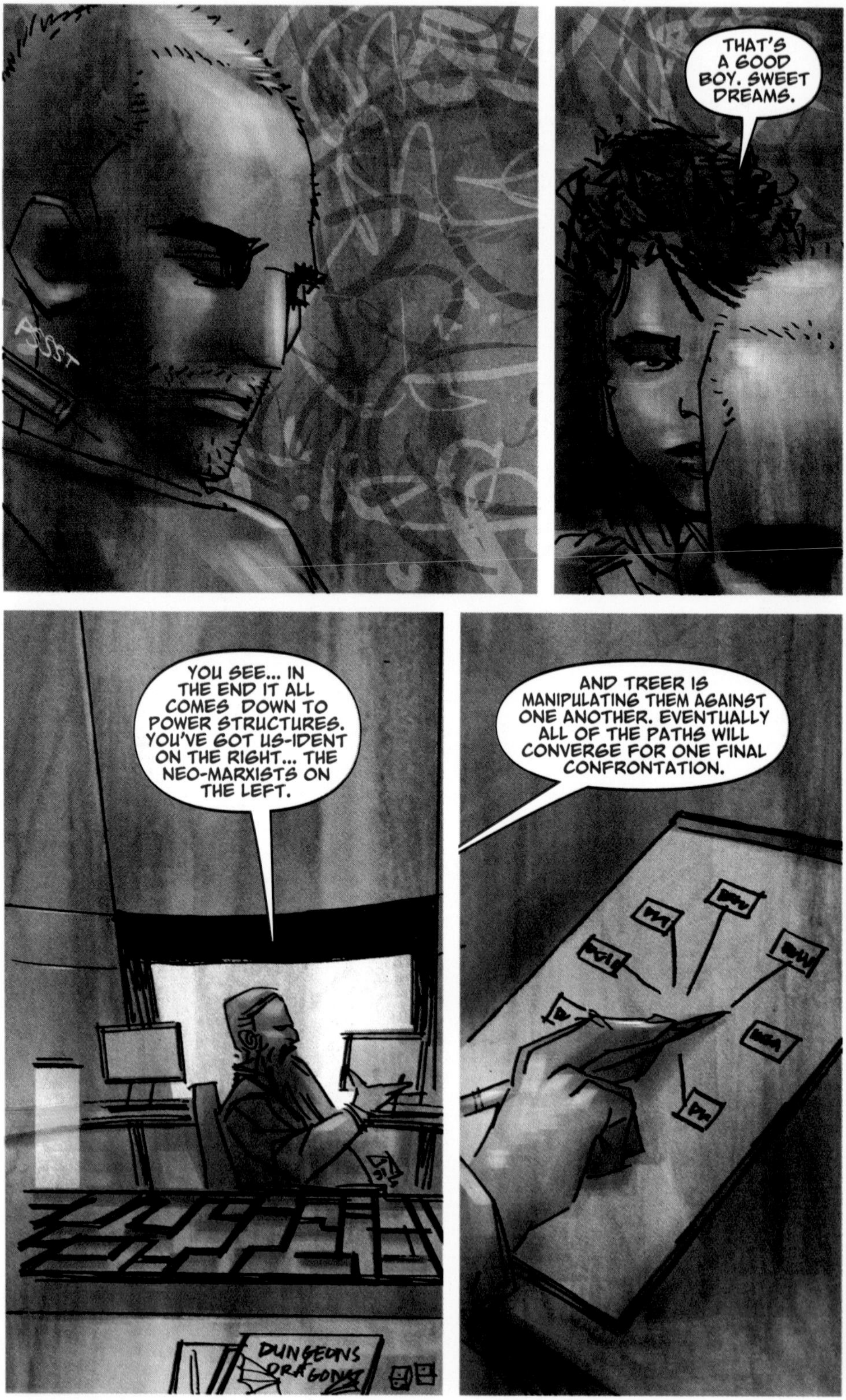
PSSST
THAT'S A GOOD BOY. SWEET DREAMS.
YOU SEE... IN THE END IT ALL COMES DOWN TO POWER STRUCTURES. YOU'VE GOT US-IDENT ON THE RIGHT... THE NEO-MARXISTS ON THE LEFT.
AND TREER IS MANIPULATING THEM AGAINST ONE ANOTHER. EVENTUALLY ALL OF THE PATHS WILL CONVERGE FOR ONE FINAL CONFRONTATION.
DUNGEONS DRAGONS

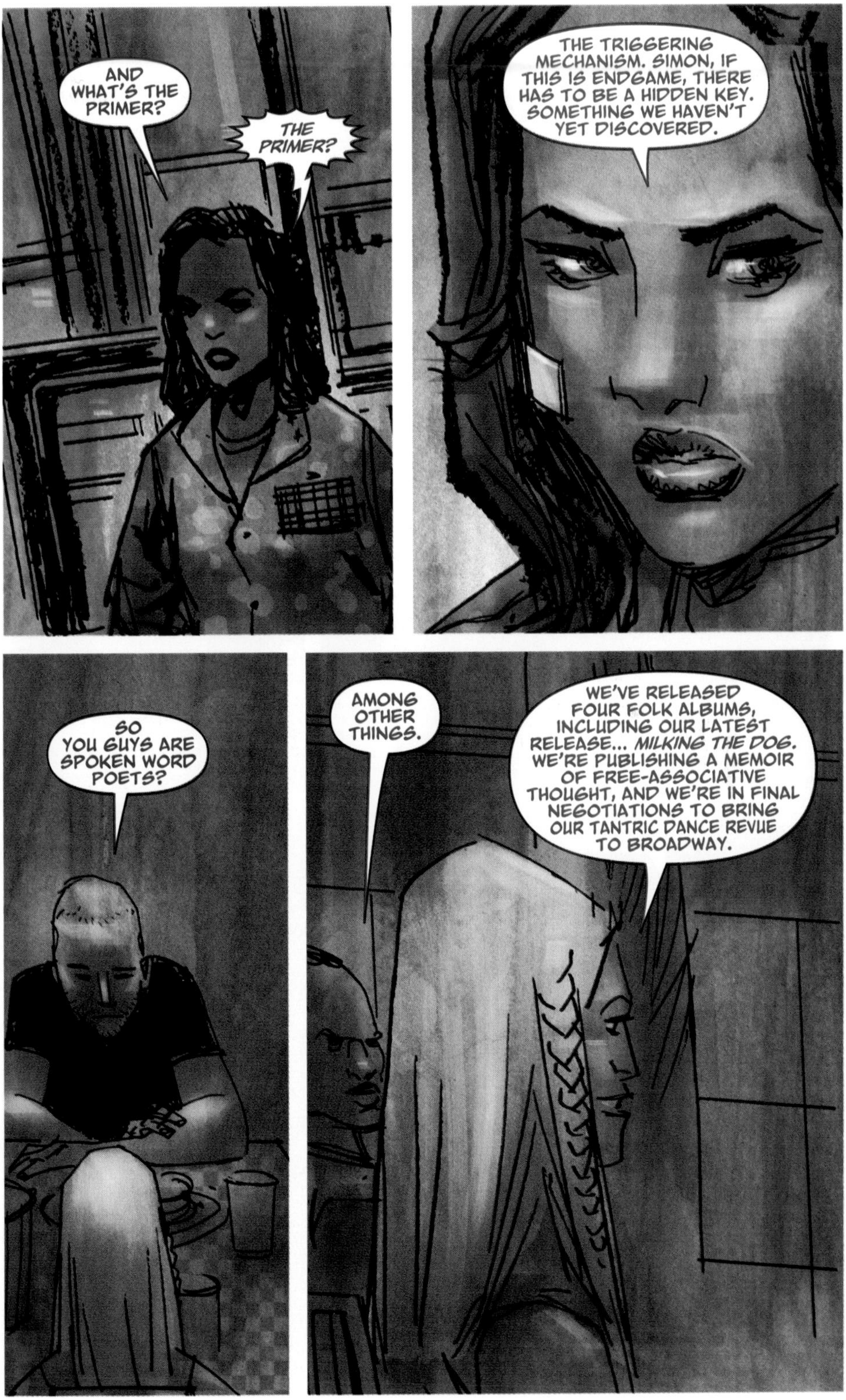
AND WHAT'S THE PRIMER?
THE PRIMER?
THE TRIGGERING MECHANISM. SIMON, IF THIS IS ENDGAME, THERE HAS TO BE A HIDDEN KEY. SOMETHING WE HAVEN'T YET DISCOVERED.
SO YOU GUYS ARE SPOKEN WORD POETS?
AMONG OTHER THINGS.
WE'VE RELEASED FOUR FOLK ALBUMS, INCLUDING OUR LATEST RELEASE... *MILKING THE DOG.* WE'RE PUBLISHING A MEMOIR OF FREE-ASSOCIATIVE THOUGHT, AND WE'RE IN FINAL NEGOTIATIONS TO BRING OUR TANTRIC DANCE REVUE TO BROADWAY.

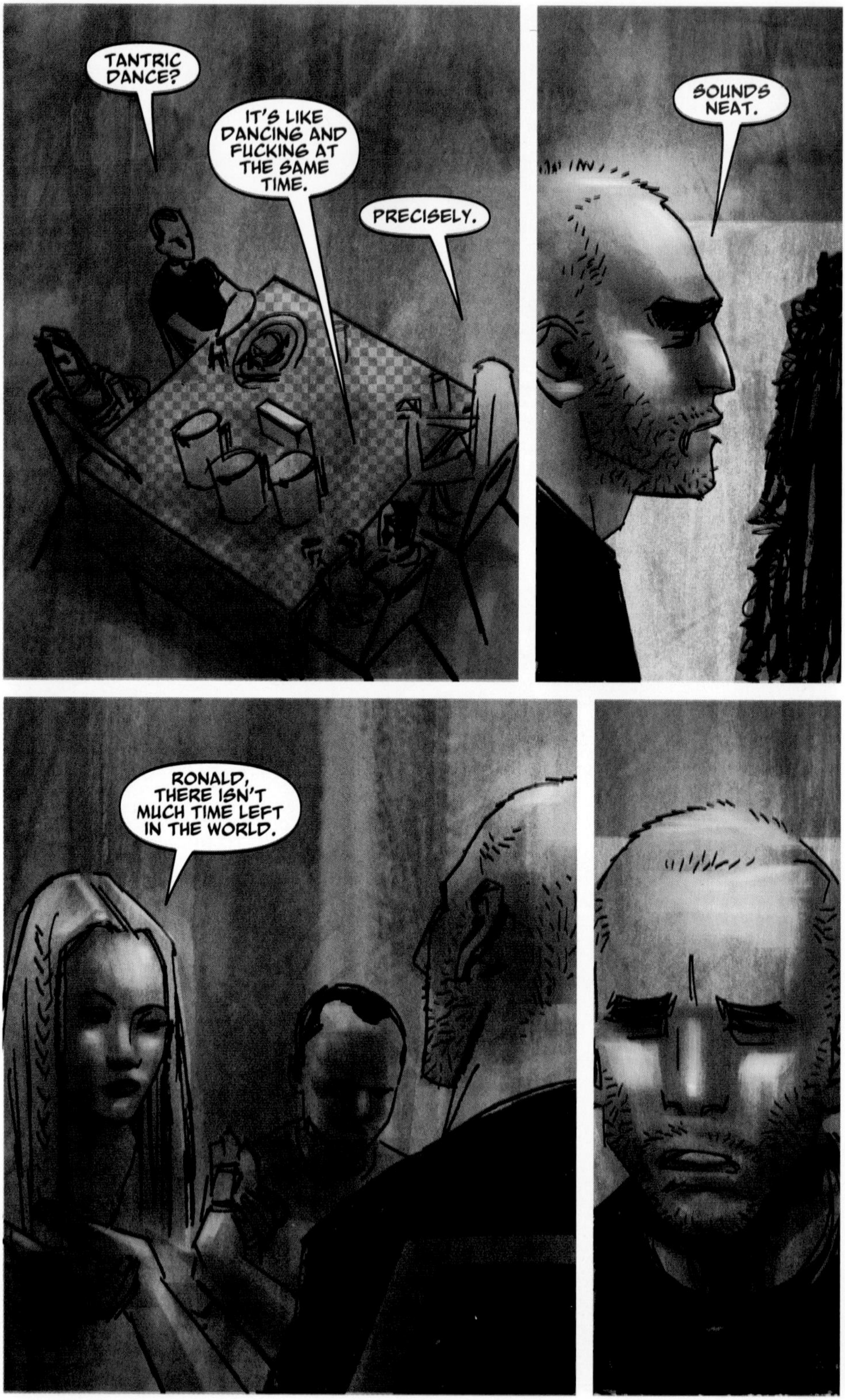
TANTRIC DANCE?
IT'S LIKE DANCING AND FUCKING AT THE SAME TIME.
PRECISELY.
SOUNDS NEAT.
RONALD, THERE ISN'T MUCH TIME LEFT IN THE WORLD.

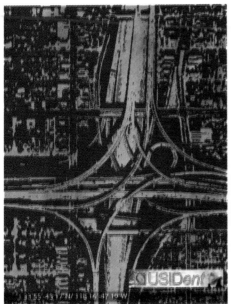

I'M HOSTING A PARTY IN THE BARON'S HONOR UP AT THE HOUSE TOMORROW NIGHT, AND IT IS IMPERATIVE THAT YOU SHOW UP.

I DON'T TRUST HIM, VAUGHN. HE'S A NEO-MARXIST.

HE DOESN'T ASSOCIATE WITH THE UNDERGROUND.

BULLSHIT.

BOBBY, WE CAN'T WIN CALIFORNIA WITHOUT AN ENDORSEMENT FROM BARON VON WESTPHALEN. HE'S TOO POWERFUL.

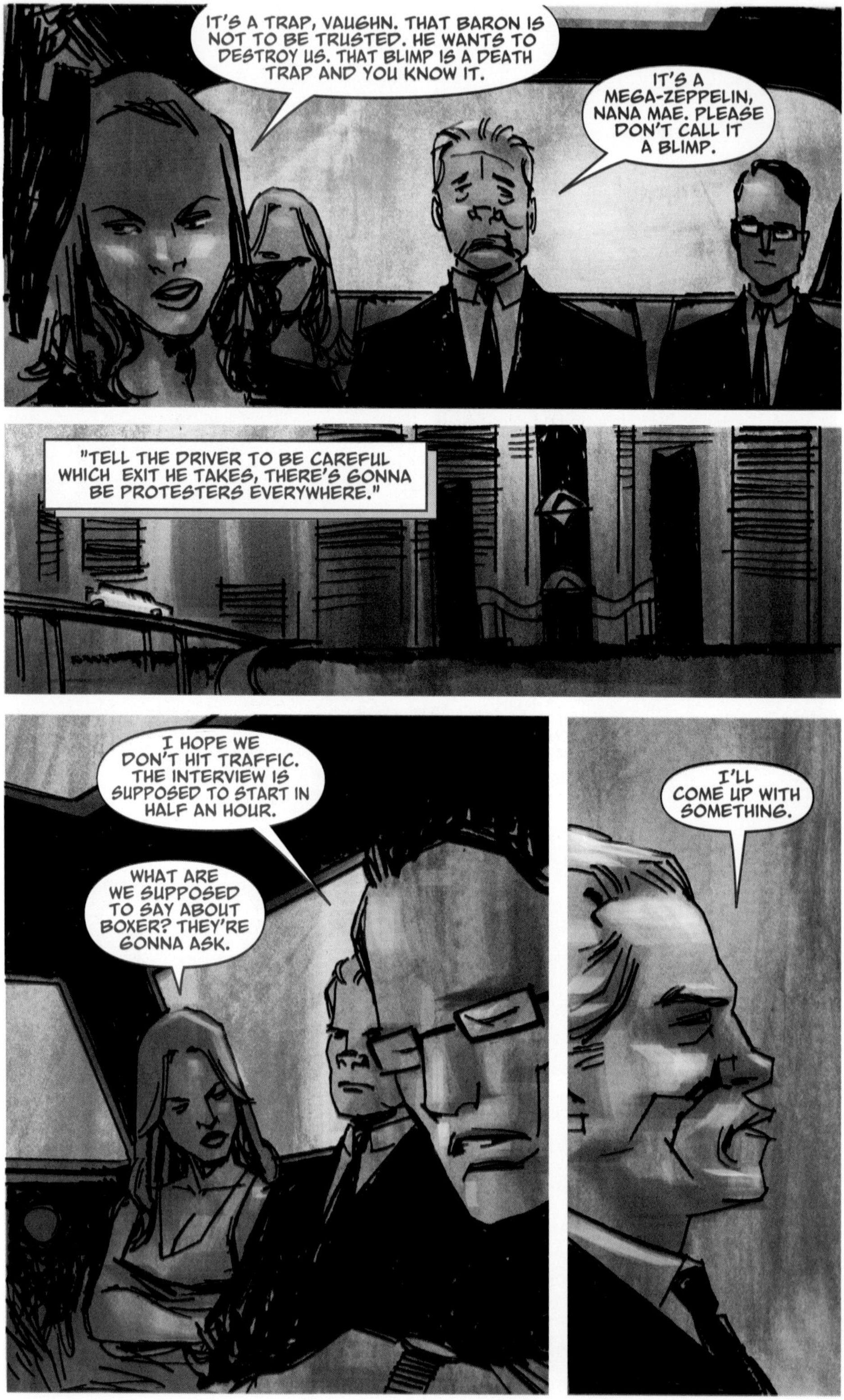
IT'S A TRAP, VAUGHN. THAT BARON IS NOT TO BE TRUSTED. HE WANTS TO DESTROY US. THAT BLIMP IS A DEATH TRAP AND YOU KNOW IT.
IT'S A MEGA-ZEPPELIN, NANA MAE. PLEASE DON'T CALL IT A BLIMP.
"TELL THE DRIVER TO BE CAREFUL WHICH EXIT HE TAKES, THERE'S GONNA BE PROTESTERS EVERYWHERE."
I HOPE WE DON'T HIT TRAFFIC. THE INTERVIEW IS SUPPOSED TO START IN HALF AN HOUR.
WHAT ARE WE SUPPOSED TO SAY ABOUT BOXER? THEY'RE GONNA ASK.
I'LL COME UP WITH SOMETHING.

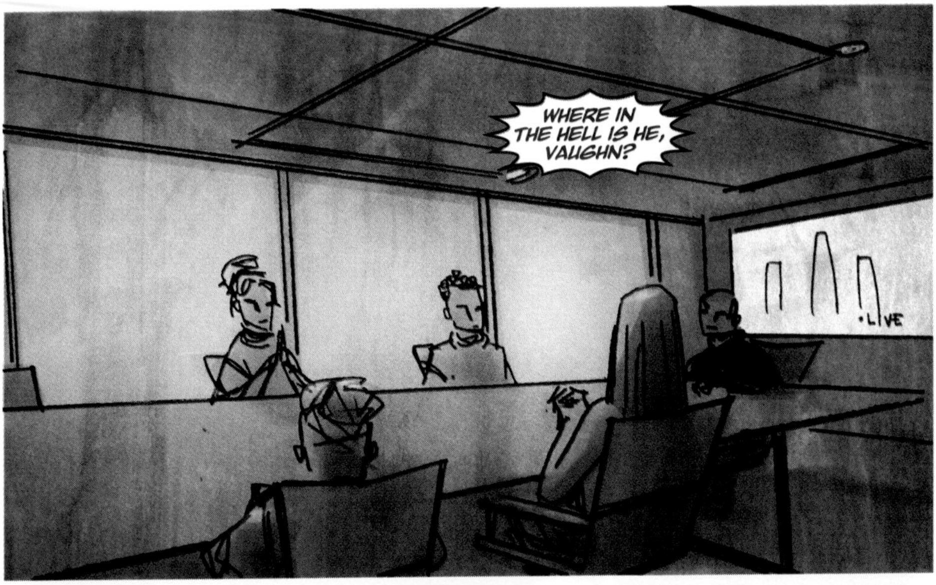

WHERE IN THE HELL IS HE, VAUGHN?
LIVE

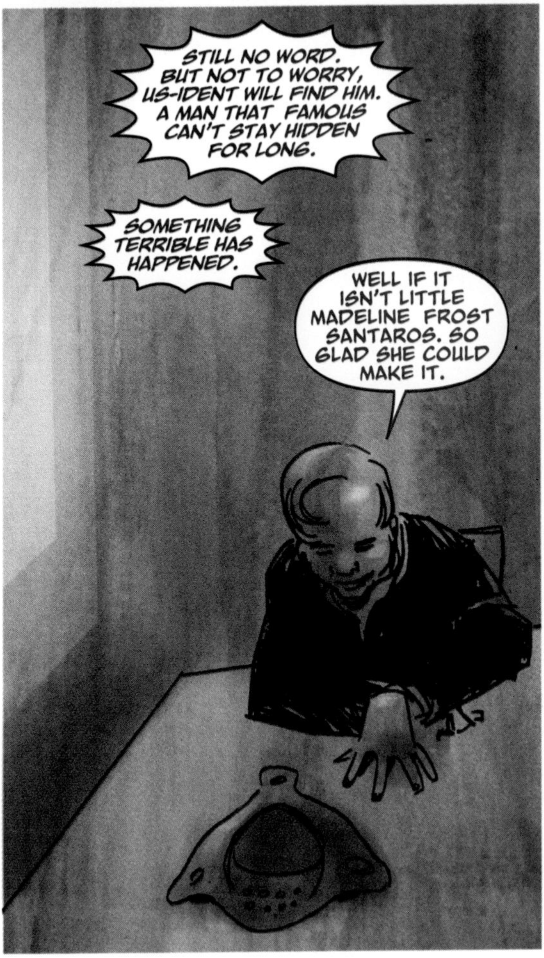

STILL NO WORD. BUT NOT TO WORRY, US-IDENT WILL FIND HIM. A MAN THAT FAMOUS CAN'T STAY HIDDEN FOR LONG.
SOMETHING TERRIBLE HAS HAPPENED.
WELL IF IT ISN'T LITTLE MADELINE FROST SANTAROS. SO GLAD SHE COULD MAKE IT.

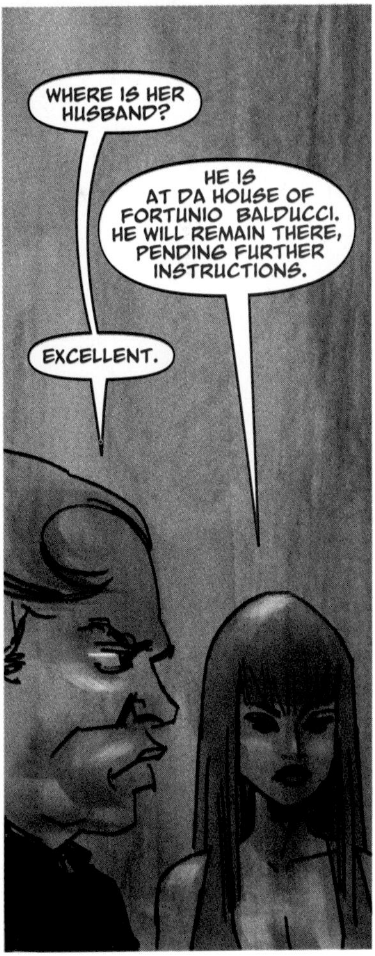

WHERE IS HER HUSBAND?
HE IS AT DA HOUSE OF FORTUNIO BALDUCCI. HE WILL REMAIN THERE, PENDING FURTHER INSTRUCTIONS.
EXCELLENT.

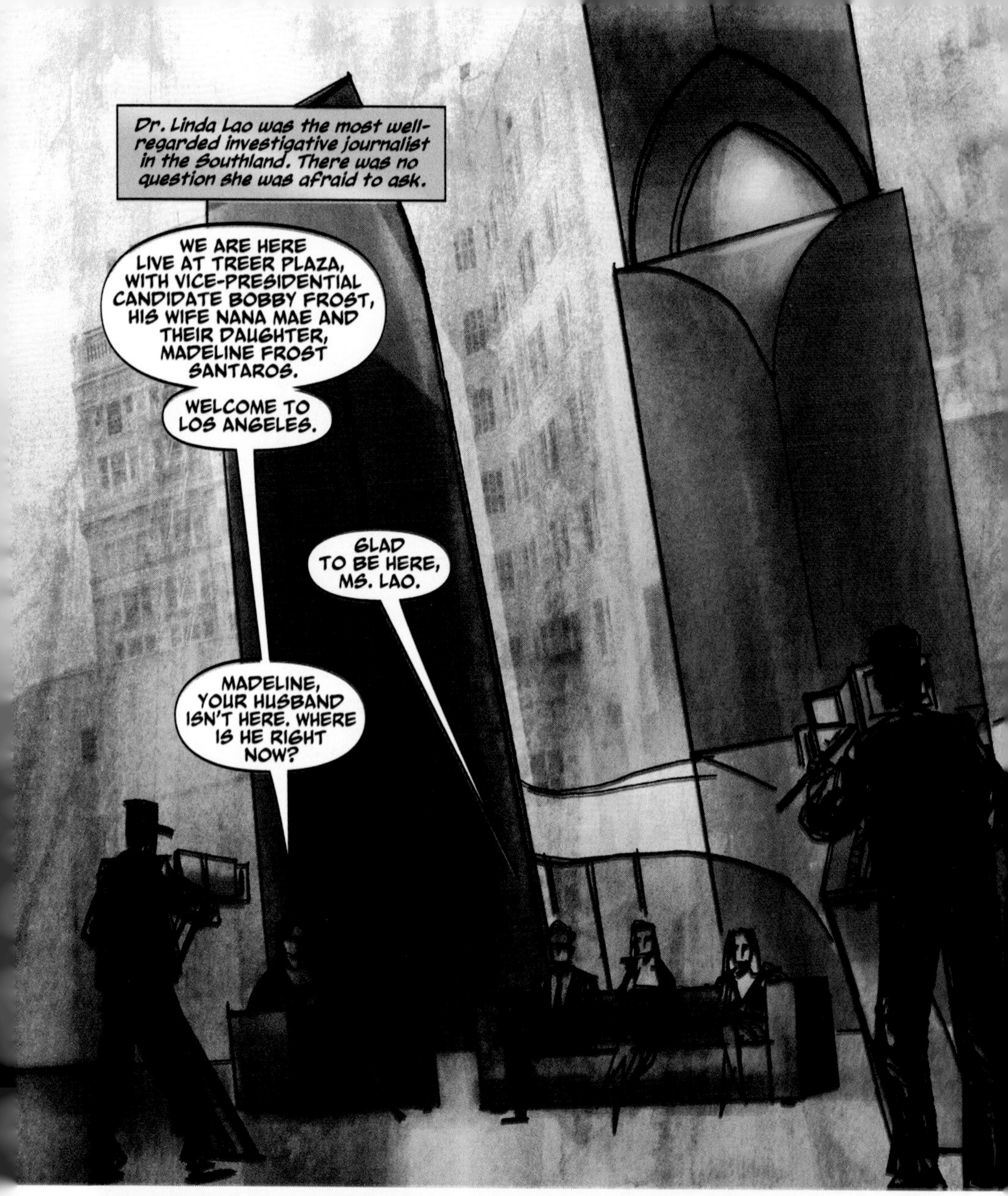
Dr. Linda Lao was the most well-regarded investigative journalist in the Southland. There was no question she was afraid to ask.
WE ARE HERE LIVE AT TREER PLAZA, WITH VICE-PRESIDENTIAL CANDIDATE BOBBY FROST, HIS WIFE NANA MAE AND THEIR DAUGHTER, MADELINE FROST SANTAROS.
WELCOME TO LOS ANGELES.
GLAD TO BE HERE, MS. LAO.
MADELINE, YOUR HUSBAND ISN'T HERE. WHERE IS HE RIGHT NOW?

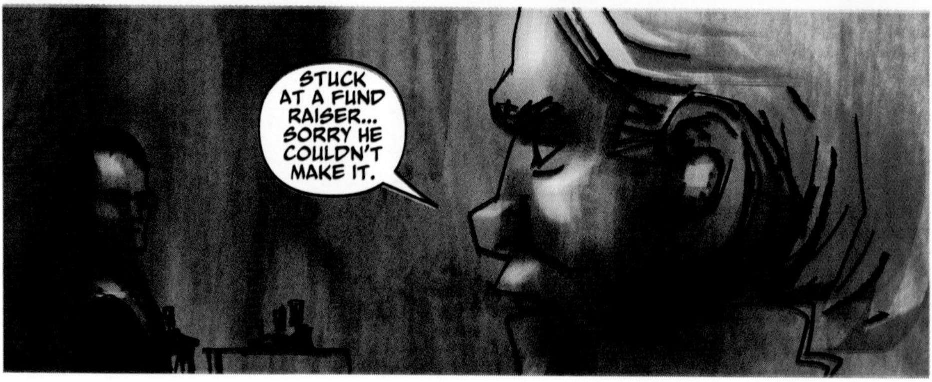
STUCK AT A FUND RAISER... SORRY HE COULDN'T MAKE IT.

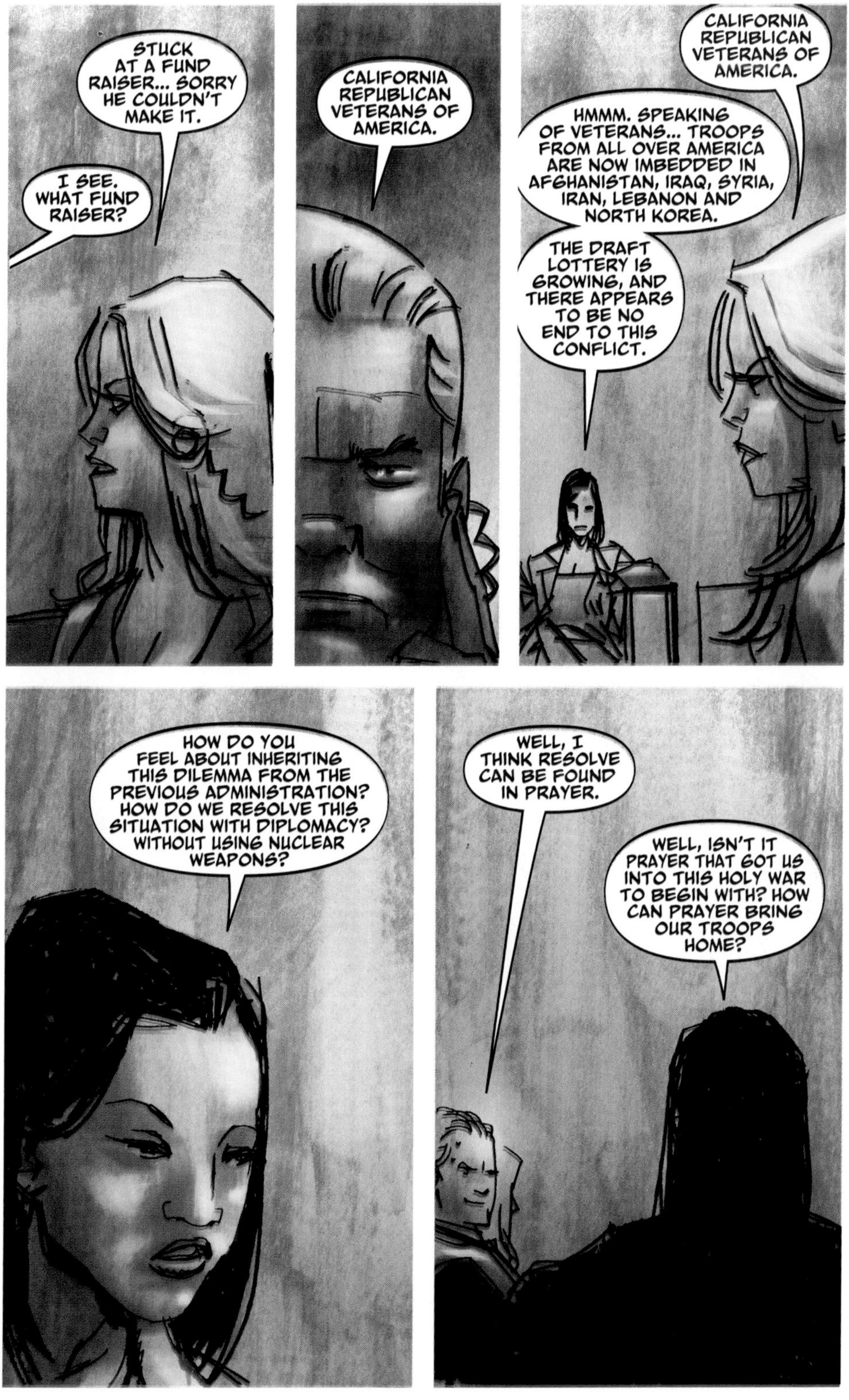
STUCK AT A FUND RAISER... SORRY HE COULDN'T MAKE IT.
I SEE. WHAT FUND RAISER?
CALIFORNIA REPUBLICAN VETERANS OF AMERICA.
CALIFORNIA REPUBLICAN VETERANS OF AMERICA.
HMMM. SPEAKING OF VETERANS... TROOPS FROM ALL OVER AMERICA ARE NOW IMBEDDED IN AFGHANISTAN, IRAQ, SYRIA, IRAN, LEBANON AND NORTH KOREA.
THE DRAFT LOTTERY IS GROWING, AND THERE APPEARS TO BE NO END TO THIS CONFLICT.
HOW DO YOU FEEL ABOUT INHERITING THIS DILEMMA FROM THE PREVIOUS ADMINISTRATION? HOW DO WE RESOLVE THIS SITUATION WITH DIPLOMACY? WITHOUT USING NUCLEAR WEAPONS?
WELL, I THINK RESOLVE CAN BE FOUND IN PRAYER.
WELL, ISN'T IT PRAYER THAT GOT US INTO THIS HOLY WAR TO BEGIN WITH? HOW CAN PRAYER BRING OUR TROOPS HOME?

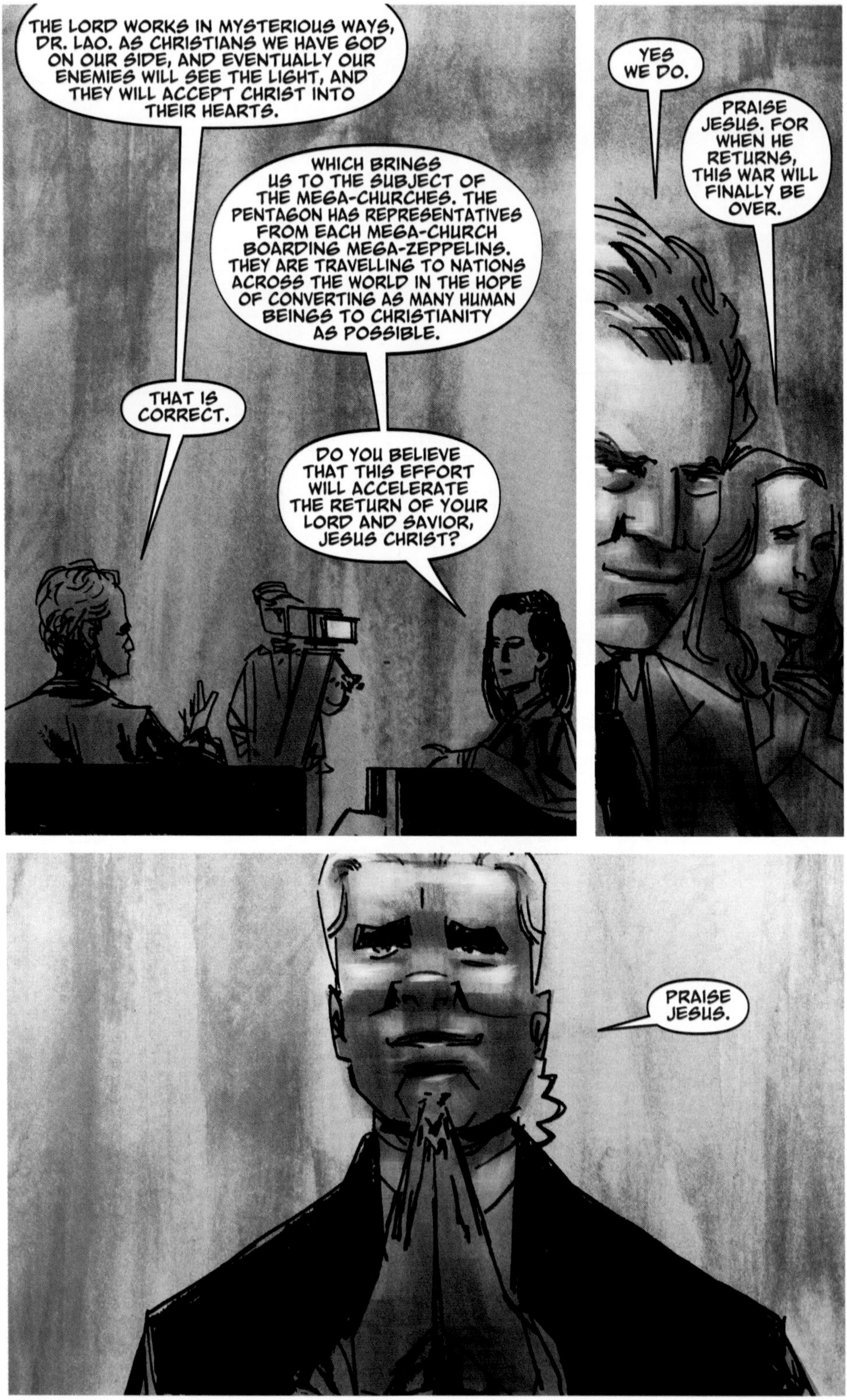
THE LORD WORKS IN MYSTERIOUS WAYS, DR. LAO. AS CHRISTIANS WE HAVE GOD ON OUR SIDE, AND EVENTUALLY OUR ENEMIES WILL SEE THE LIGHT, AND THEY WILL ACCEPT CHRIST INTO THEIR HEARTS.
WHICH BRINGS US TO THE SUBJECT OF THE MEGA-CHURCHES. THE PENTAGON HAS REPRESENTATIVES FROM EACH MEGA-CHURCH BOARDING MEGA-ZEPPELINS. THEY ARE TRAVELLING TO NATIONS ACROSS THE WORLD IN THE HOPE OF CONVERTING AS MANY HUMAN BEINGS TO CHRISTIANITY AS POSSIBLE.
THAT IS CORRECT.
DO YOU BELIEVE THAT THIS EFFORT WILL ACCELERATE THE RETURN OF YOUR LORD AND SAVIOR, JESUS CHRIST?
YES WE DO.
PRAISE JESUS. FOR WHEN HE RETURNS, THIS WAR WILL FINALLY BE OVER.
PRAISE JESUS.

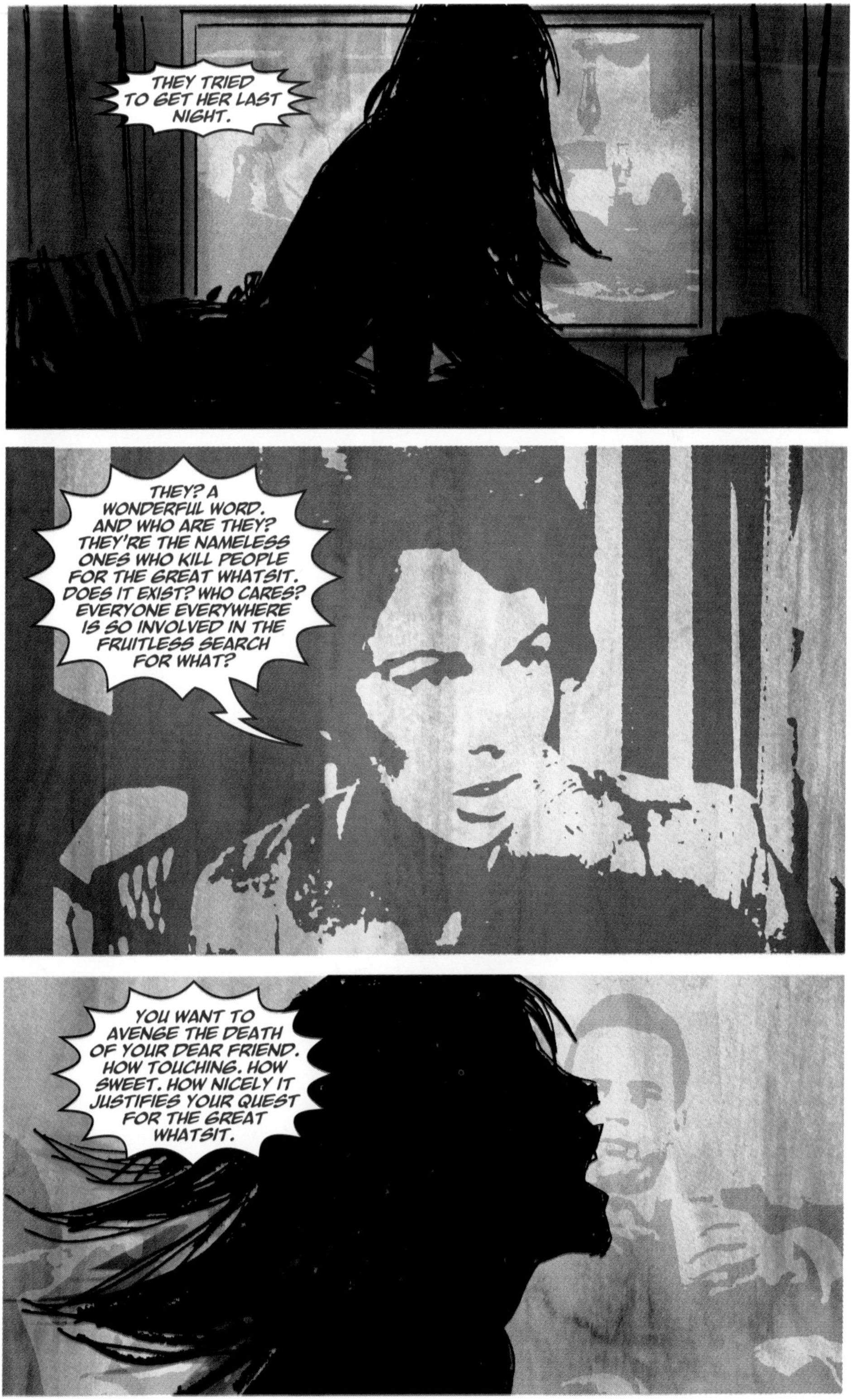
THEY TRIED TO GET HER LAST NIGHT.
THEY? A WONDERFUL WORD. AND WHO ARE THEY? THEY'RE THE NAMELESS ONES WHO KILL PEOPLE FOR THE GREAT WHATSIT. DOES IT EXIST? WHO CARES? EVERYONE EVERYWHERE IS SO INVOLVED IN THE FRUITLESS SEARCH FOR WHAT?
YOU WANT TO AVENGE THE DEATH OF YOUR DEAR FRIEND. HOW TOUCHING. HOW SWEET. HOW NICELY IT JUSTIFIES YOUR QUEST FOR THE GREAT WHATSIT.

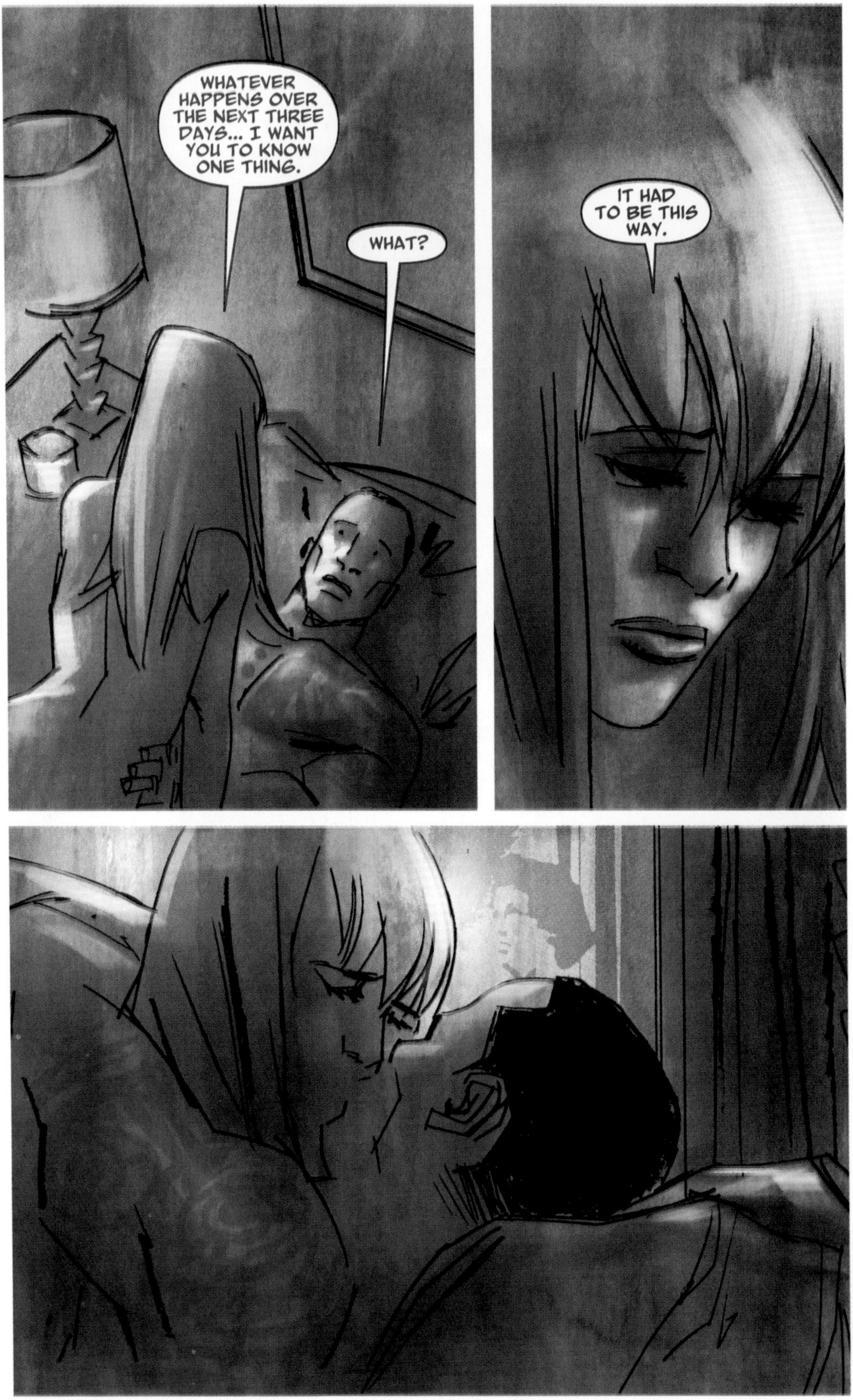
WHATEVER HAPPENS OVER THE NEXT THREE DAYS... I WANT YOU TO KNOW ONE THING.
WHAT?
IT HAD TO BE THIS WAY.

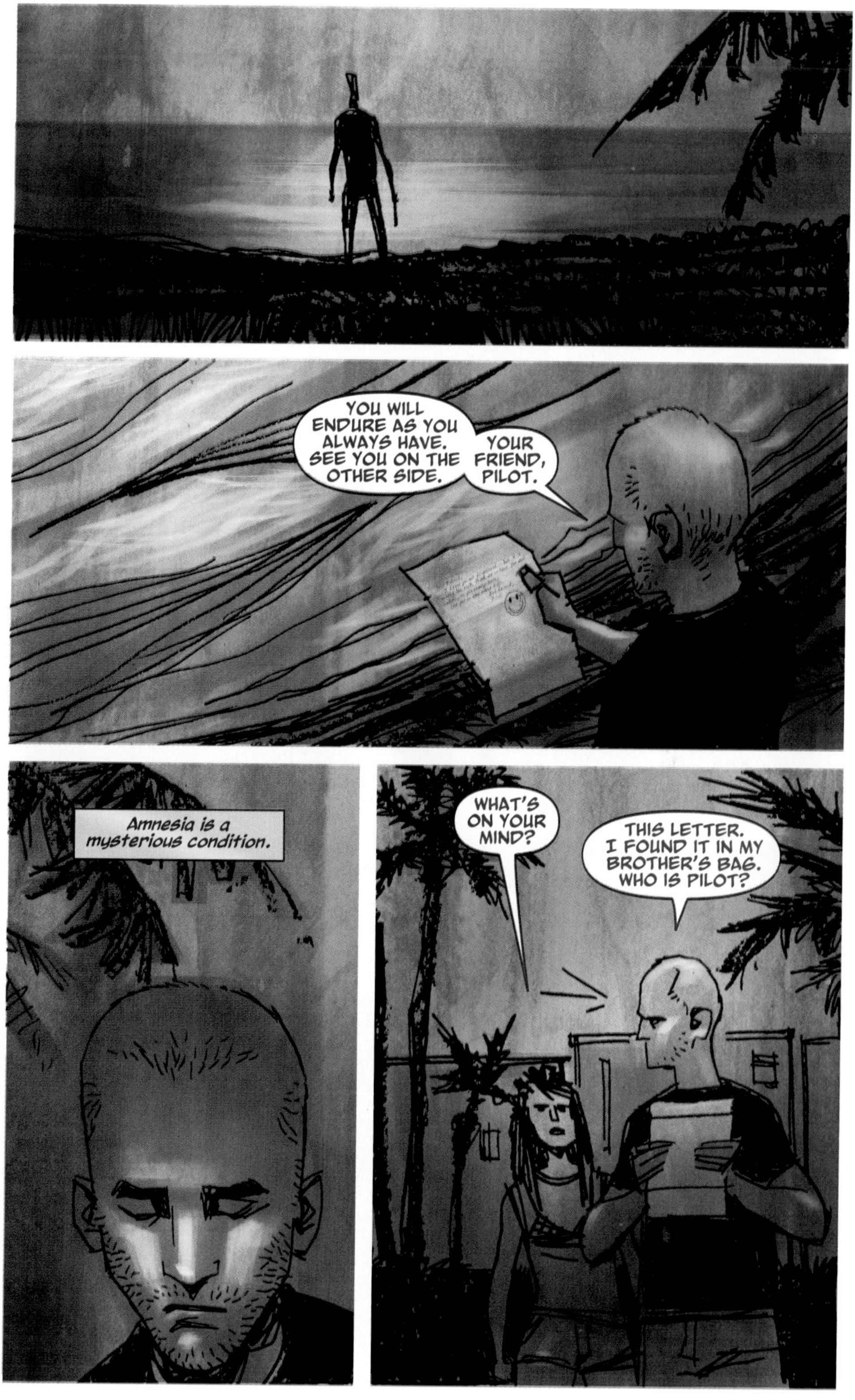
YOU WILL ENDURE AS YOU ALWAYS HAVE. SEE YOU ON THE OTHER SIDE.
YOUR FRIEND, PILOT.
Amnesia is a mysterious condition.
WHAT'S ON YOUR MIND?
THIS LETTER. I FOUND IT IN MY BROTHER'S BAG. WHO IS PILOT?

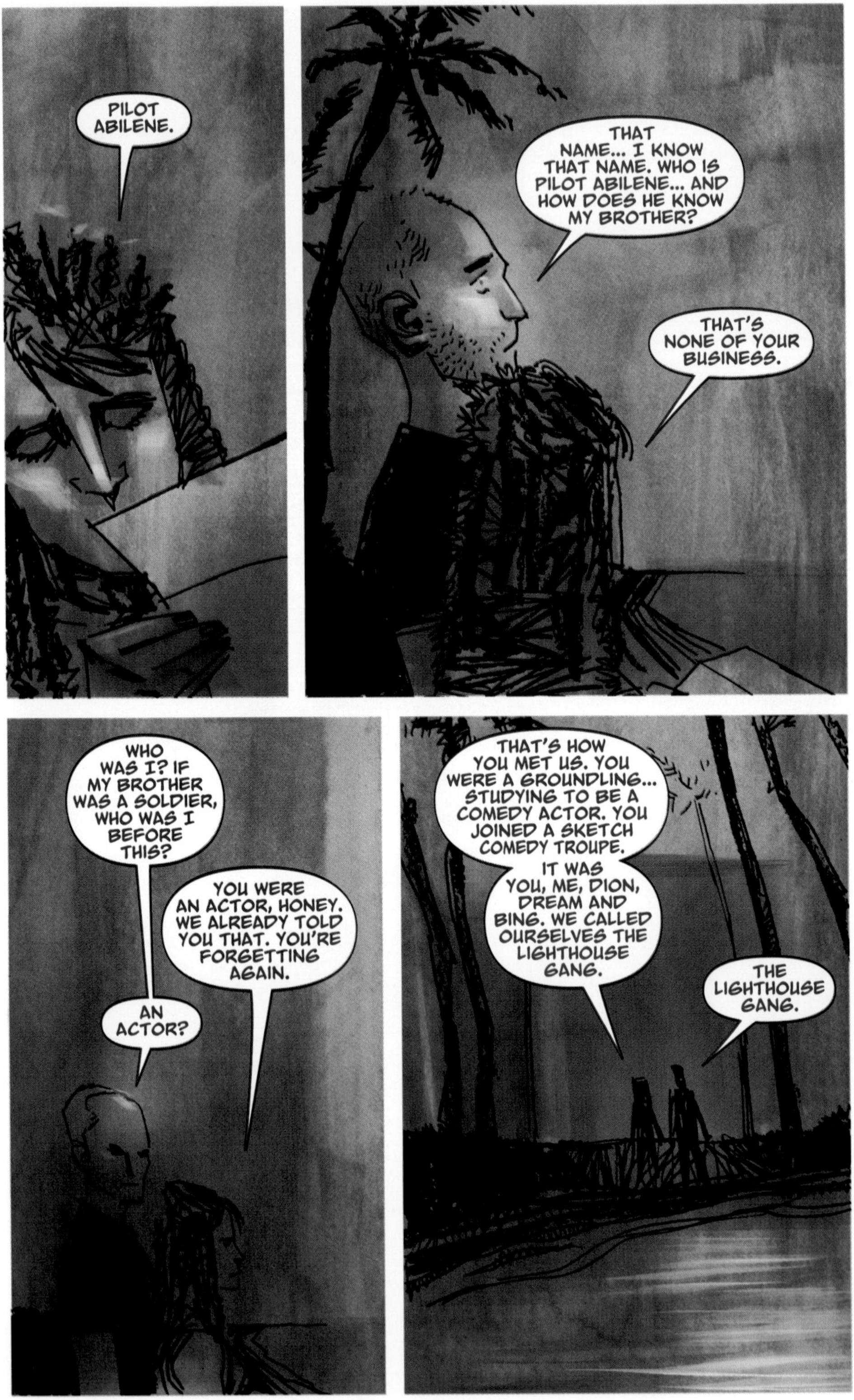
PILOT ABILENE.
THAT NAME... I KNOW THAT NAME. WHO IS PILOT ABILENE... AND HOW DOES HE KNOW MY BROTHER?
THAT'S NONE OF YOUR BUSINESS.
WHO WAS I? IF MY BROTHER WAS A SOLDIER, WHO WAS I BEFORE THIS?
YOU WERE AN ACTOR, HONEY. WE ALREADY TOLD YOU THAT. YOU'RE FORGETTING AGAIN.
AN ACTOR?
THAT'S HOW YOU MET US. YOU WERE A GROUNDLING... STUDYING TO BE A COMEDY ACTOR. YOU JOINED A SKETCH COMEDY TROUPE.
IT WAS YOU, ME, DION, DREAM AND BING. WE CALLED OURSELVES THE LIGHTHOUSE GANG.
THE LIGHTHOUSE GANG.

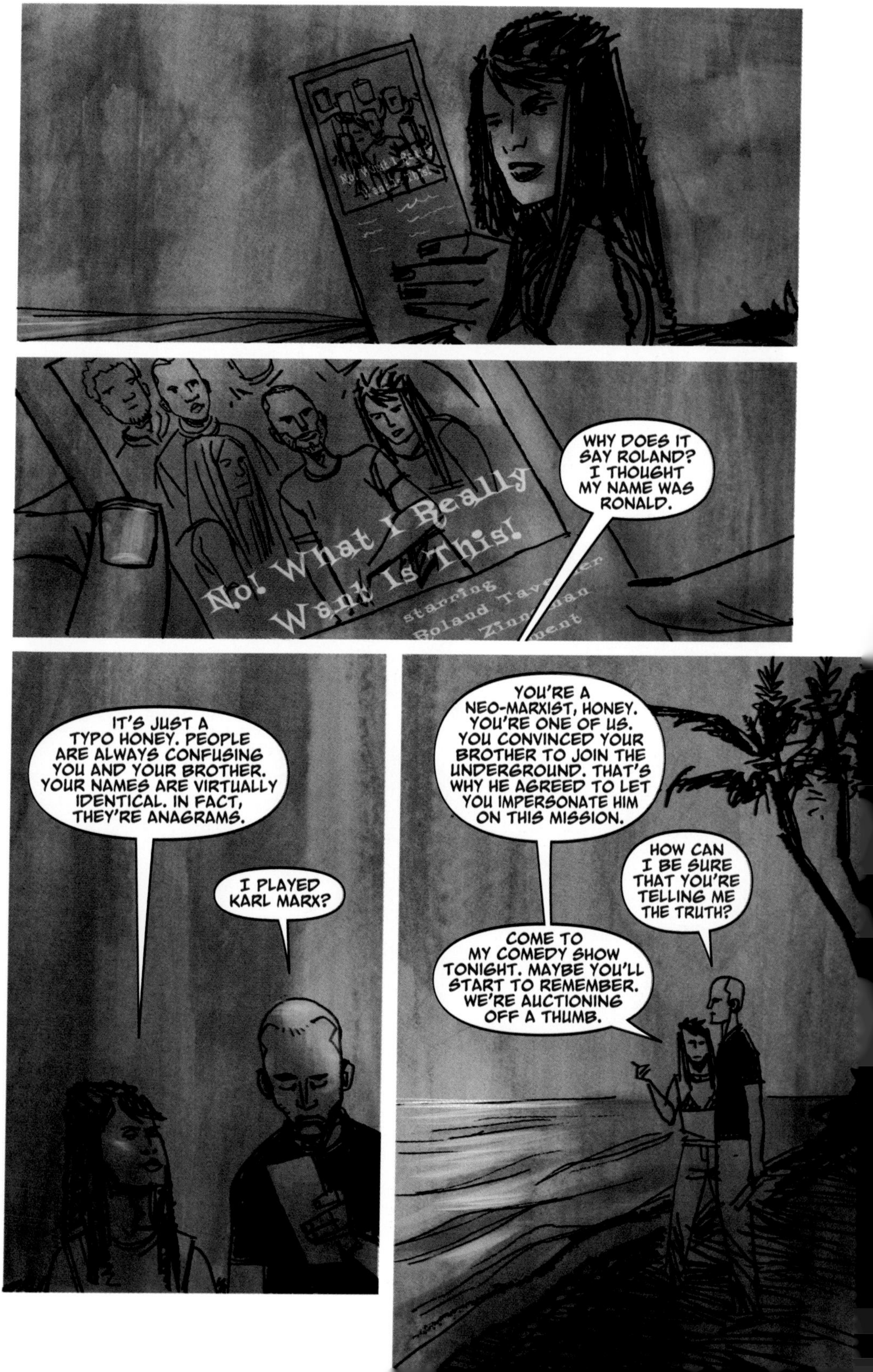
No! What I Really Want Is This!
starring
Roland Tav
WHY DOES IT SAY ROLAND? I THOUGHT MY NAME WAS RONALD.
IT'S JUST A TYPO HONEY. PEOPLE ARE ALWAYS CONFUSING YOU AND YOUR BROTHER. YOUR NAMES ARE VIRTUALLY IDENTICAL. IN FACT, THEY'RE ANAGRAMS.
I PLAYED KARL MARX?
YOU'RE A NEO-MARXIST, HONEY. YOU'RE ONE OF US. YOU CONVINCED YOUR BROTHER TO JOIN THE UNDERGROUND. THAT'S WHY HE AGREED TO LET YOU IMPERSONATE HIM ON THIS MISSION.
HOW CAN I BE SURE THAT YOU'RE TELLING ME THE TRUTH?
COME TO MY COMEDY SHOW TONIGHT. MAYBE YOU'LL START TO REMEMBER. WE'RE AUCTIONING OFF A THUMB.

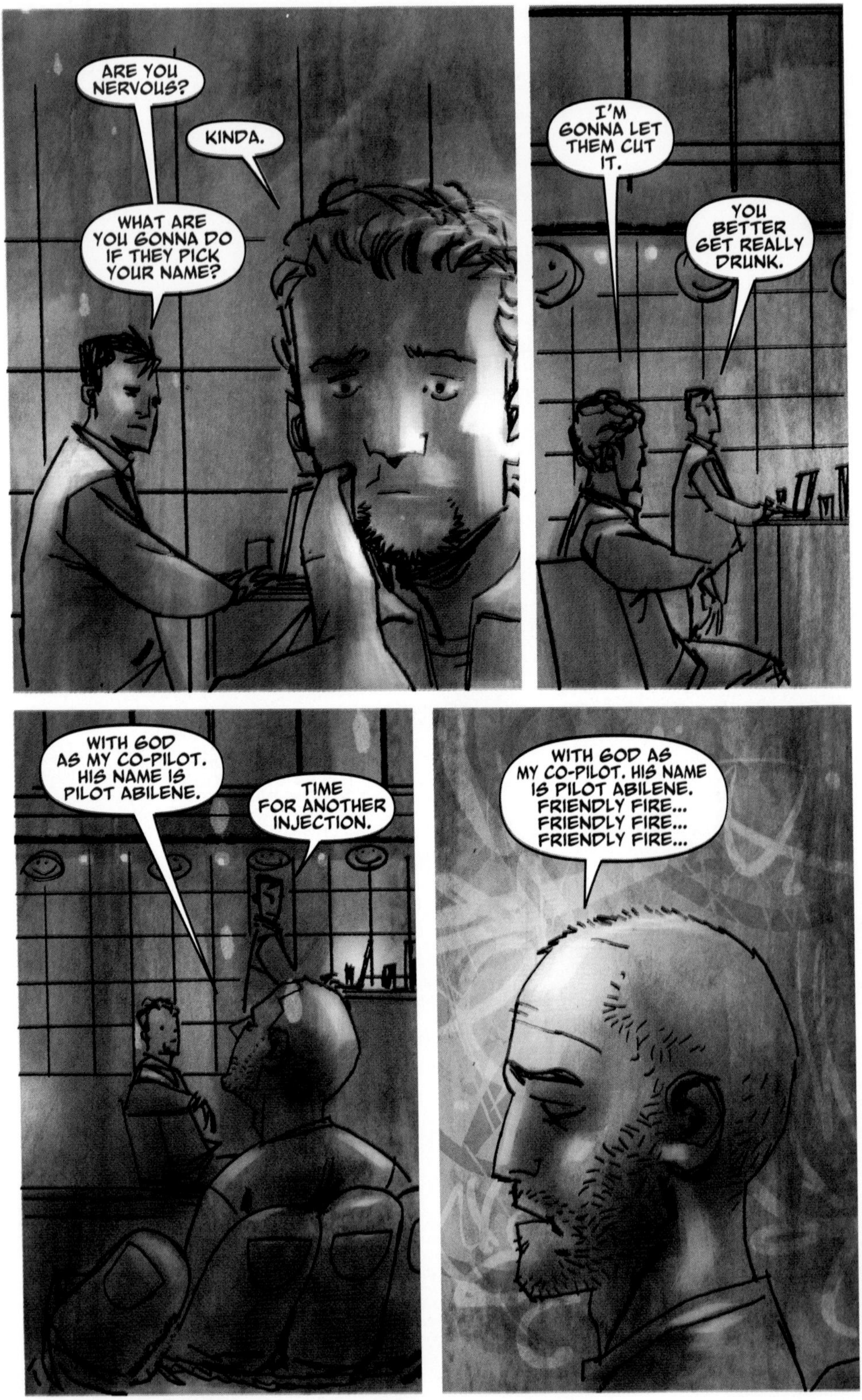
ARE YOU NERVOUS?
KINDA.
WHAT ARE YOU GONNA DO IF THEY PICK YOUR NAME?
I'M GONNA LET THEM CUT IT.
YOU BETTER GET REALLY DRUNK.
WITH GOD AS MY CO-PILOT. HIS NAME IS PILOT ABILENE.
TIME FOR ANOTHER INJECTION.
WITH GOD AS MY CO-PILOT. HIS NAME IS PILOT ABILENE. FRIENDLY FIRE... FRIENDLY FIRE... FRIENDLY FIRE...

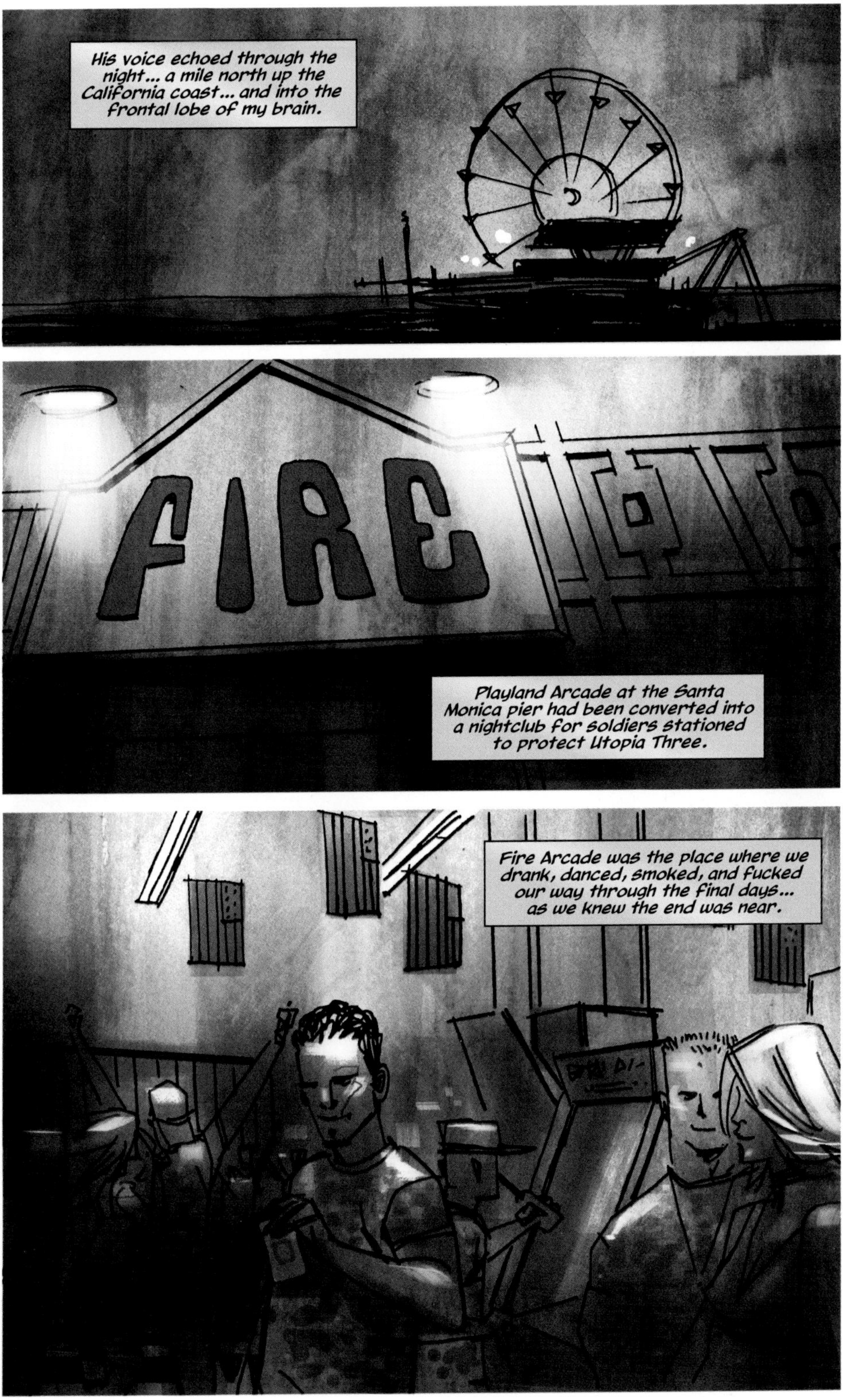
His voice echoed through the night... a mile north up the California coast... and into the frontal lobe of my brain.
FIRE
Playland Arcade at the Santa Monica pier had been converted into a nightclub for soldiers stationed to protect Utopia Three.
Fire Arcade was the place where we drank, danced, smoked, and fucked our way through the final days... as we knew the end was near.

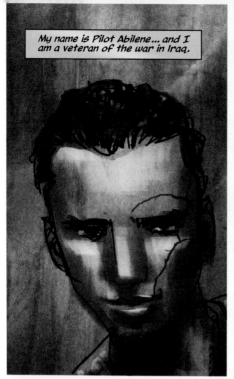

My name is Pilot Abilene... and I am a veteran of the war in Iraq.

I was born in Abilene, Texas.

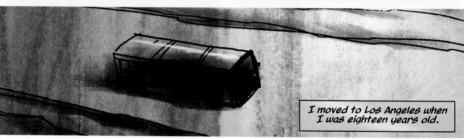

I moved to Los Angeles when I was eighteen years old.

I always wanted to act... and I was always a lucky bastard.

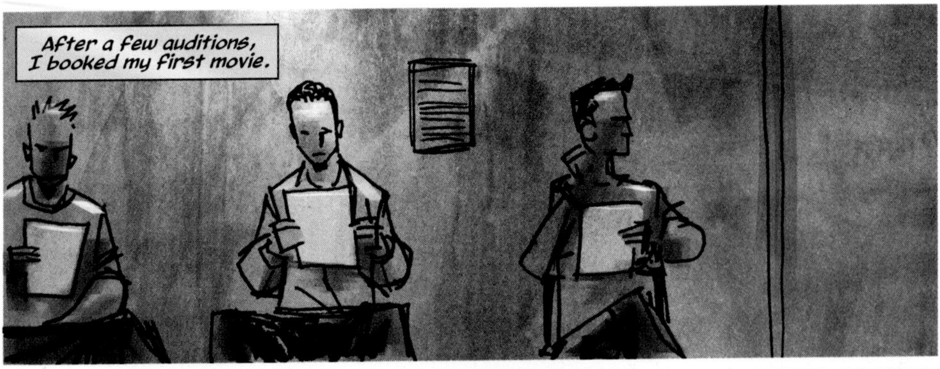
After a few auditions, I booked my first movie.

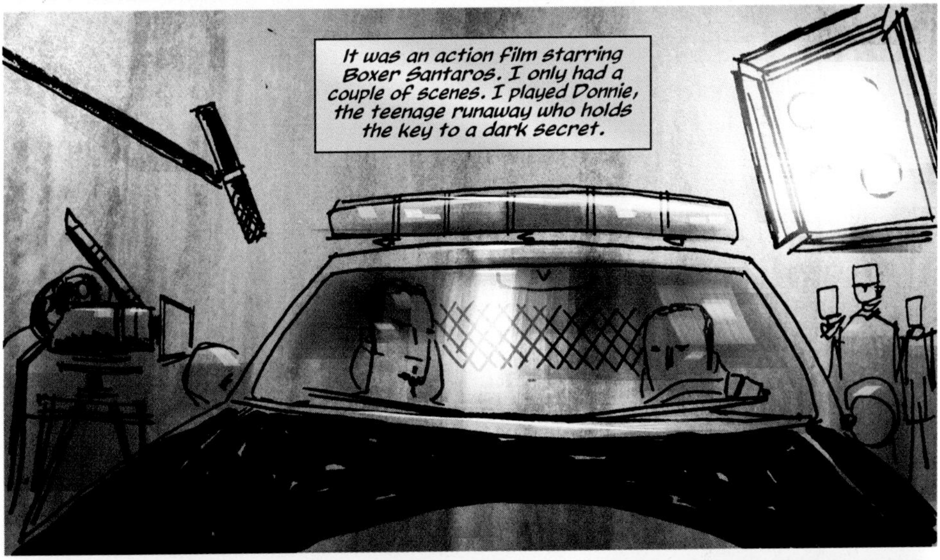
It was an action film starring Boxer Santaros. I only had a couple of scenes. I played Donnie, the teenage runaway who holds the key to a dark secret.

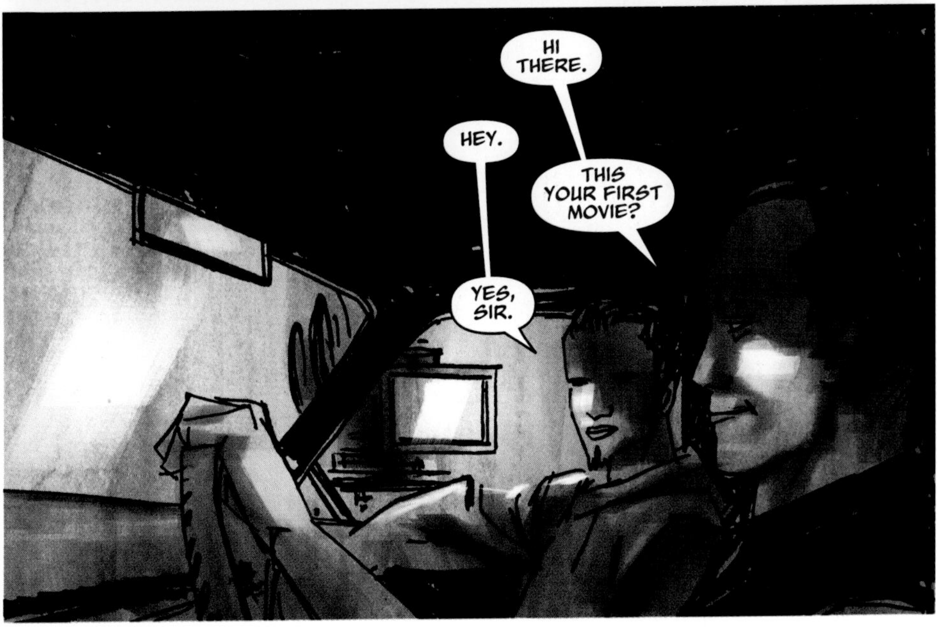
HI THERE.
HEY.
THIS YOUR FIRST MOVIE?
YES, SIR.

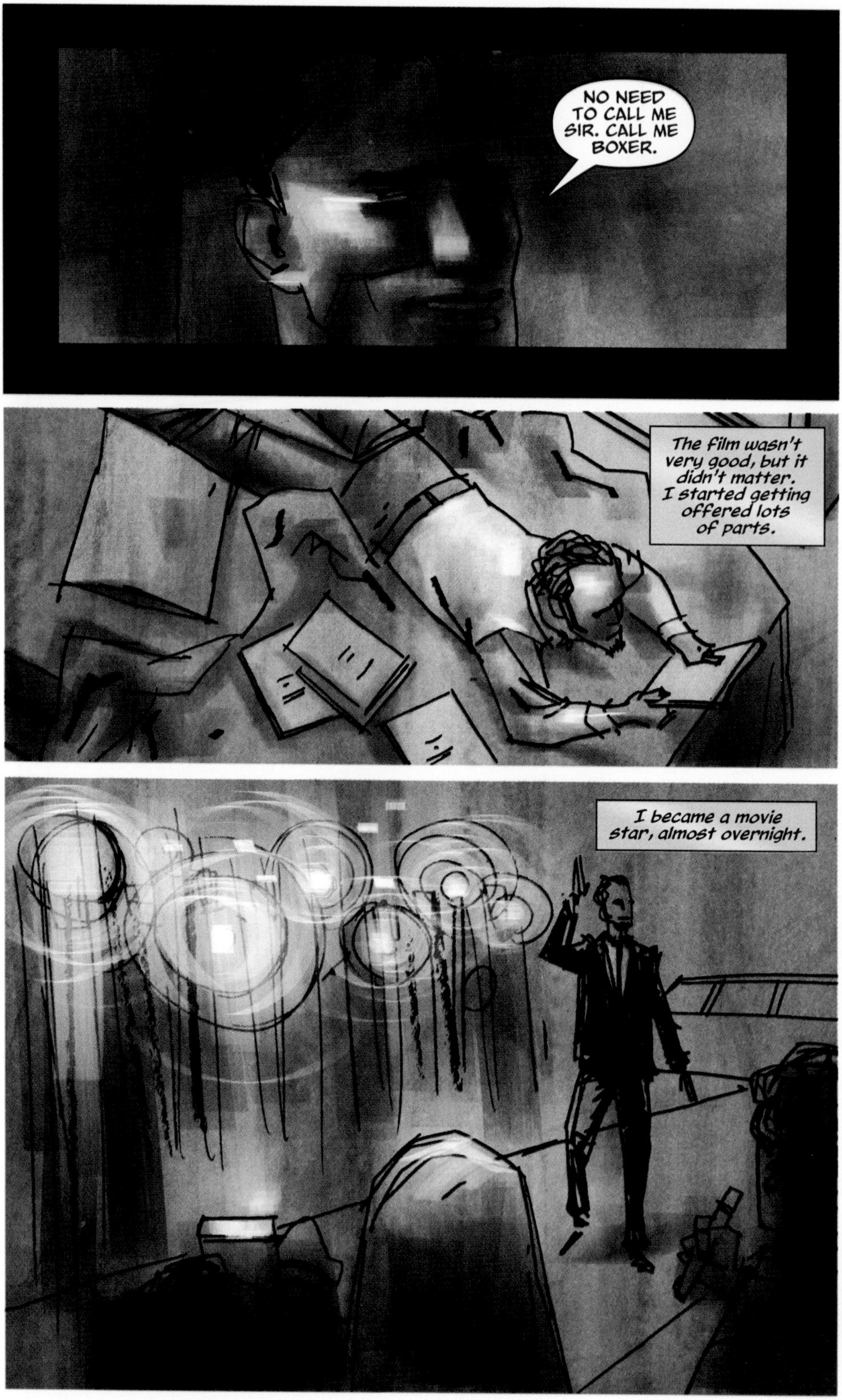
NO NEED TO CALL ME SIR. CALL ME BOXER.
The film wasn't very good, but it didn't matter. I started getting offered lots of parts.
I became a movie star, almost overnight.

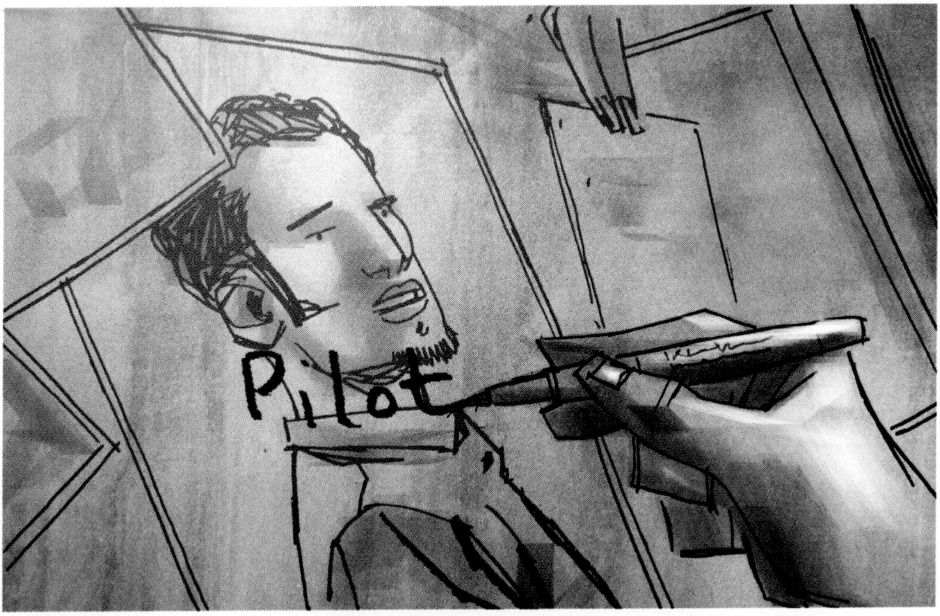
Pilot

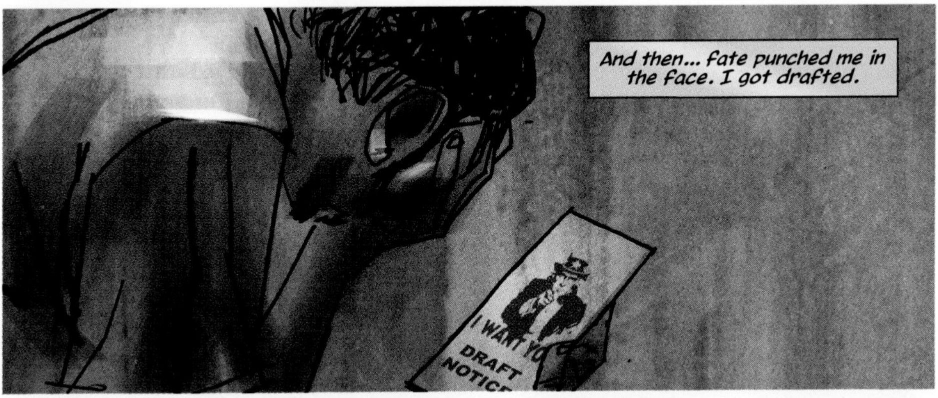
And then... fate punched me in the face. I got drafted.
DRAFT

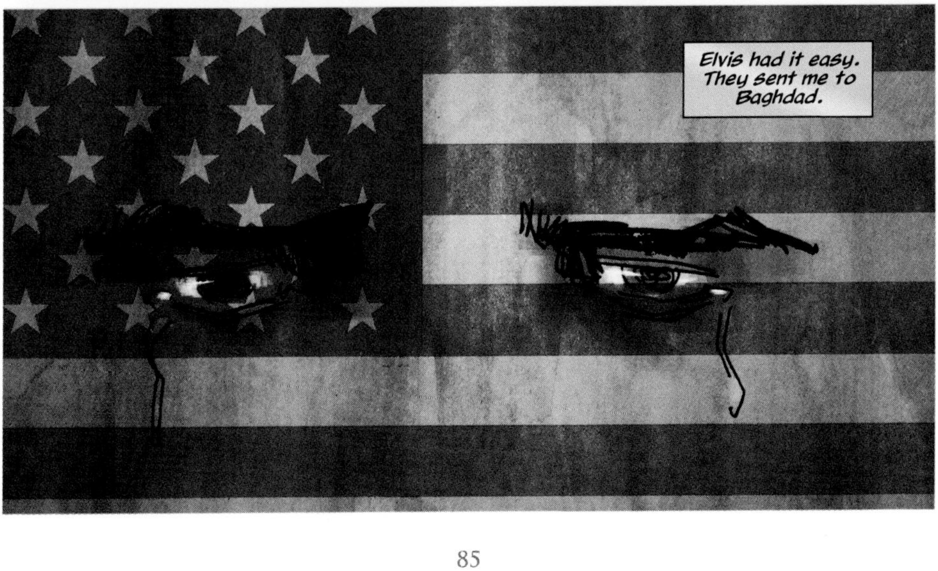
Elvis had it easy. They sent me to Baghdad.

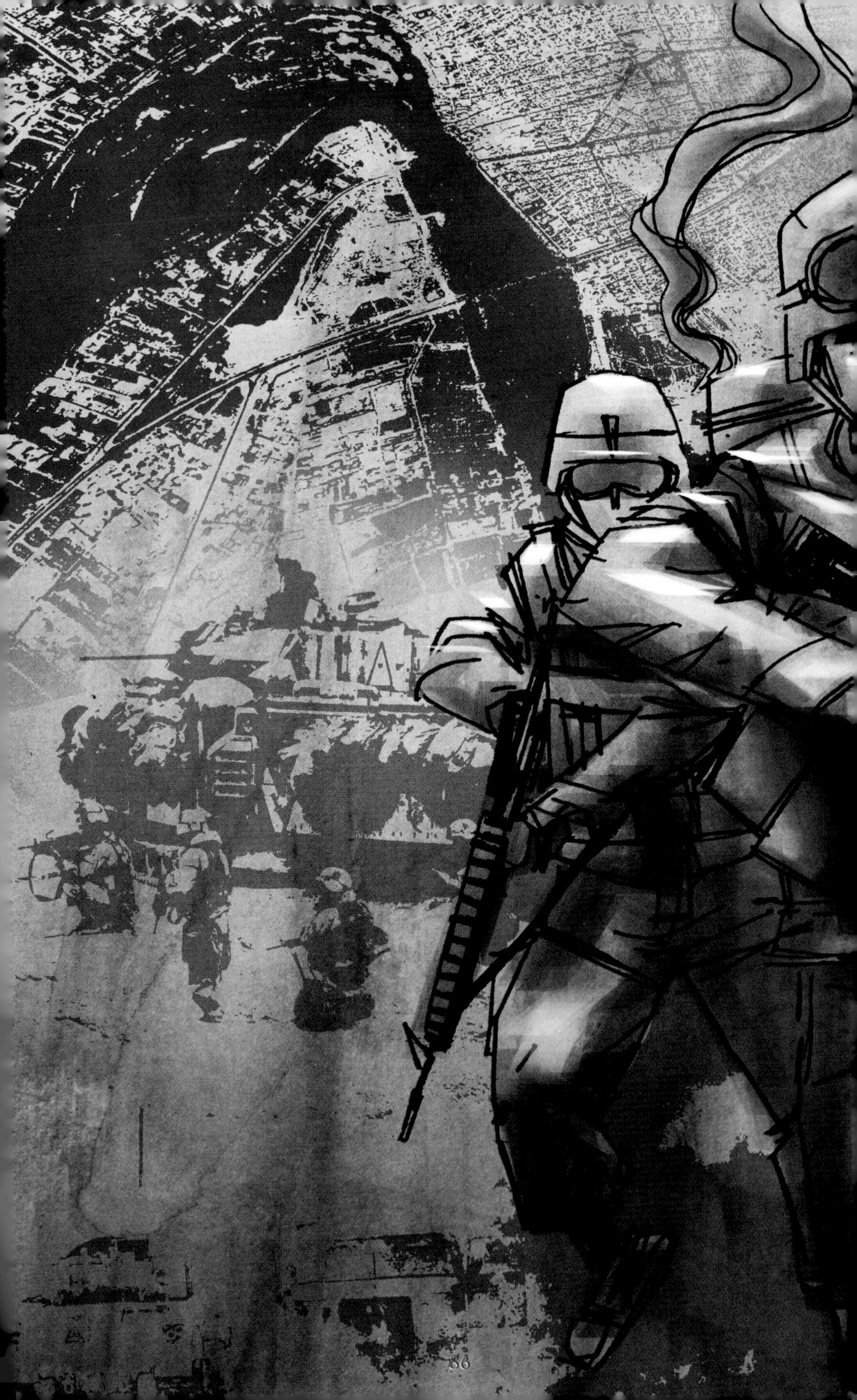

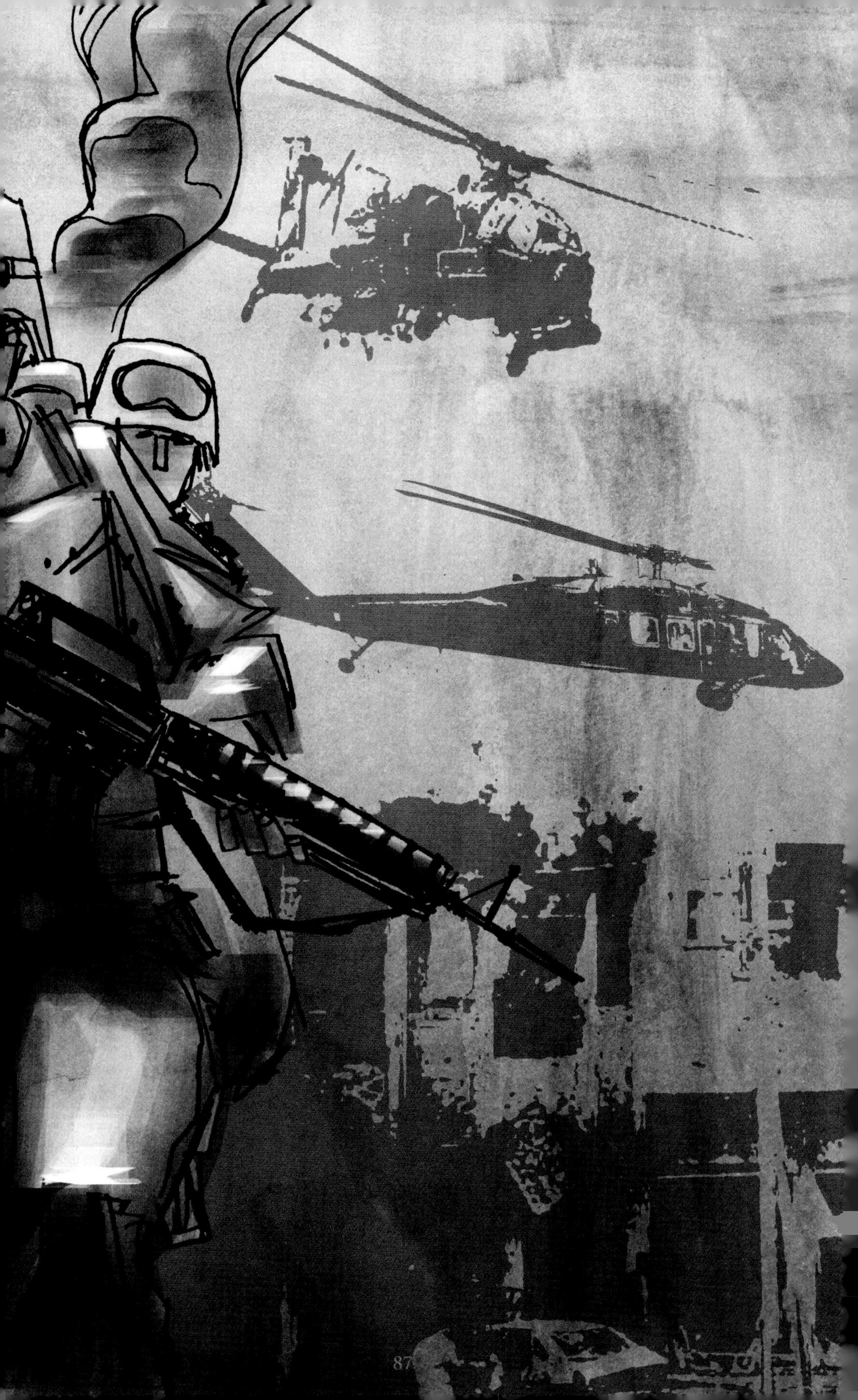

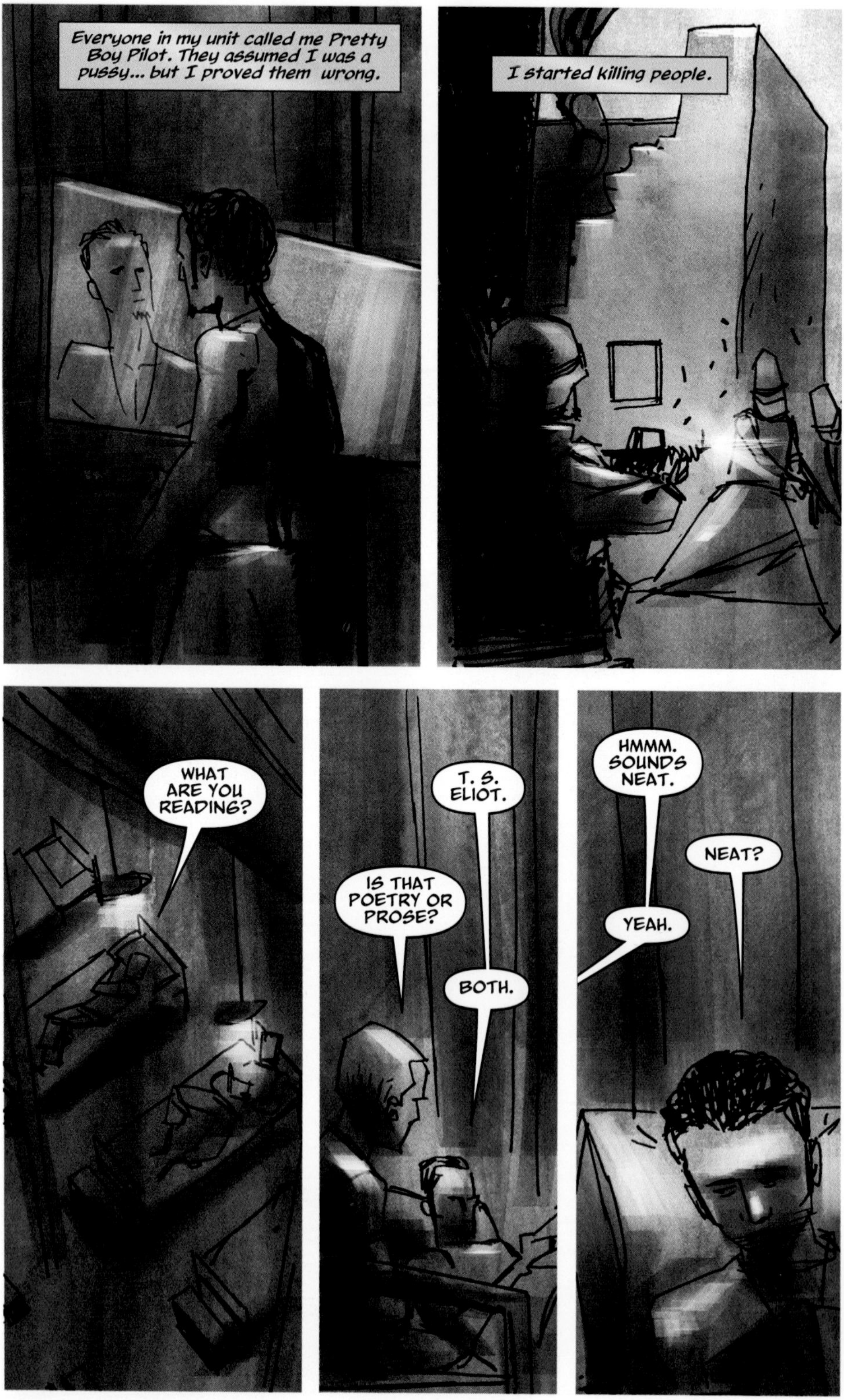
Everyone in my unit called me Pretty Boy Pilot. They assumed I was a pussy... but I proved them wrong.
I started killing people.
WHAT ARE YOU READING?
T. S. ELIOT.
IS THAT POETRY OR PROSE?
BOTH.
HMMM. SOUNDS NEAT.
NEAT?
YEAH.

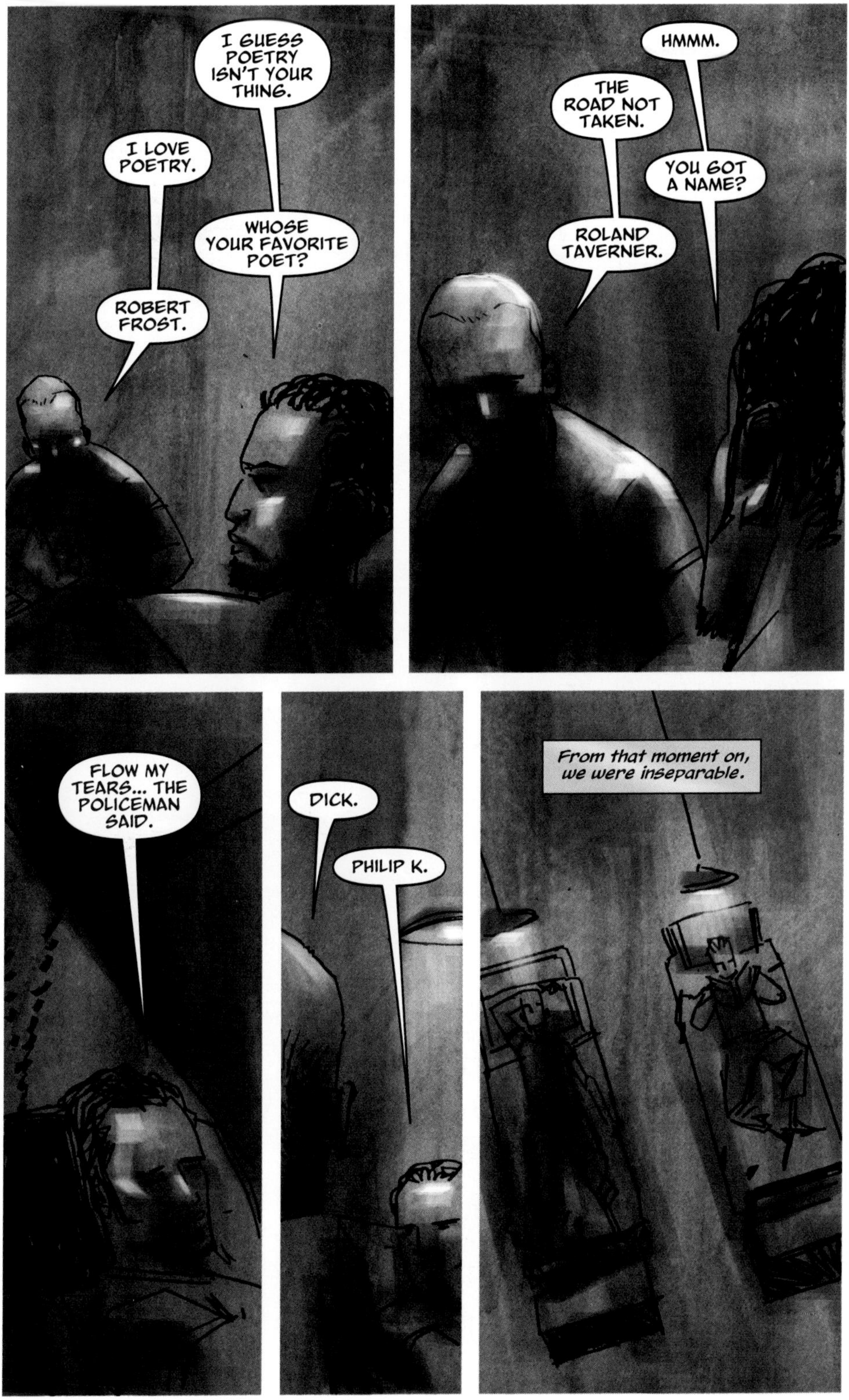
I GUESS POETRY ISN'T YOUR THING.
I LOVE POETRY.
WHOSE YOUR FAVORITE POET?
ROBERT FROST.
HMMM.
THE ROAD NOT TAKEN.
YOU GOT A NAME?
ROLAND TAVERNER.
FLOW MY TEARS... THE POLICEMAN SAID.
DICK.
PHILIP K.
From that moment on, we were inseparable.

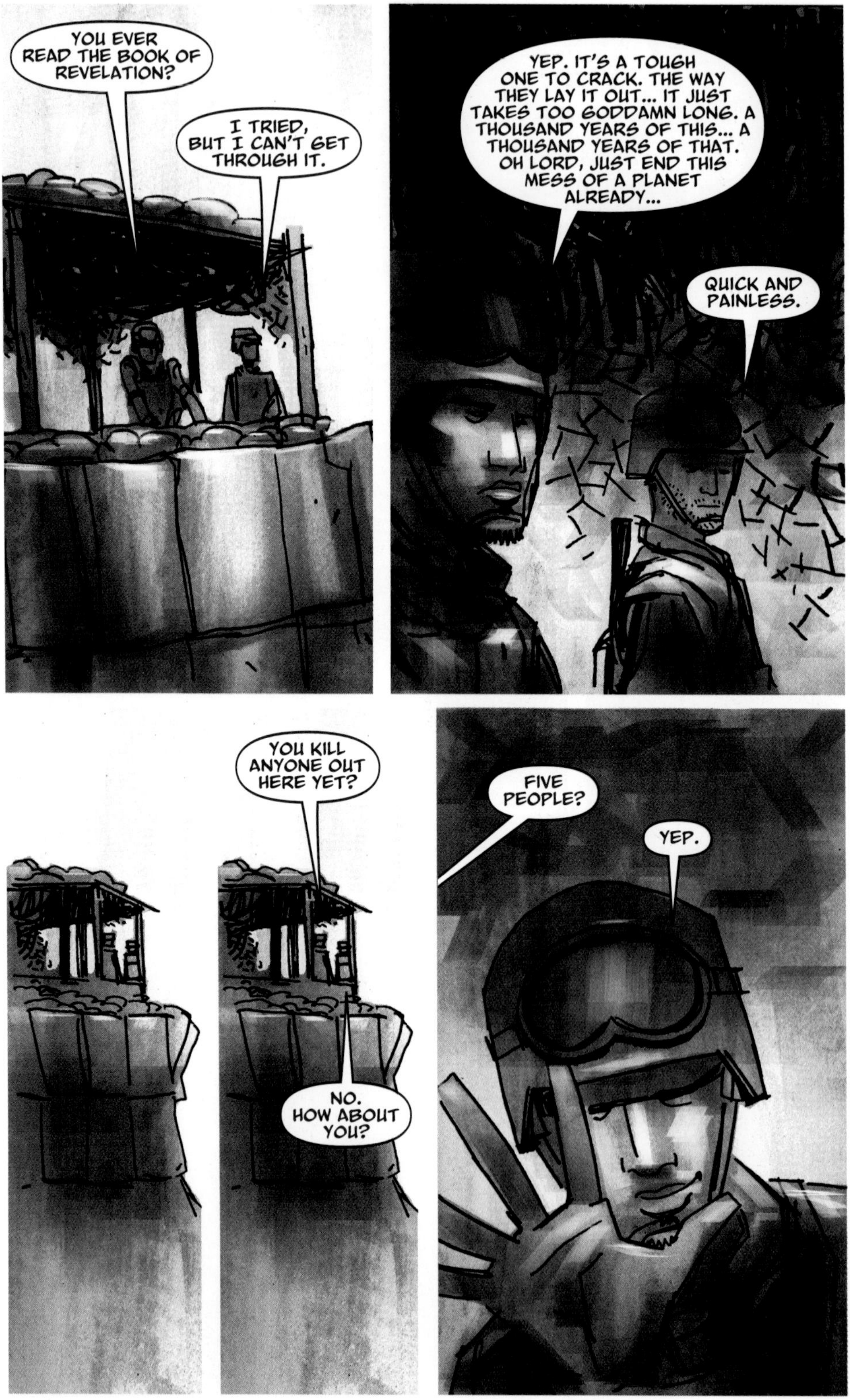
YOU EVER READ THE BOOK OF REVELATION?
I TRIED, BUT I CAN'T GET THROUGH IT.
YEP. IT'S A TOUGH ONE TO CRACK. THE WAY THEY LAY IT OUT... IT JUST TAKES TOO GODDAMN LONG. A THOUSAND YEARS OF THIS... A THOUSAND YEARS OF THAT. OH LORD, JUST END THIS MESS OF A PLANET ALREADY...
QUICK AND PAINLESS.
YOU KILL ANYONE OUT HERE YET?
NO. HOW ABOUT YOU?
FIVE PEOPLE?
YEP.

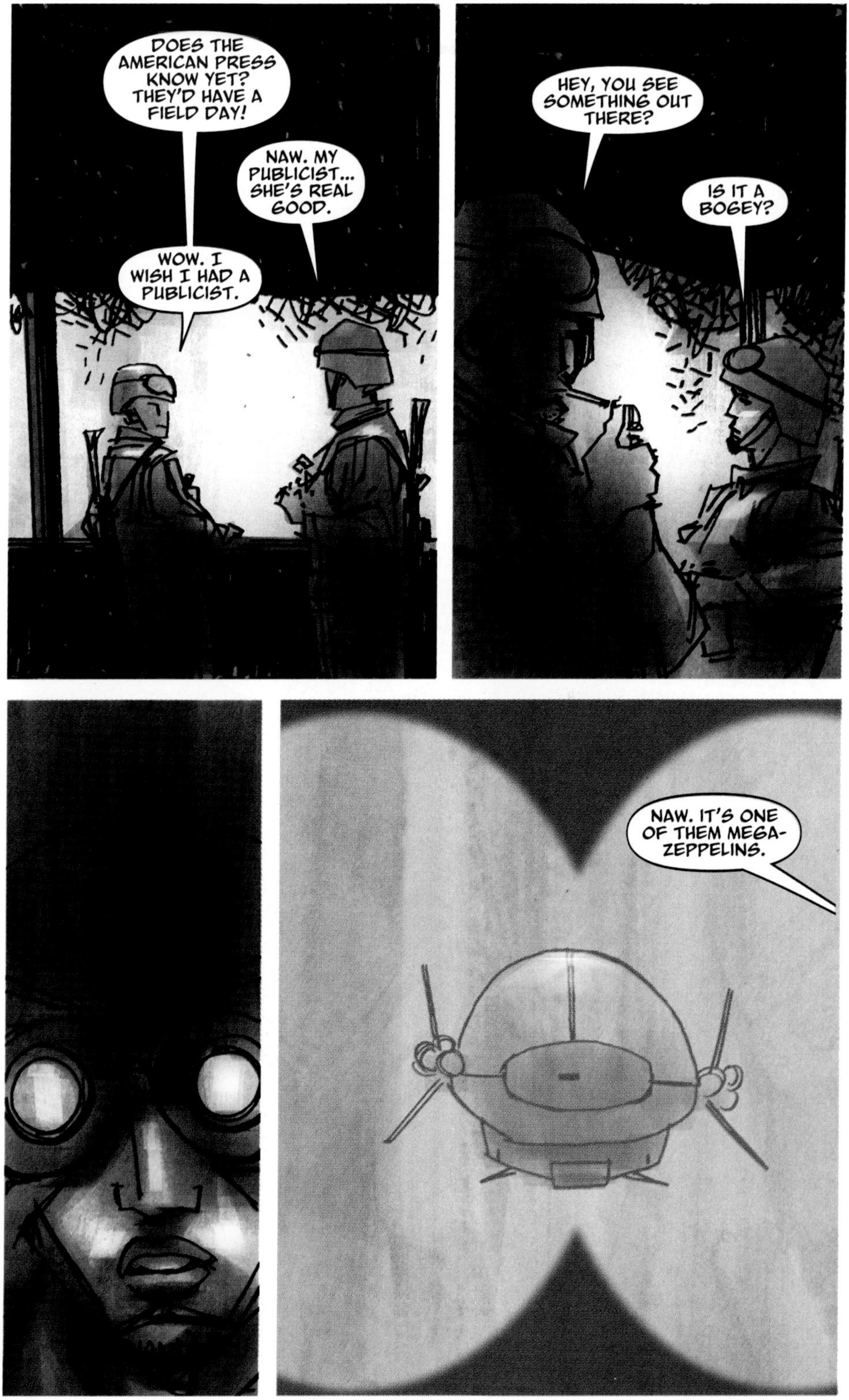
DOES THE AMERICAN PRESS KNOW YET? THEY'D HAVE A FIELD DAY!
NAW. MY PUBLICIST... SHE'S REAL GOOD.
WOW. I WISH I HAD A PUBLICIST.
HEY, YOU SEE SOMETHING OUT THERE?
IS IT A BOGEY?
NAW. IT'S ONE OF THEM MEGA-ZEPPELINS.

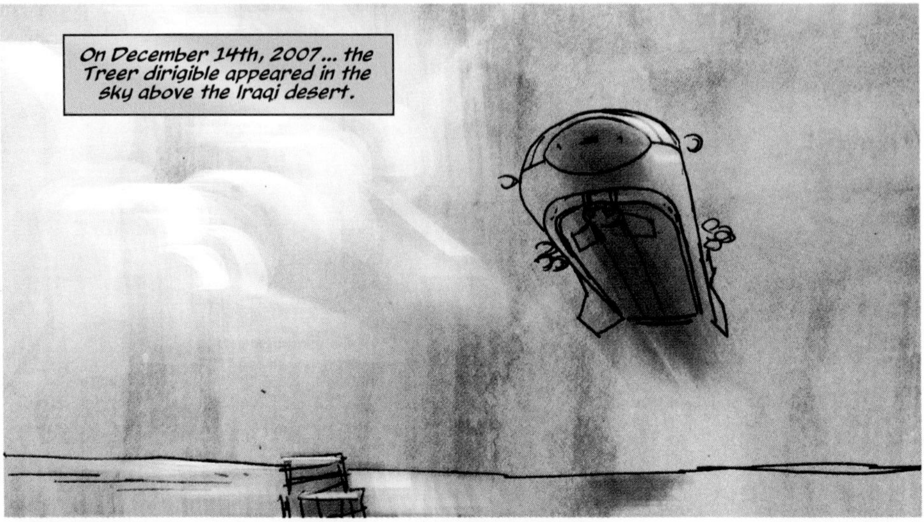
On December 14th, 2007... the Treer dirigible appeared in the sky above the Iraqi desert.

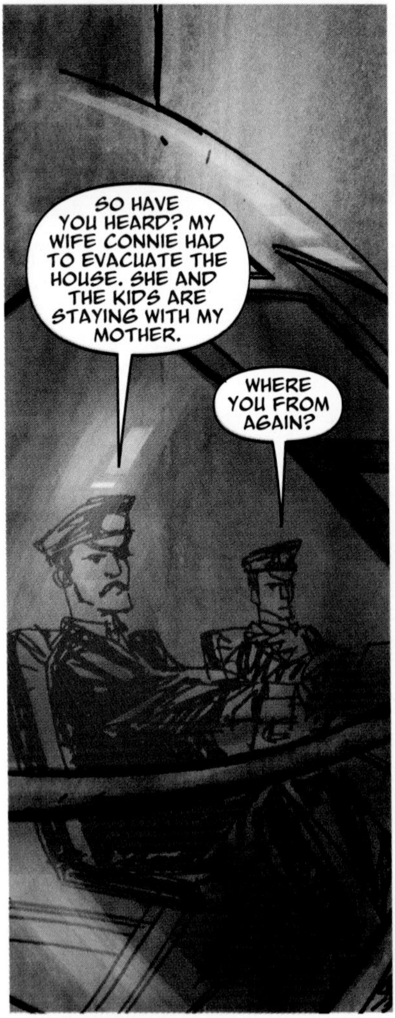
SO HAVE YOU HEARD? MY WIFE CONNIE HAD TO EVACUATE THE HOUSE. SHE AND THE KIDS ARE STAYING WITH MY MOTHER.
WHERE YOU FROM AGAIN?

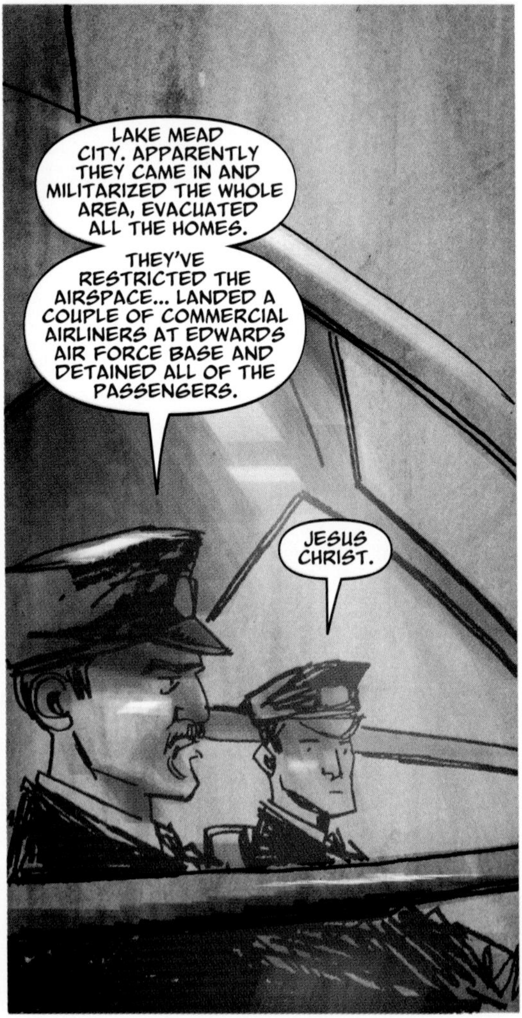
LAKE MEAD CITY. APPARENTLY THEY CAME IN AND MILITARIZED THE WHOLE AREA, EVACUATED ALL THE HOMES.
THEY'VE RESTRICTED THE AIRSPACE... LANDED A COUPLE OF COMMERCIAL AIRLINERS AT EDWARDS AIR FORCE BASE AND DETAINED ALL OF THE PASSENGERS.
JESUS CHRIST.

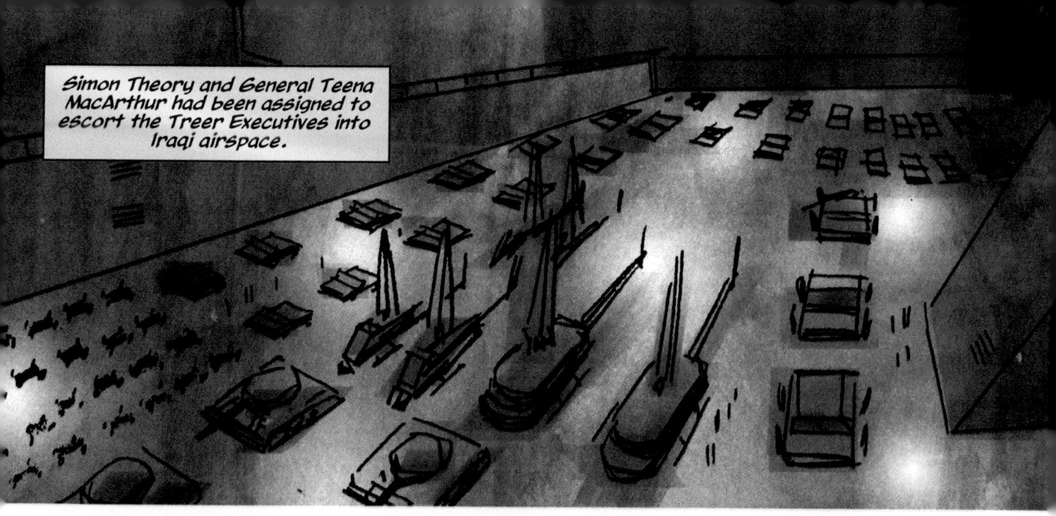
Simon Theory and General Teena MacArthur had been assigned to escort the Treer Executives into Iraqi airspace.

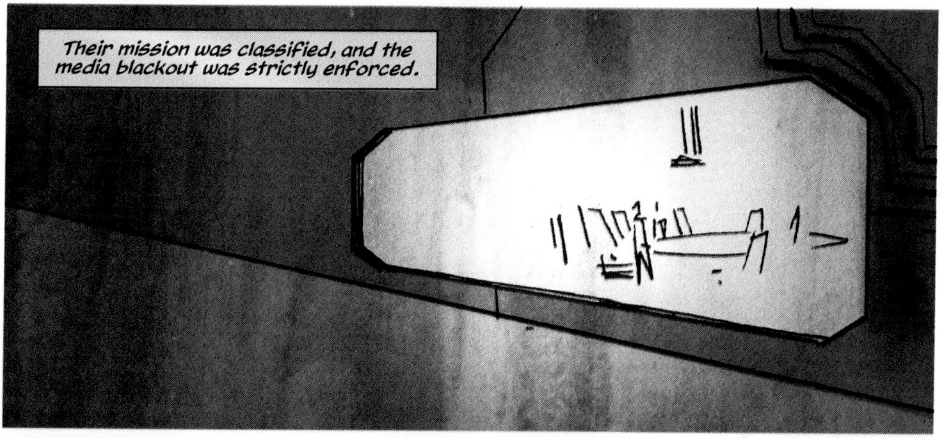
Their mission was classified, and the media blackout was strictly enforced.

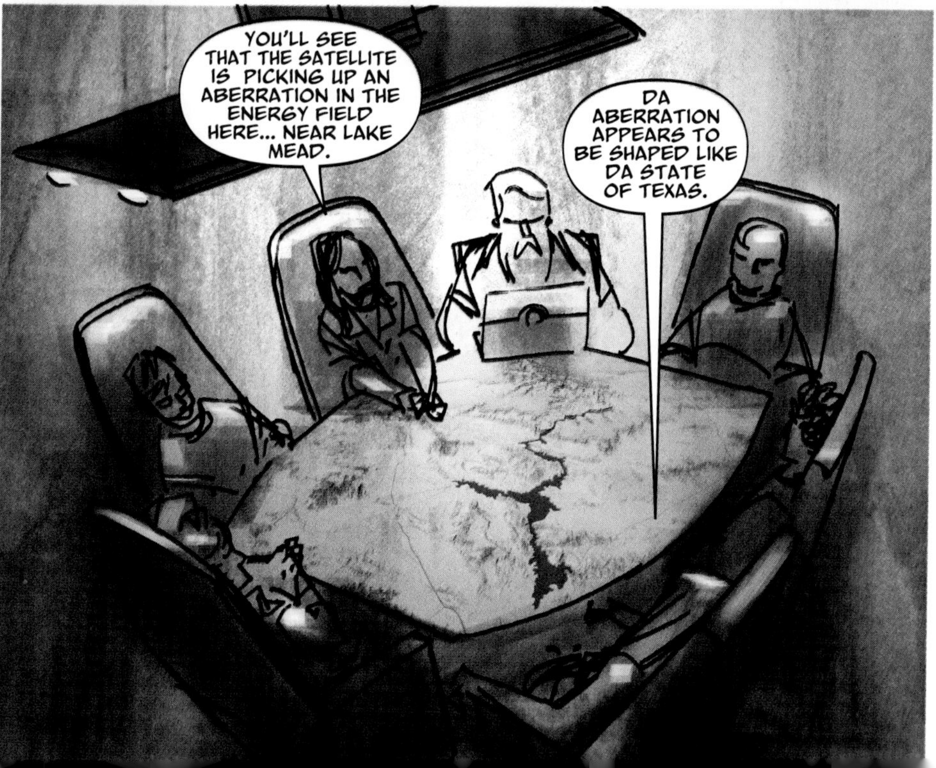
YOU'LL SEE THAT THE SATELLITE IS PICKING UP AN ABERRATION IN THE ENERGY FIELD HERE... NEAR LAKE MEAD.
DA ABERRATION APPEARS TO BE SHAPED LIKE DA STATE OF TEXAS.

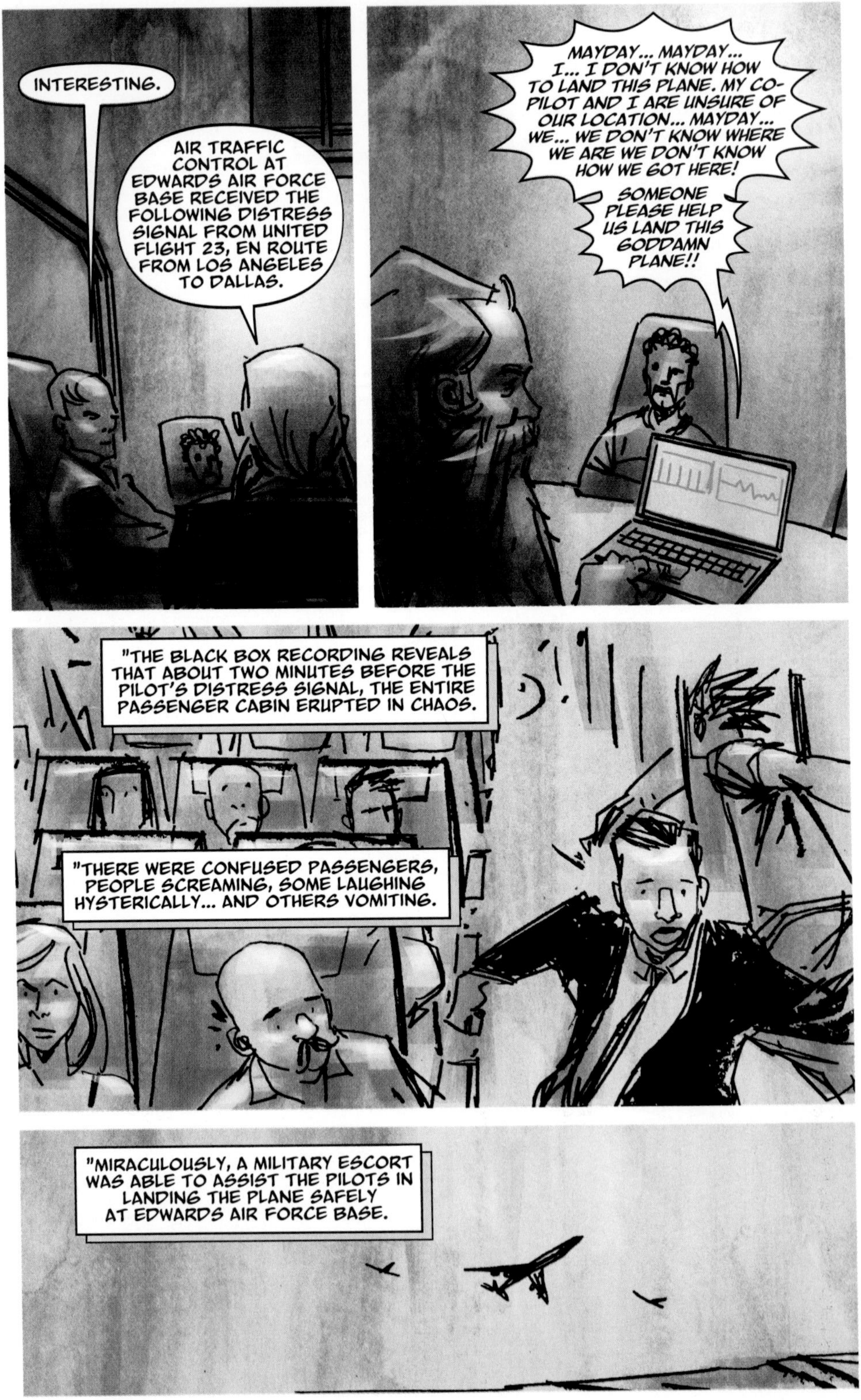
INTERESTING.
AIR TRAFFIC CONTROL AT EDWARDS AIR FORCE BASE RECEIVED THE FOLLOWING DISTRESS SIGNAL FROM UNITED FLIGHT 23, EN ROUTE FROM LOS ANGELES TO DALLAS.
MAYDAY... MAYDAY... I... I DON'T KNOW HOW TO LAND THIS PLANE. MY CO-PILOT AND I ARE UNSURE OF OUR LOCATION... MAYDAY... WE... WE DON'T KNOW WHERE WE ARE WE DON'T KNOW HOW WE GOT HERE!
SOMEONE PLEASE HELP US LAND THIS GODDAMN PLANE!!
"THE BLACK BOX RECORDING REVEALS THAT ABOUT TWO MINUTES BEFORE THE PILOT'S DISTRESS SIGNAL, THE ENTIRE PASSENGER CABIN ERUPTED IN CHAOS.
"THERE WERE CONFUSED PASSENGERS, PEOPLE SCREAMING, SOME LAUGHING HYSTERICALLY... AND OTHERS VOMITING.
"MIRACULOUSLY, A MILITARY ESCORT WAS ABLE TO ASSIST THE PILOTS IN LANDING THE PLANE SAFELY AT EDWARDS AIR FORCE BASE.

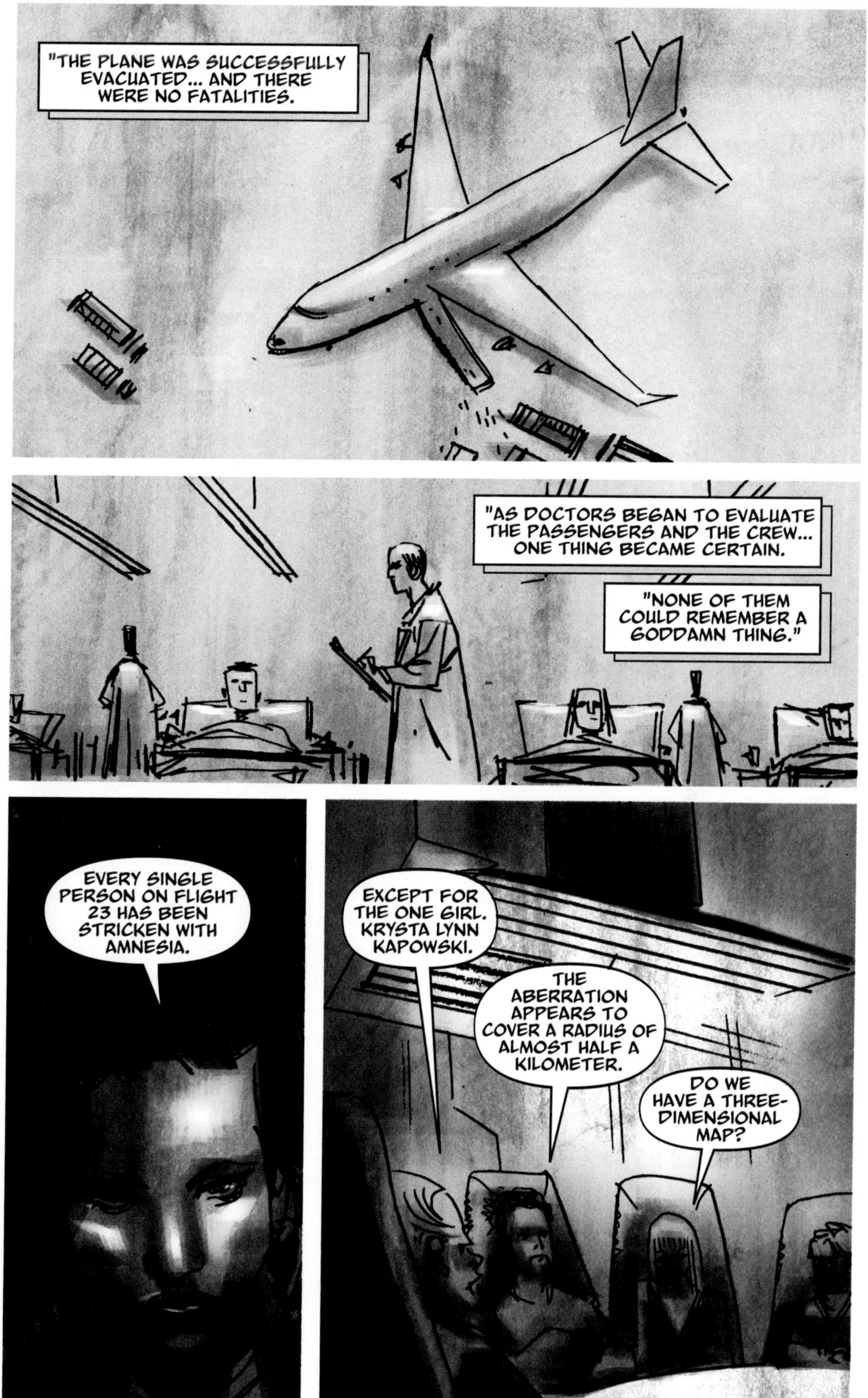
"THE PLANE WAS SUCCESSFULLY EVACUATED... AND THERE WERE NO FATALITIES.
"AS DOCTORS BEGAN TO EVALUATE THE PASSENGERS AND THE CREW... ONE THING BECAME CERTAIN.
"NONE OF THEM COULD REMEMBER A GODDAMN THING."
EVERY SINGLE PERSON ON FLIGHT 23 HAS BEEN STRICKEN WITH AMNESIA.
EXCEPT FOR THE ONE GIRL. KRYSTA LYNN KAPOWSKI.
THE ABERRATION APPEARS TO COVER A RADIUS OF ALMOST HALF A KILOMETER.
DO WE HAVE A THREE-DIMENSIONAL MAP?

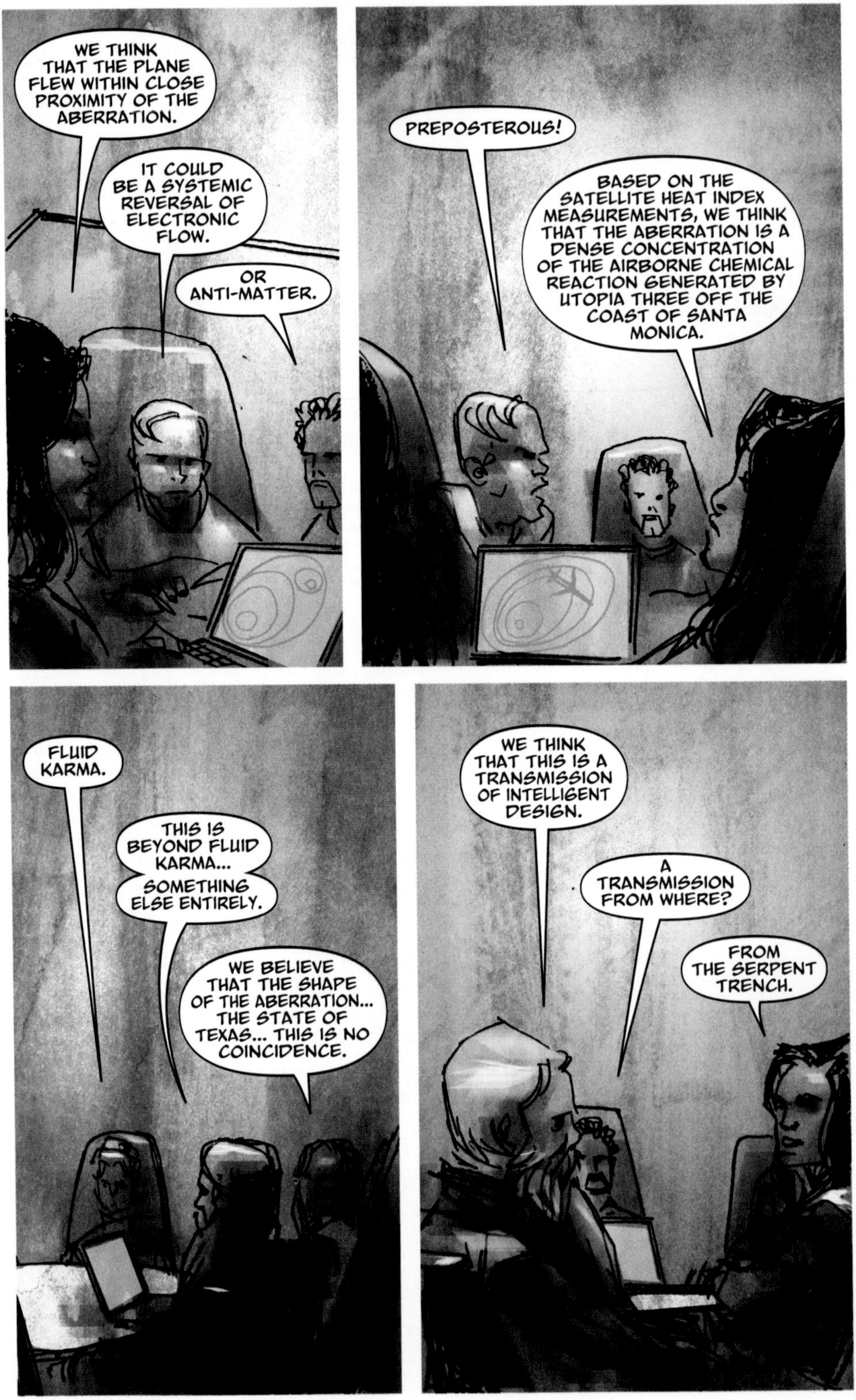
WE THINK THAT THE PLANE FLEW WITHIN CLOSE PROXIMITY OF THE ABERRATION.
IT COULD BE A SYSTEMIC REVERSAL OF ELECTRONIC FLOW.
OR ANTI-MATTER.
PREPOSTEROUS!
BASED ON THE SATELLITE HEAT INDEX MEASUREMENTS, WE THINK THAT THE ABERRATION IS A DENSE CONCENTRATION OF THE AIRBORNE CHEMICAL REACTION GENERATED BY UTOPIA THREE OFF THE COAST OF SANTA MONICA.
FLUID KARMA.
THIS IS BEYOND FLUID KARMA...
SOMETHING ELSE ENTIRELY.
WE BELIEVE THAT THE SHAPE OF THE ABERRATION... THE STATE OF TEXAS... THIS IS NO COINCIDENCE.
WE THINK THAT THIS IS A TRANSMISSION OF INTELLIGENT DESIGN.
A TRANSMISSION FROM WHERE?
FROM THE SERPENT TRENCH.

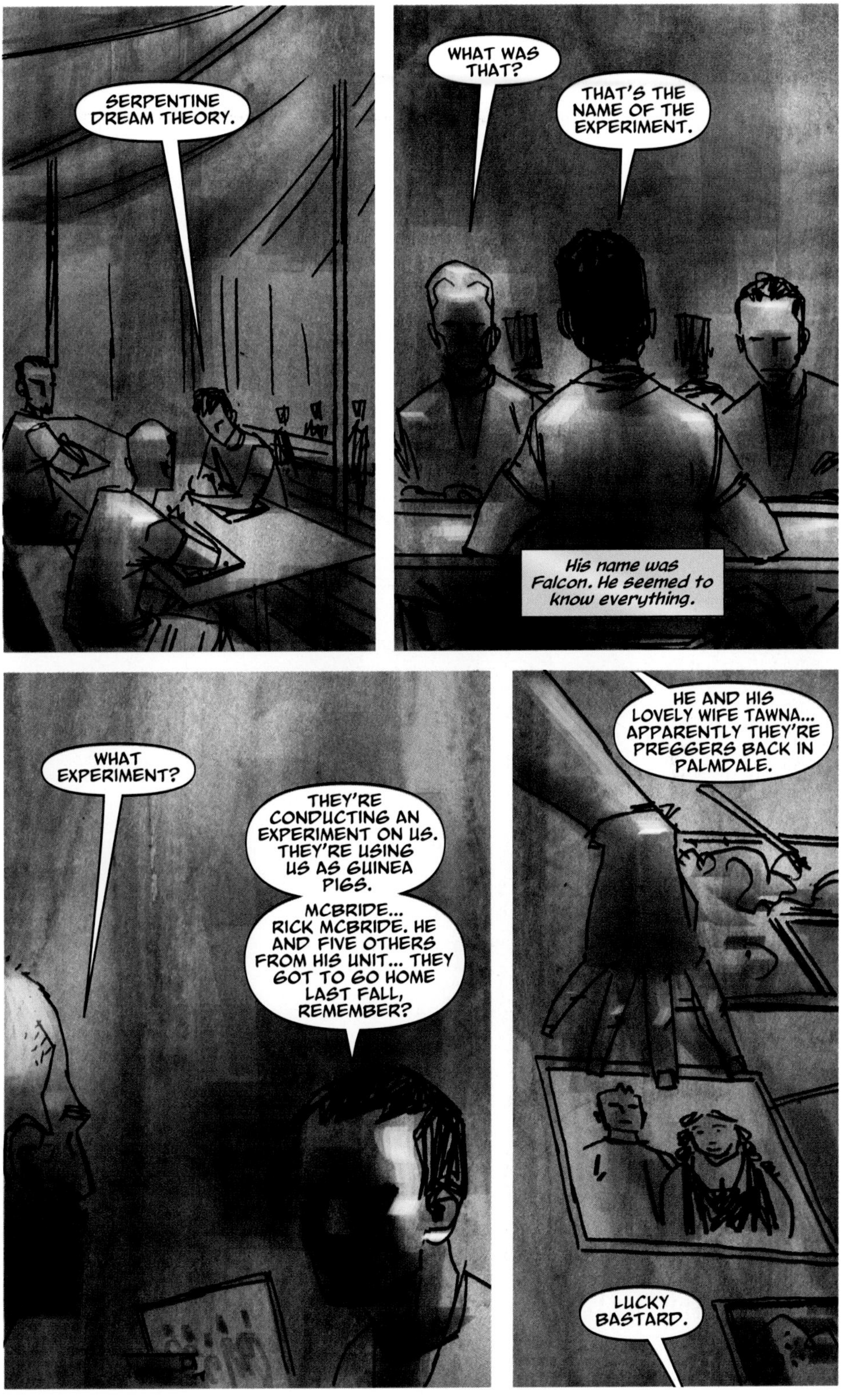
SERPENTINE DREAM THEORY.
WHAT WAS THAT?
THAT'S THE NAME OF THE EXPERIMENT.
His name was Falcon. He seemed to know everything.
WHAT EXPERIMENT?
THEY'RE CONDUCTING AN EXPERIMENT ON US. THEY'RE USING US AS GUINEA PIGS.
MCBRIDE... RICK MCBRIDE. HE AND FIVE OTHERS FROM HIS UNIT... THEY GOT TO GO HOME LAST FALL, REMEMBER?
HE AND HIS LOVELY WIFE TAWNA... APPARENTLY THEY'RE PREGGERS BACK IN PALMDALE.
LUCKY BASTARD.

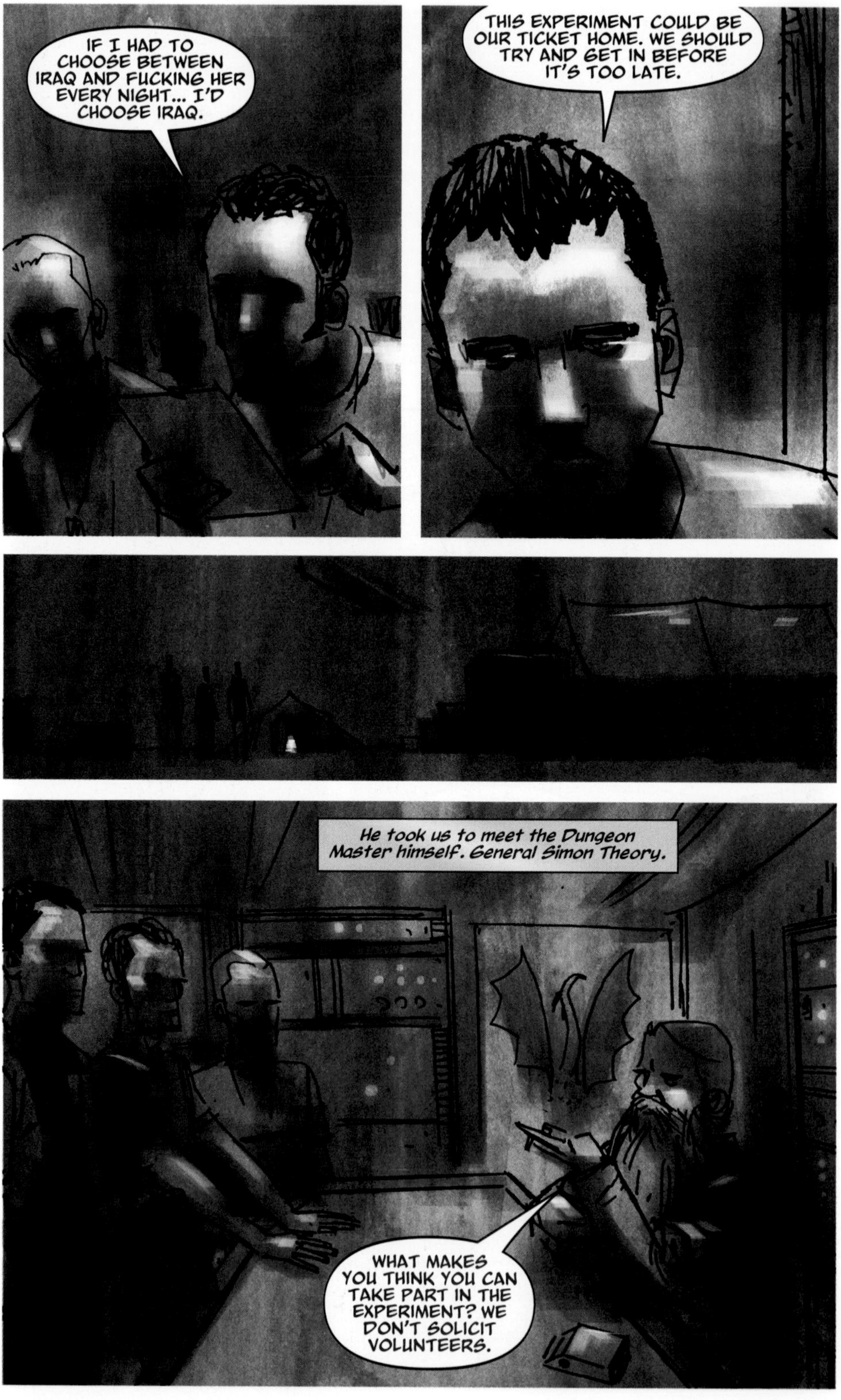
IF I HAD TO CHOOSE BETWEEN IRAQ AND FUCKING HER EVERY NIGHT... I'D CHOOSE IRAQ.
THIS EXPERIMENT COULD BE OUR TICKET HOME. WE SHOULD TRY AND GET IN BEFORE IT'S TOO LATE.
He took us to meet the Dungeon Master himself. General Simon Theory.
WHAT MAKES YOU THINK YOU CAN TAKE PART IN THE EXPERIMENT? WE DON'T SOLICIT VOLUNTEERS.

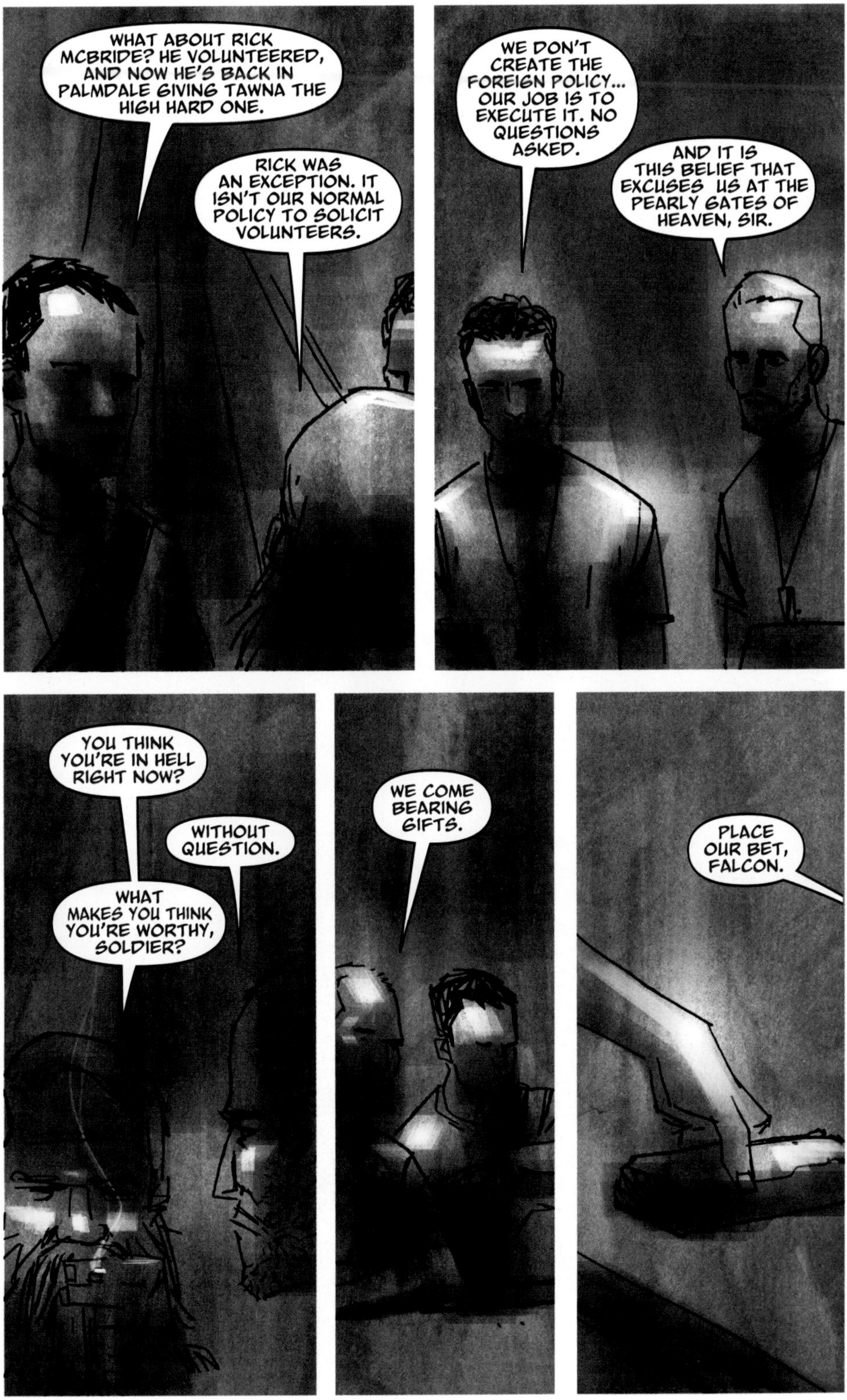
WHAT ABOUT RICK MCBRIDE? HE VOLUNTEERED, AND NOW HE'S BACK IN PALMDALE GIVING TAWNA THE HIGH HARD ONE.
RICK WAS AN EXCEPTION. IT ISN'T OUR NORMAL POLICY TO SOLICIT VOLUNTEERS.
WE DON'T CREATE THE FOREIGN POLICY... OUR JOB IS TO EXECUTE IT. NO QUESTIONS ASKED.
AND IT IS THIS BELIEF THAT EXCUSES US AT THE PEARLY GATES OF HEAVEN, SIR.
YOU THINK YOU'RE IN HELL RIGHT NOW?
WITHOUT QUESTION.
WHAT MAKES YOU THINK YOU'RE WORTHY, SOLDIER?
WE COME BEARING GIFTS.
PLACE OUR BET, FALCON.

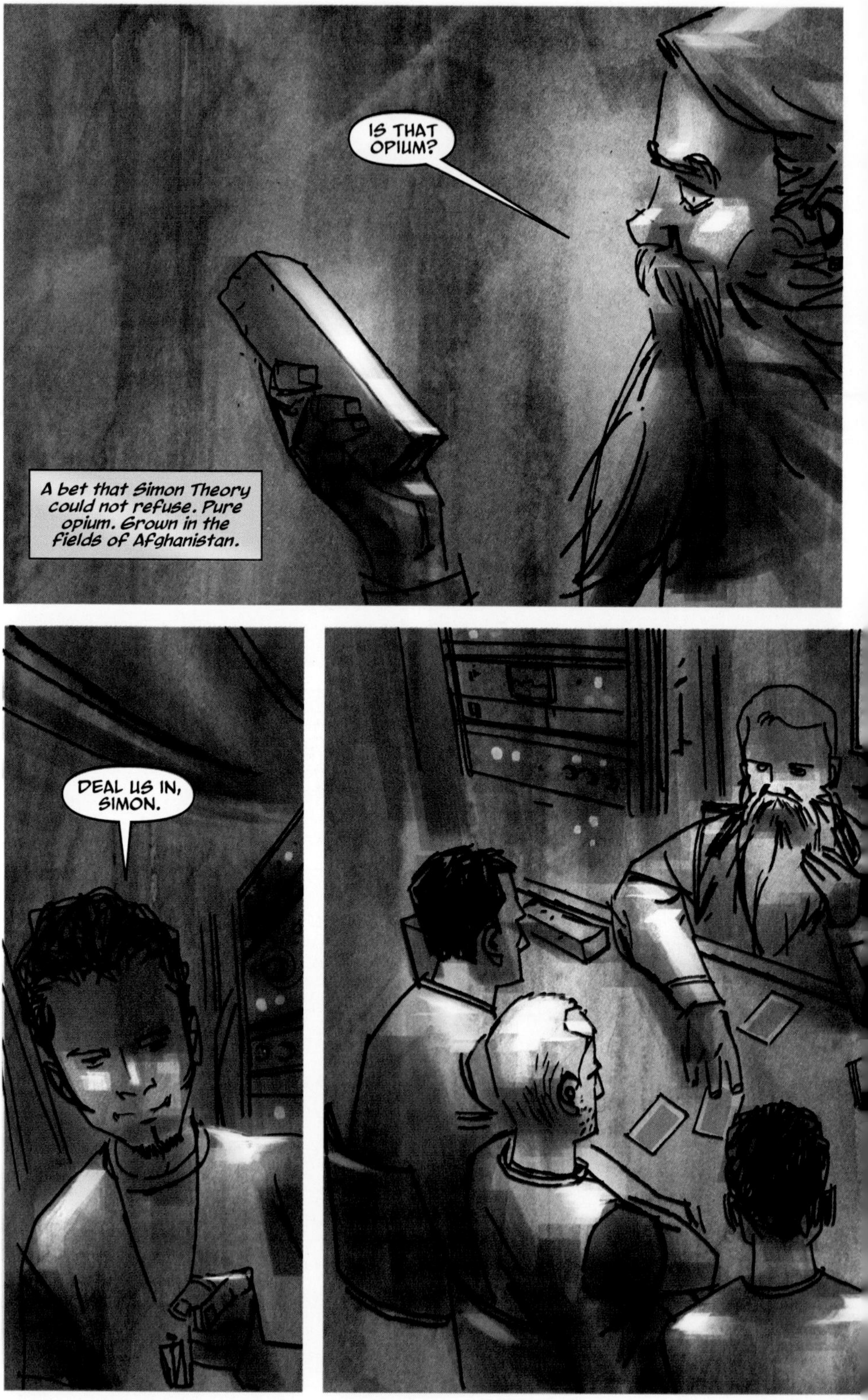
IS THAT OPIUM?
A bet that Simon Theory could not refuse. Pure opium. Grown in the fields of Afghanistan.
DEAL US IN, SIMON.

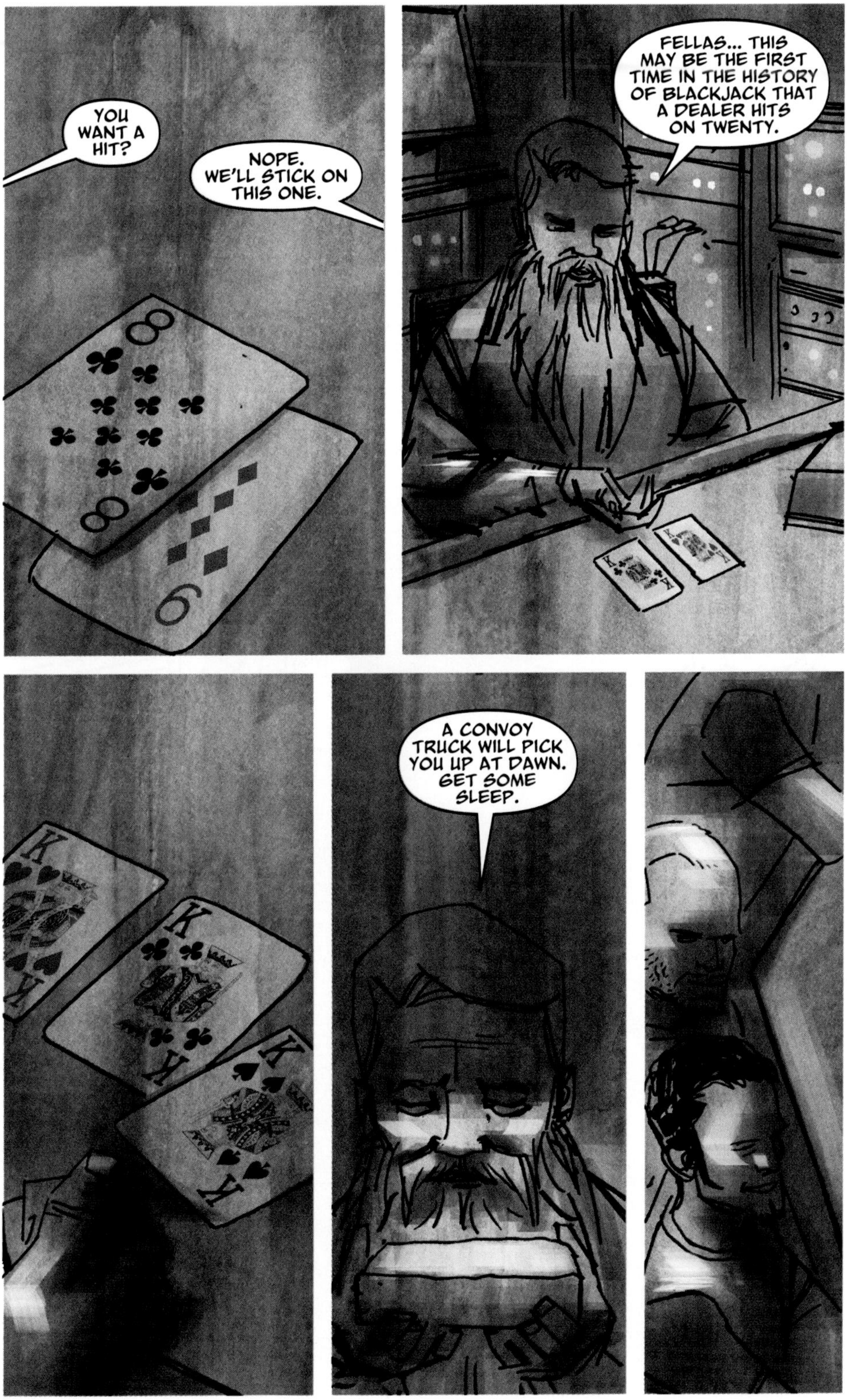
YOU WANT A HIT?
NOPE. WE'LL STICK ON THIS ONE.
FELLAS... THIS MAY BE THE FIRST TIME IN THE HISTORY OF BLACKJACK THAT A DEALER HITS ON TWENTY.
A CONVOY TRUCK WILL PICK YOU UP AT DAWN. GET SOME SLEEP.

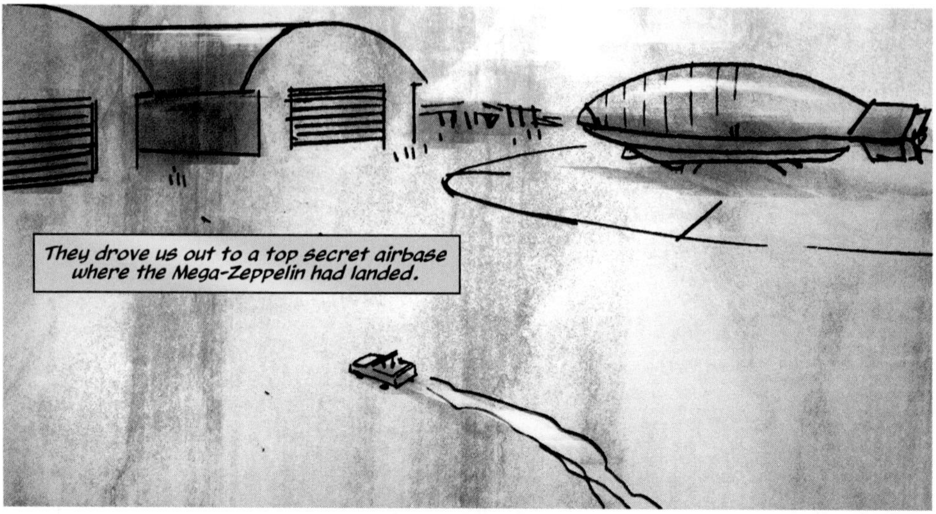
They drove us out to a top secret airbase where the Mega-Zeppelin had landed.

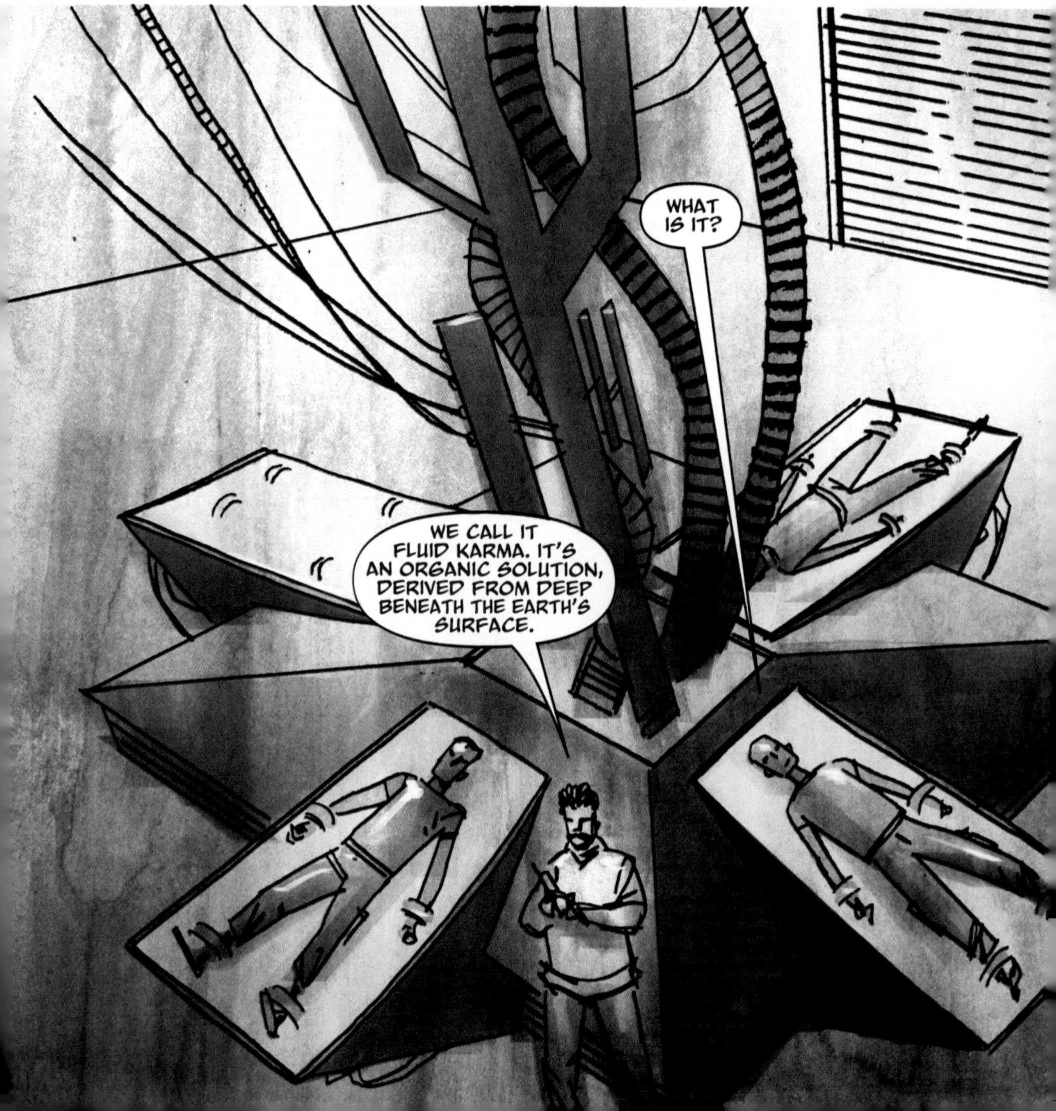
WHAT IS IT?
WE CALL IT FLUID KARMA. IT'S AN ORGANIC SOLUTION, DERIVED FROM DEEP BENEATH THE EARTH'S SURFACE.

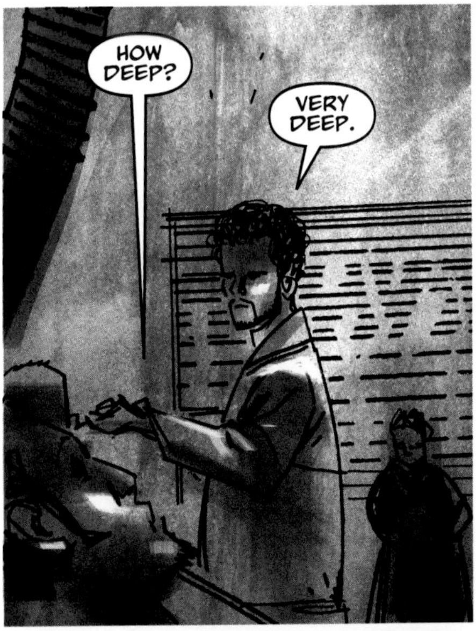
HOW DEEP?
VERY DEEP.

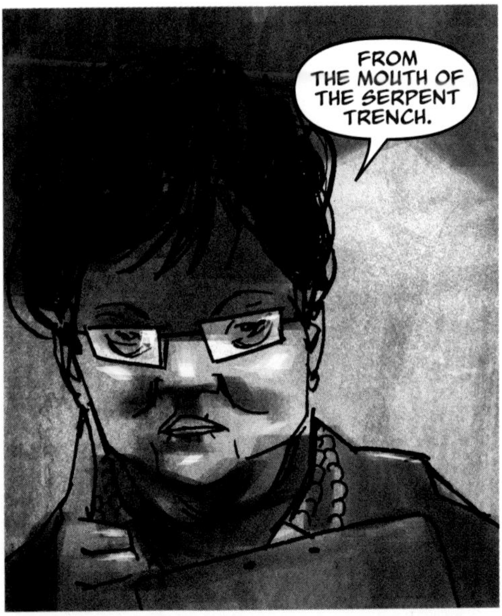
FROM THE MOUTH OF THE SERPENT TRENCH.

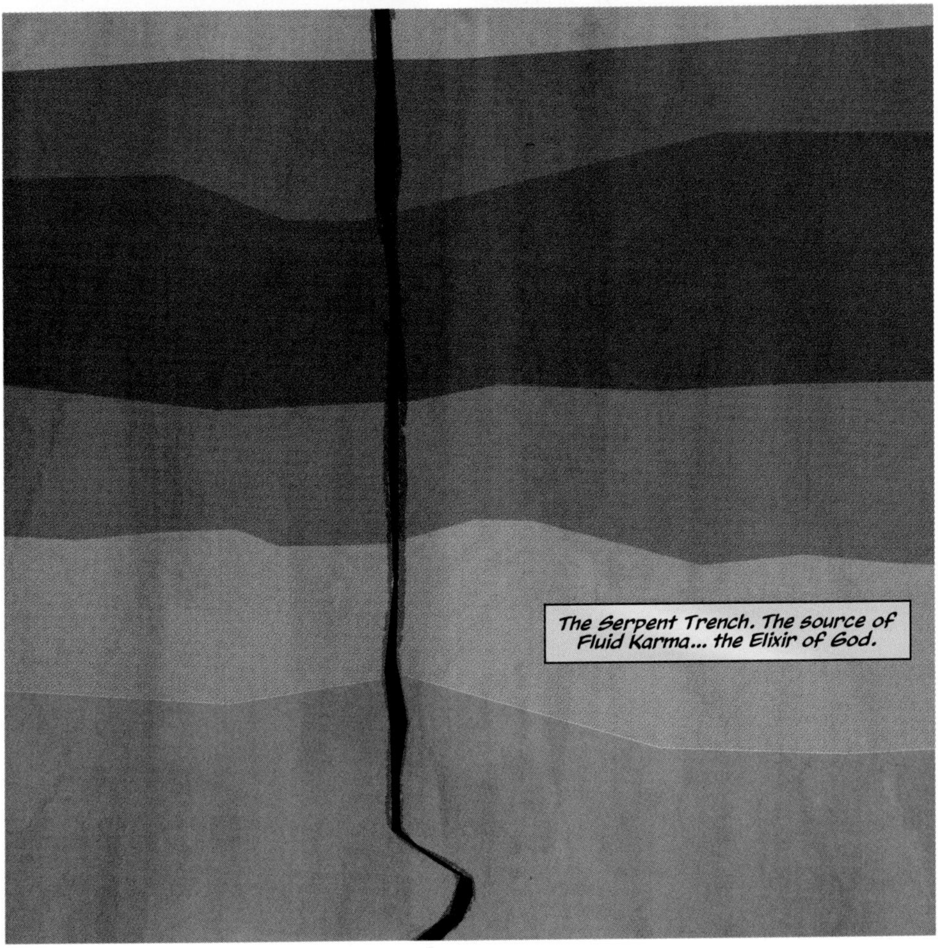
The Serpent Trench. The source of Fluid Karma... the Elixir of God.

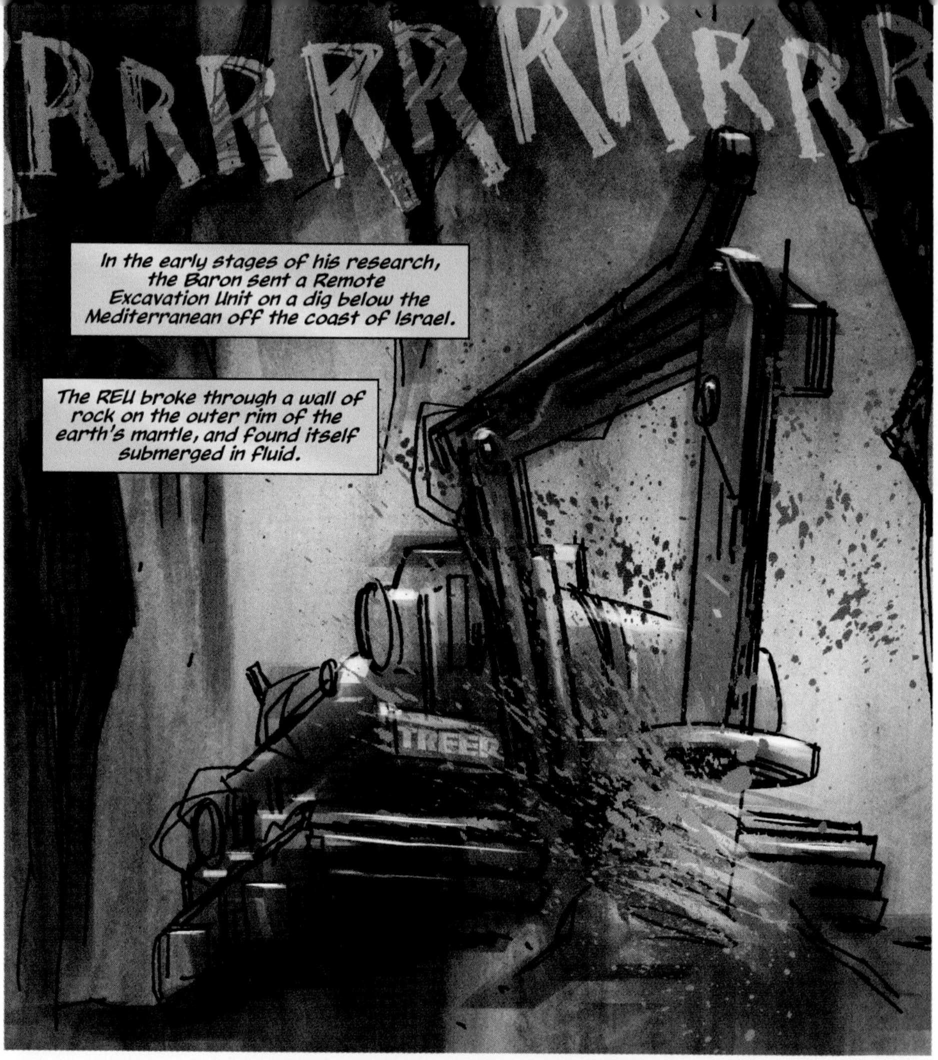
RRRRRRRRRR
In the early stages of his research, the Baron sent a Remote Excavation Unit on a dig below the Mediterranean off the coast of Israel.
The REU broke through a wall of rock on the outer rim of the earth's mantle, and found itself submerged in fluid.

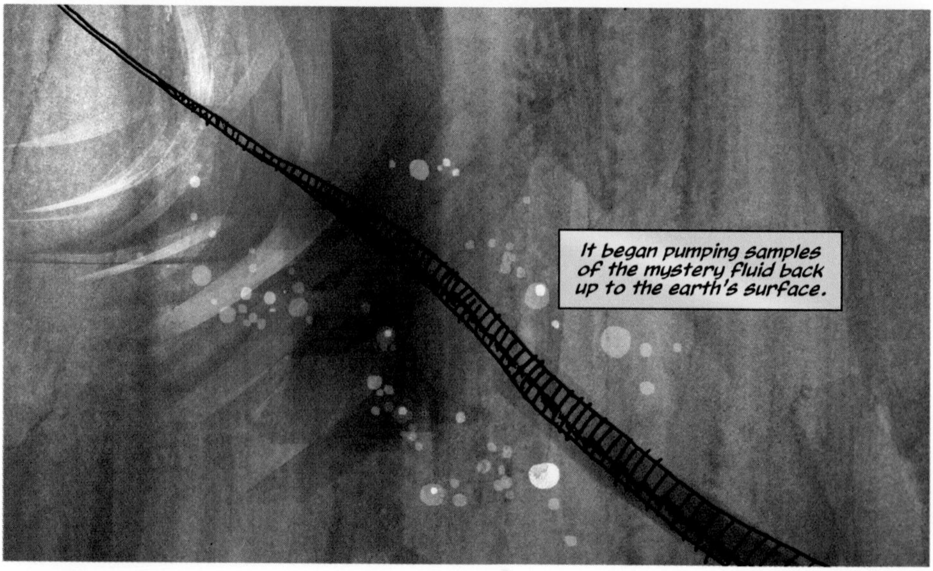
It began pumping samples of the mystery fluid back up to the earth's surface.

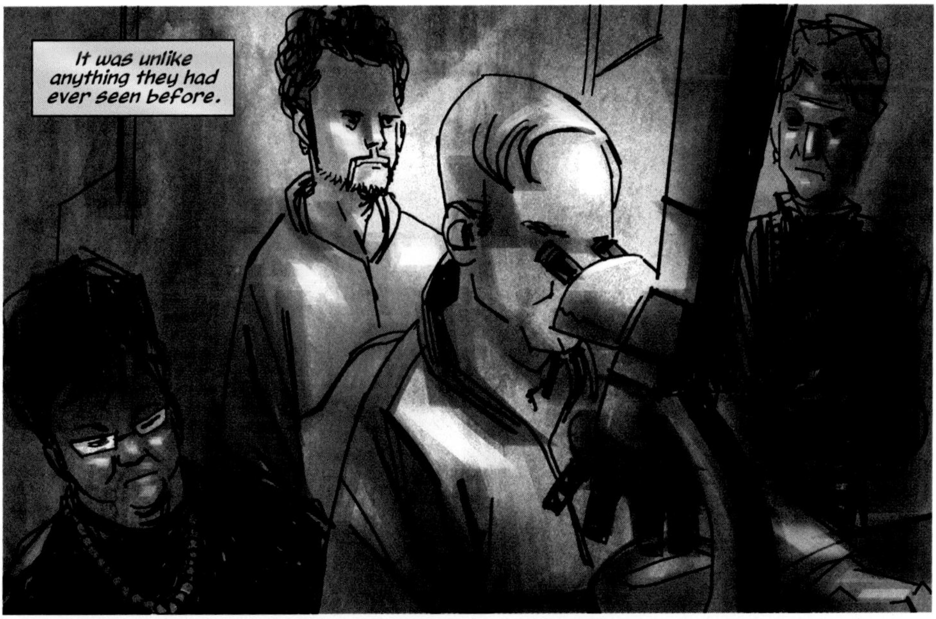
It was unlike anything they had ever seen before.

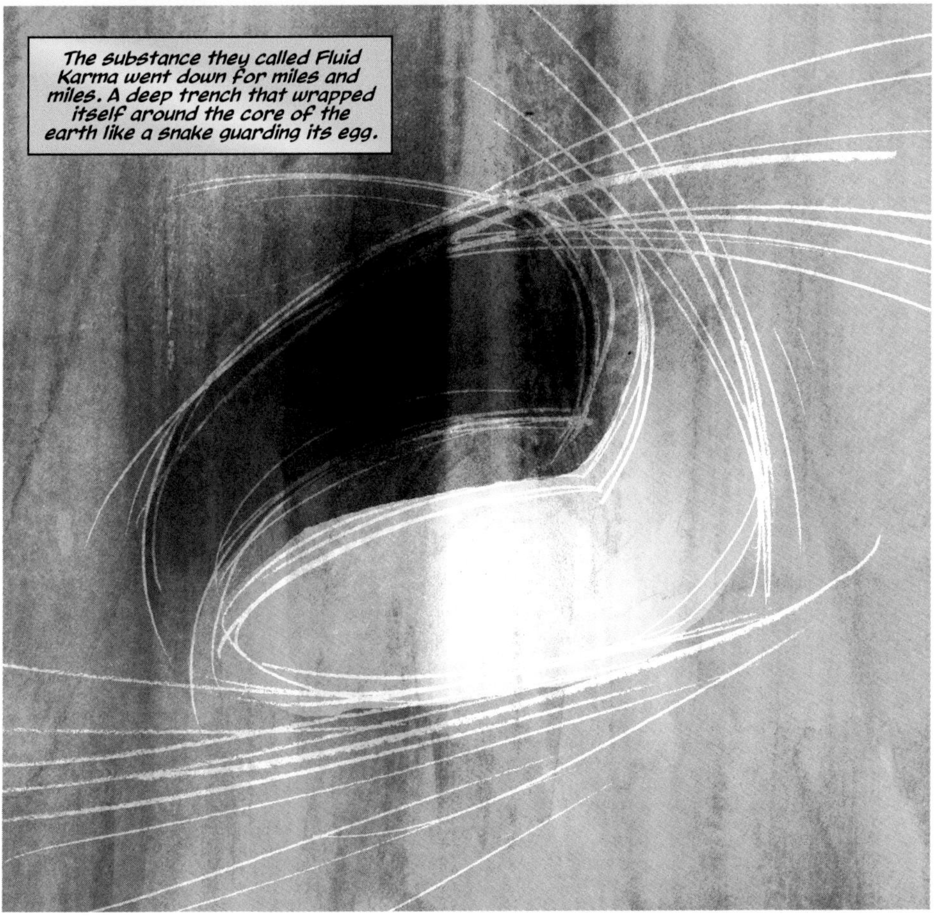
The substance they called Fluid Karma went down for miles and miles. A deep trench that wrapped itself around the core of the earth like a snake guarding its egg.

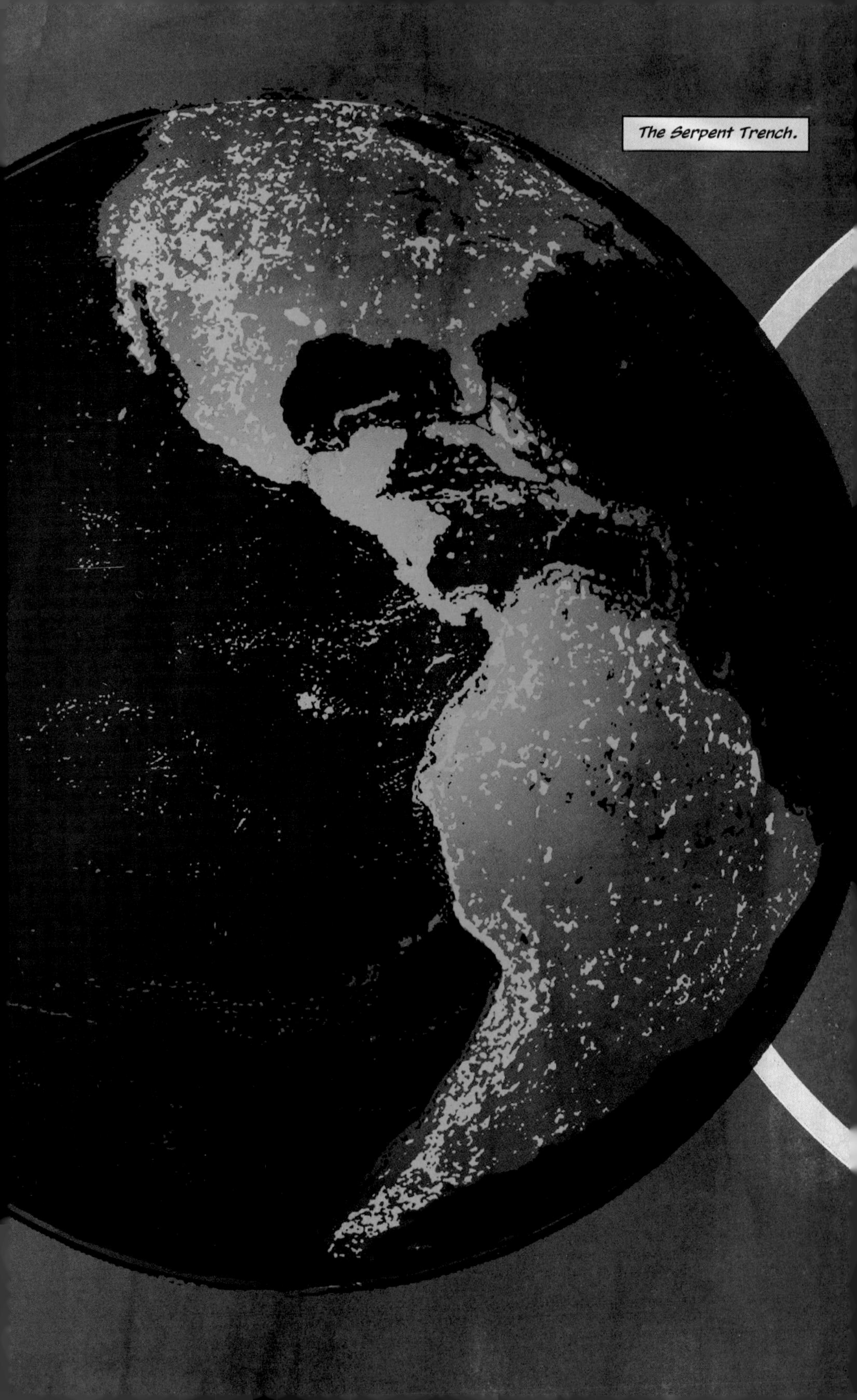
The Serpent Trench.

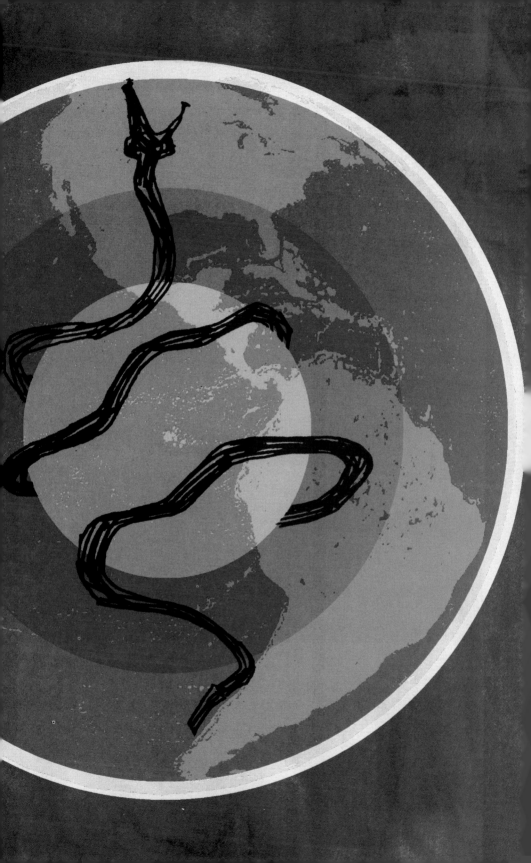

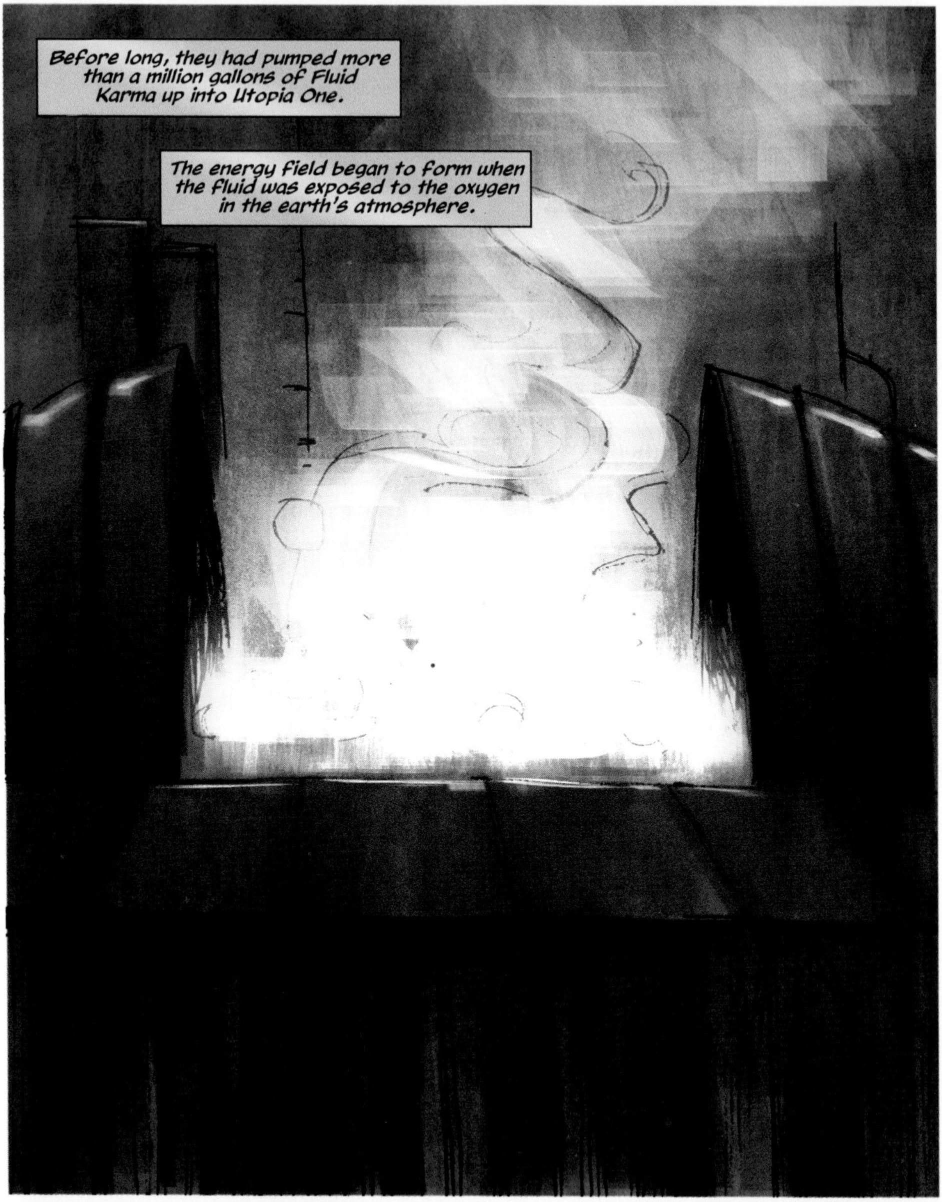
Before long, they had pumped more than a million gallons of Fluid Karma up into Utopia One.
The energy field began to form when the fluid was exposed to the oxygen in the earth's atmosphere.

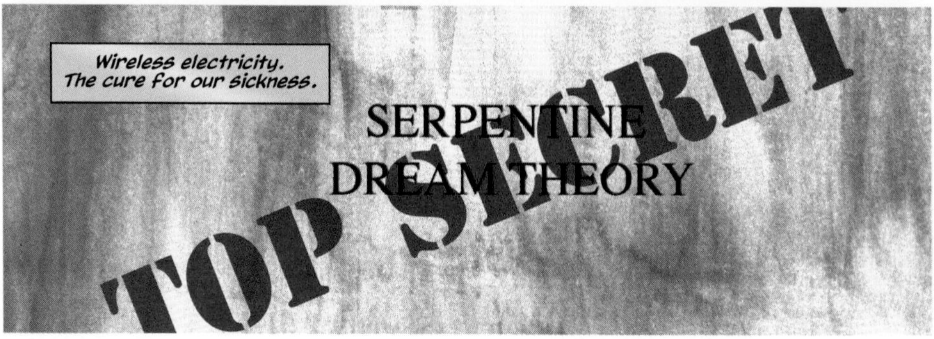
Wireless electricity. The cure for our sickness.
SERPENTINE
DREAM THEORY
TOP SECRET

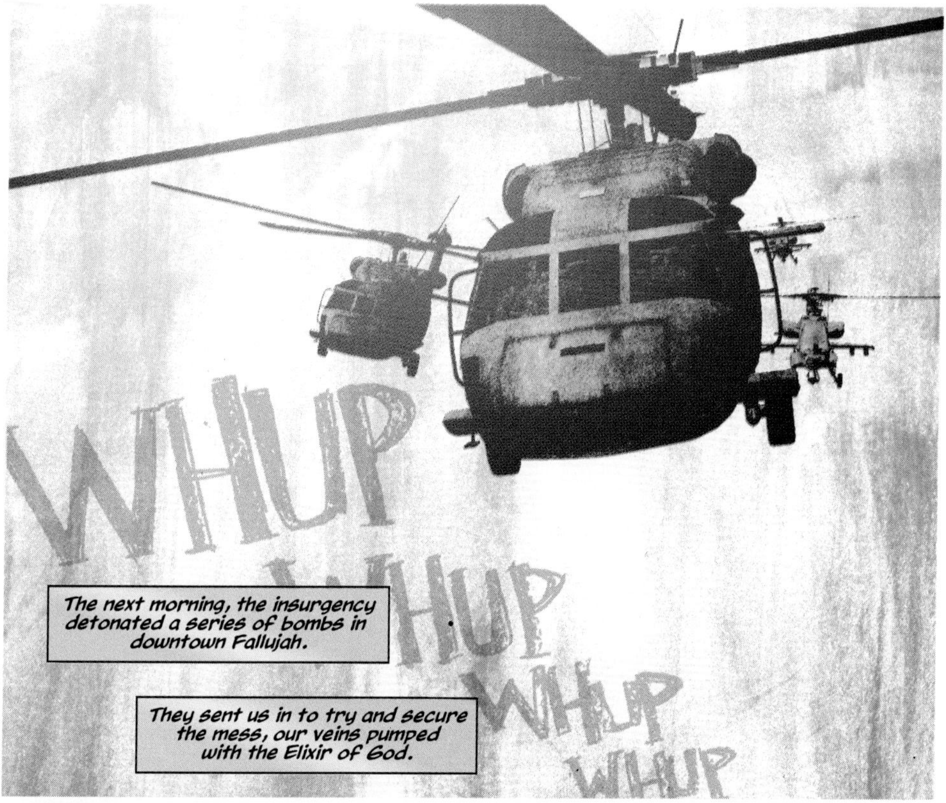
WHUP
WHUP
WHUP
WHUP
The next morning, the insurgency detonated a series of bombs in downtown Fallujah.
They sent us in to try and secure the mess, our veins pumped with the Elixir of God.

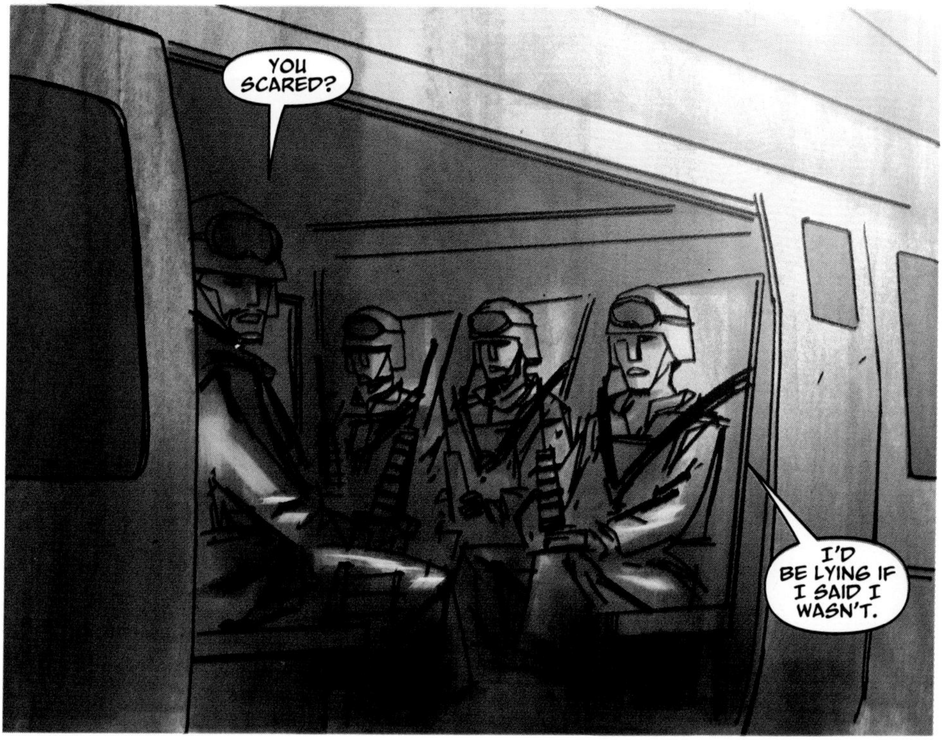
YOU SCARED?
I'D BE LYING IF I SAID I WASN'T.

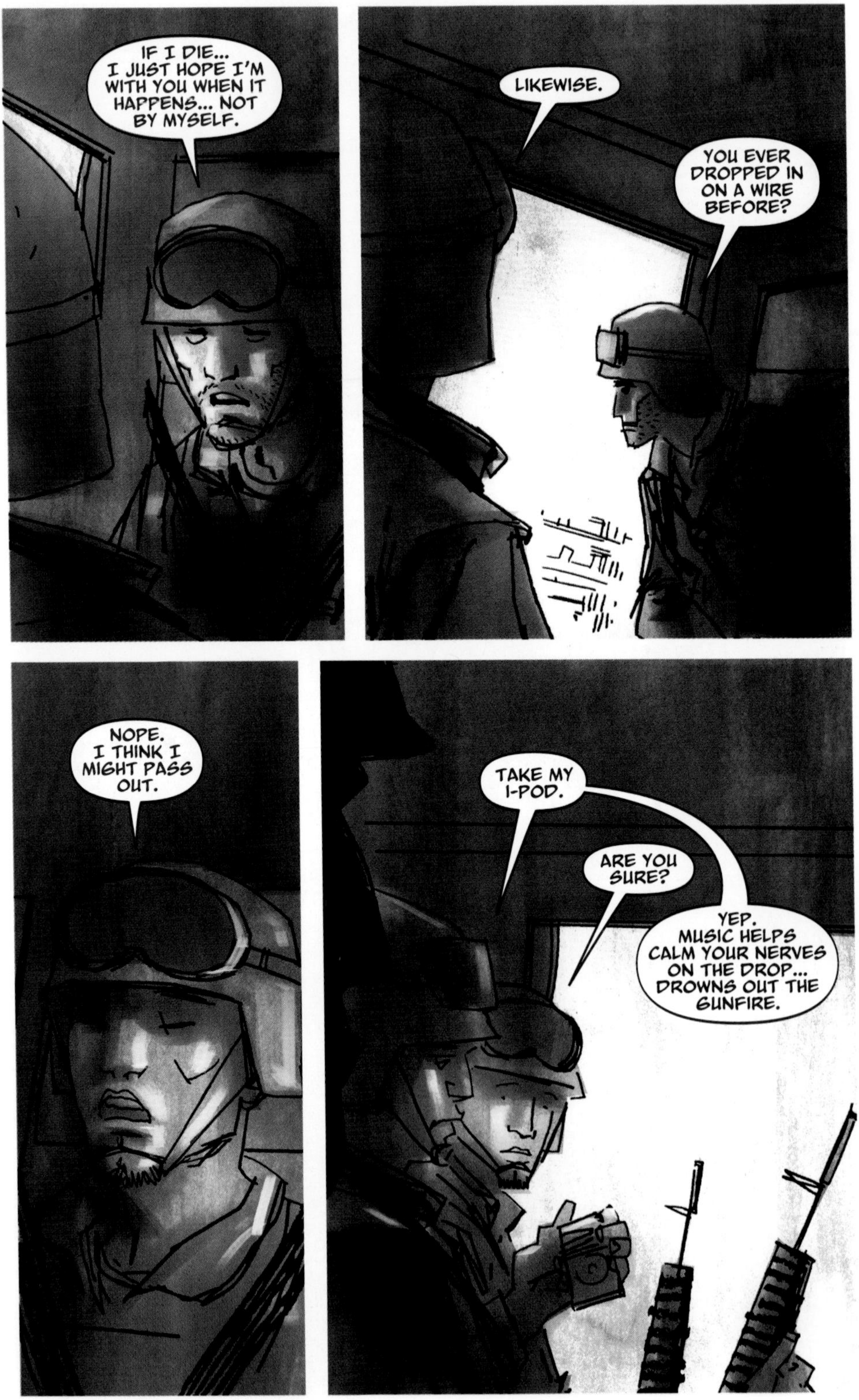
IF I DIE...
I JUST HOPE I'M WITH YOU WHEN IT HAPPENS... NOT BY MYSELF.
LIKEWISE.
YOU EVER DROPPED IN ON A WIRE BEFORE?
NOPE. I THINK I MIGHT PASS OUT.
TAKE MY I-POD.
ARE YOU SURE?
YEP. MUSIC HELPS CALM YOUR NERVES ON THE DROP... DROWNS OUT THE GUNFIRE.

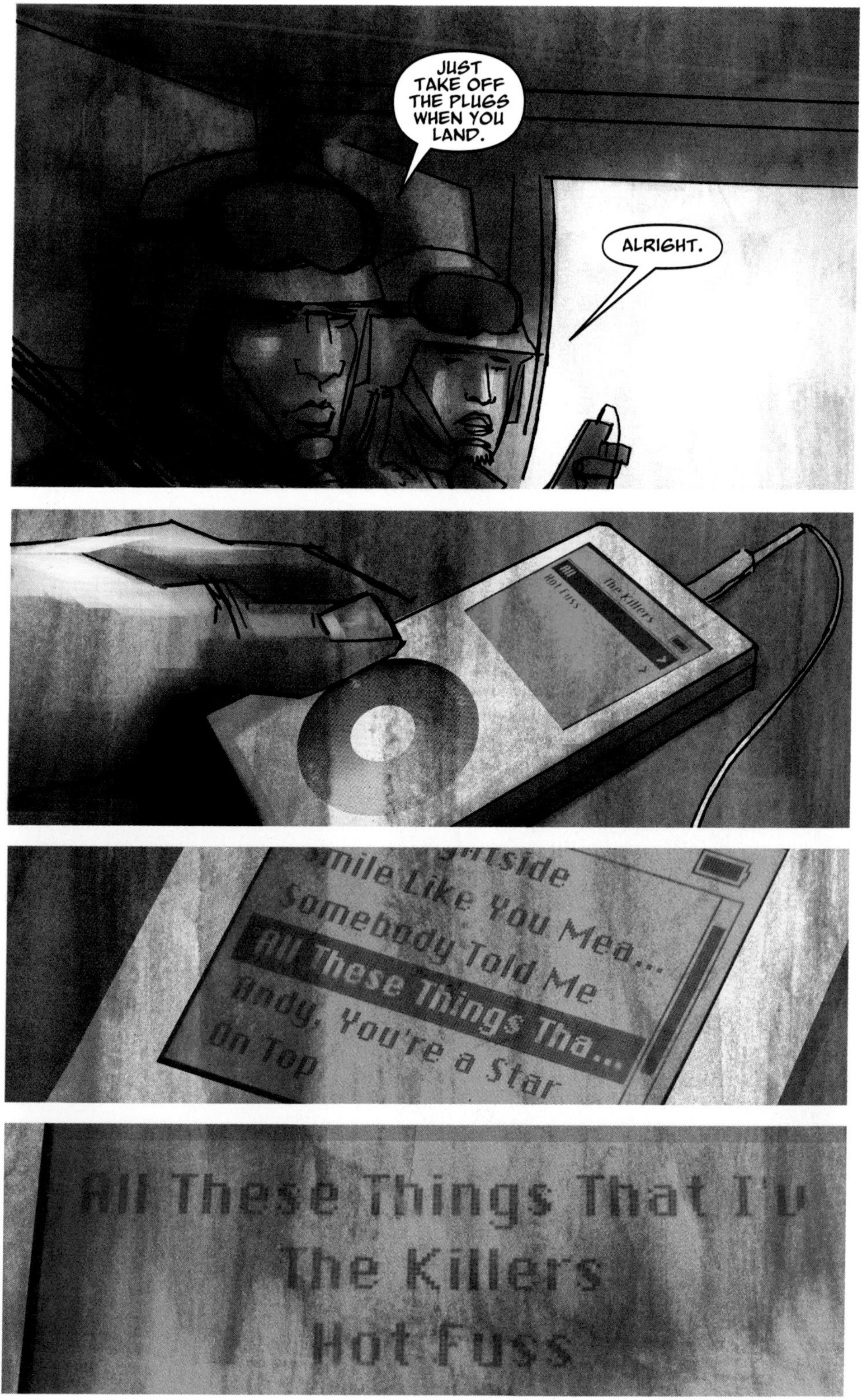
JUST TAKE OFF THE PLUGS WHEN YOU LAND.
ALRIGHT.
The Killers
Hot Fuss
Smile Like You Mea...
Somebody Told Me
All These Things Tha...
Andy, You're a Star
On Top
All These Things That I'v
The Killers
Hot Fuss

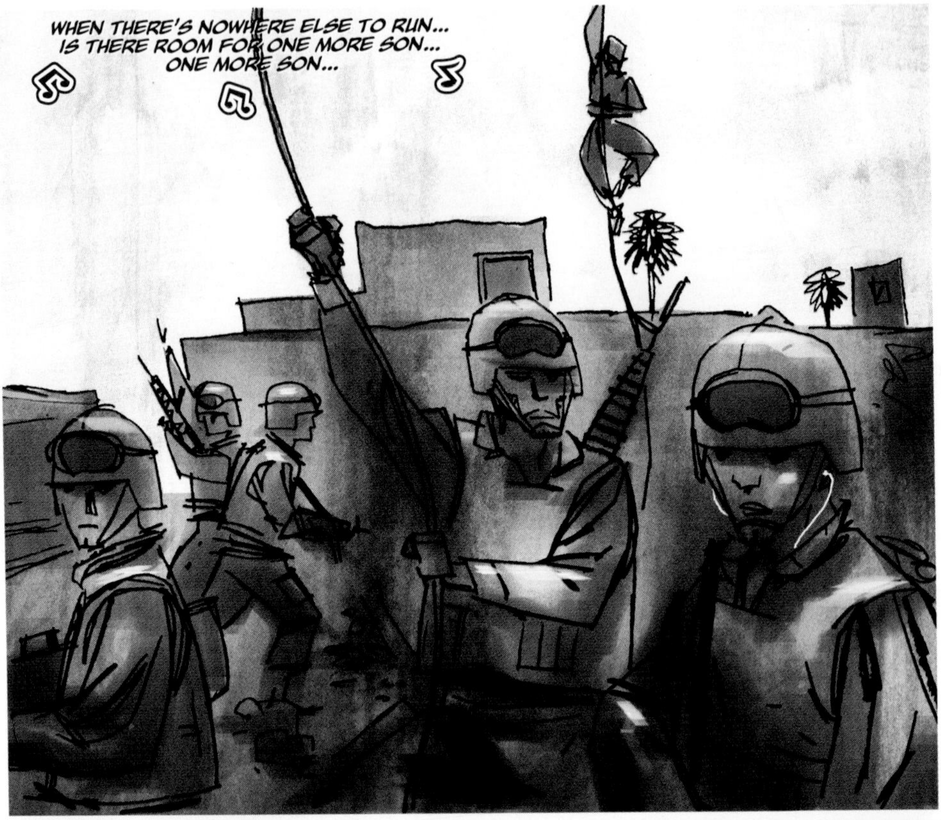
WHEN THERE'S NOWHERE ELSE TO RUN... IS THERE ROOM FOR ONE MORE SON... ONE MORE SON...

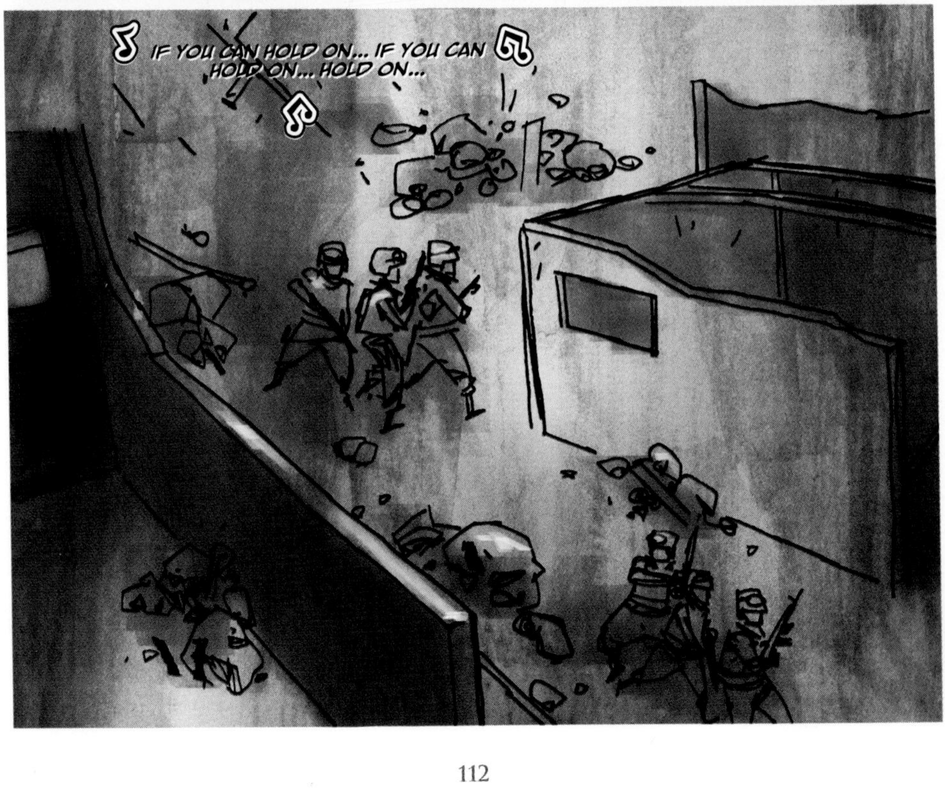
IF YOU CAN HOLD ON... IF YOU CAN HOLD ON... HOLD ON...

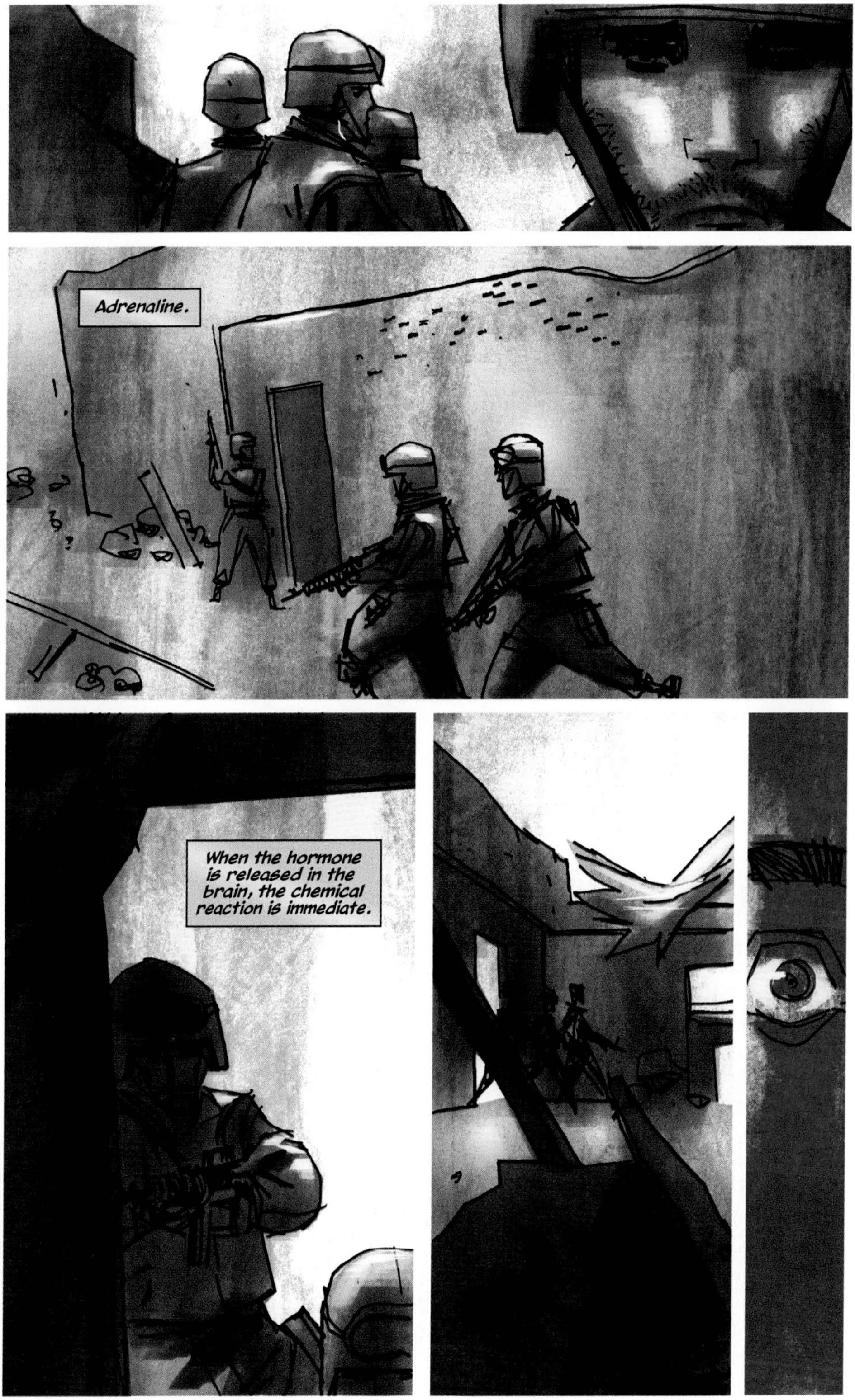
Adrenaline.
When the hormone is released in the brain, the chemical reaction is immediate.

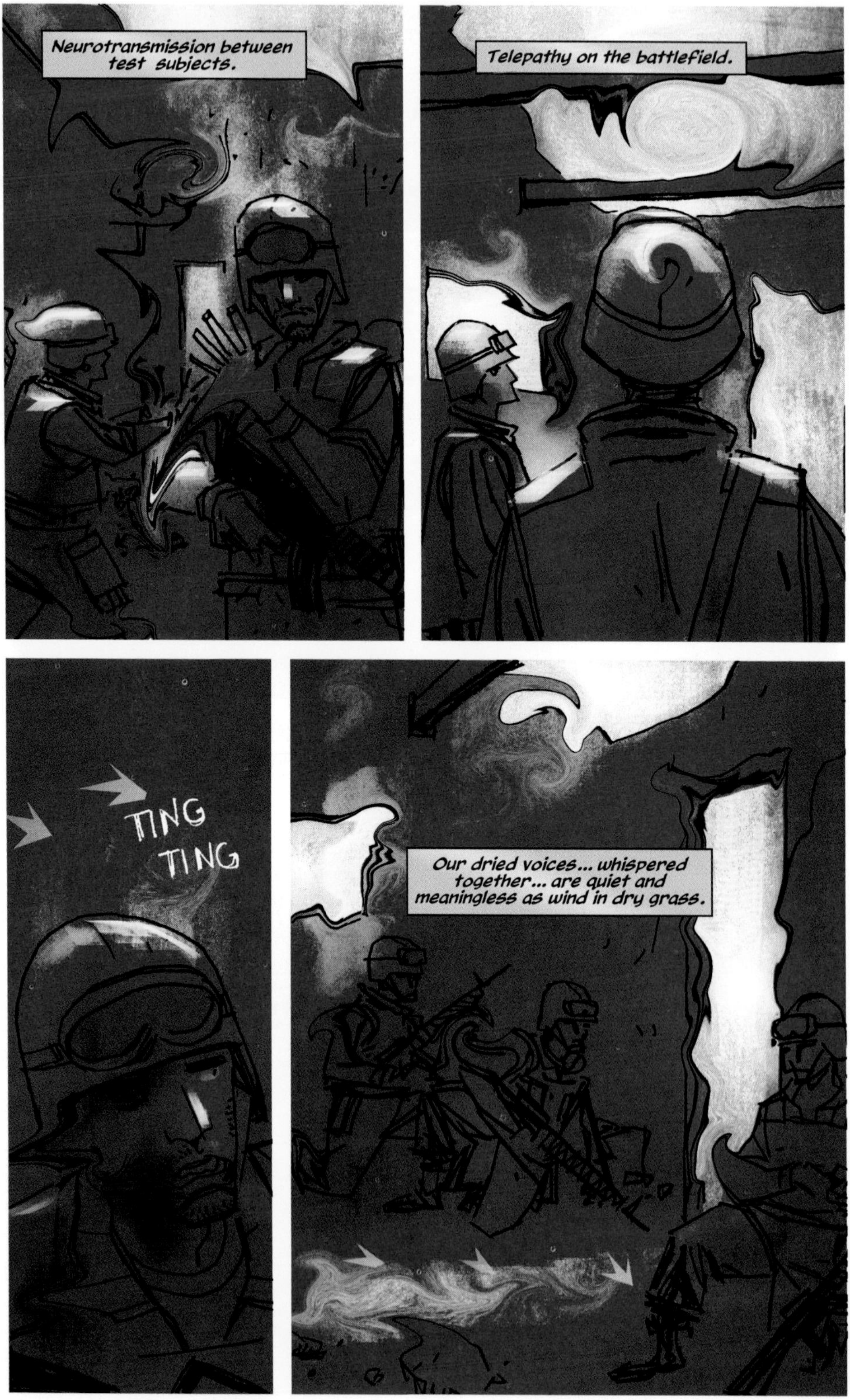
Neurotransmission between test subjects.
Telepathy on the battlefield.
TING
TING
Our dried voices... whispered together... are quiet and meaningless as wind in dry grass.

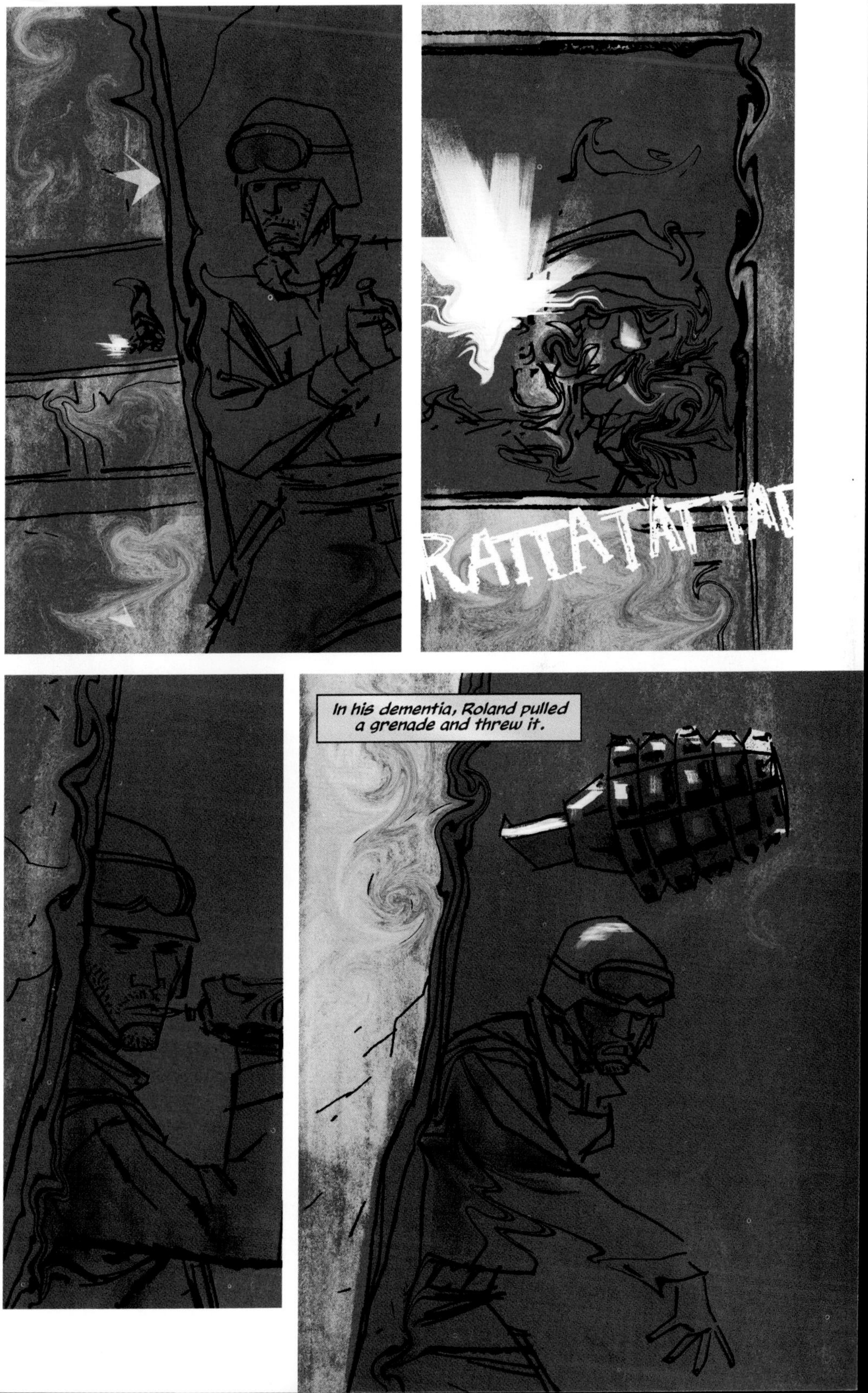
RATTATATTAT
In his dementia, Roland pulled a grenade and threw it.

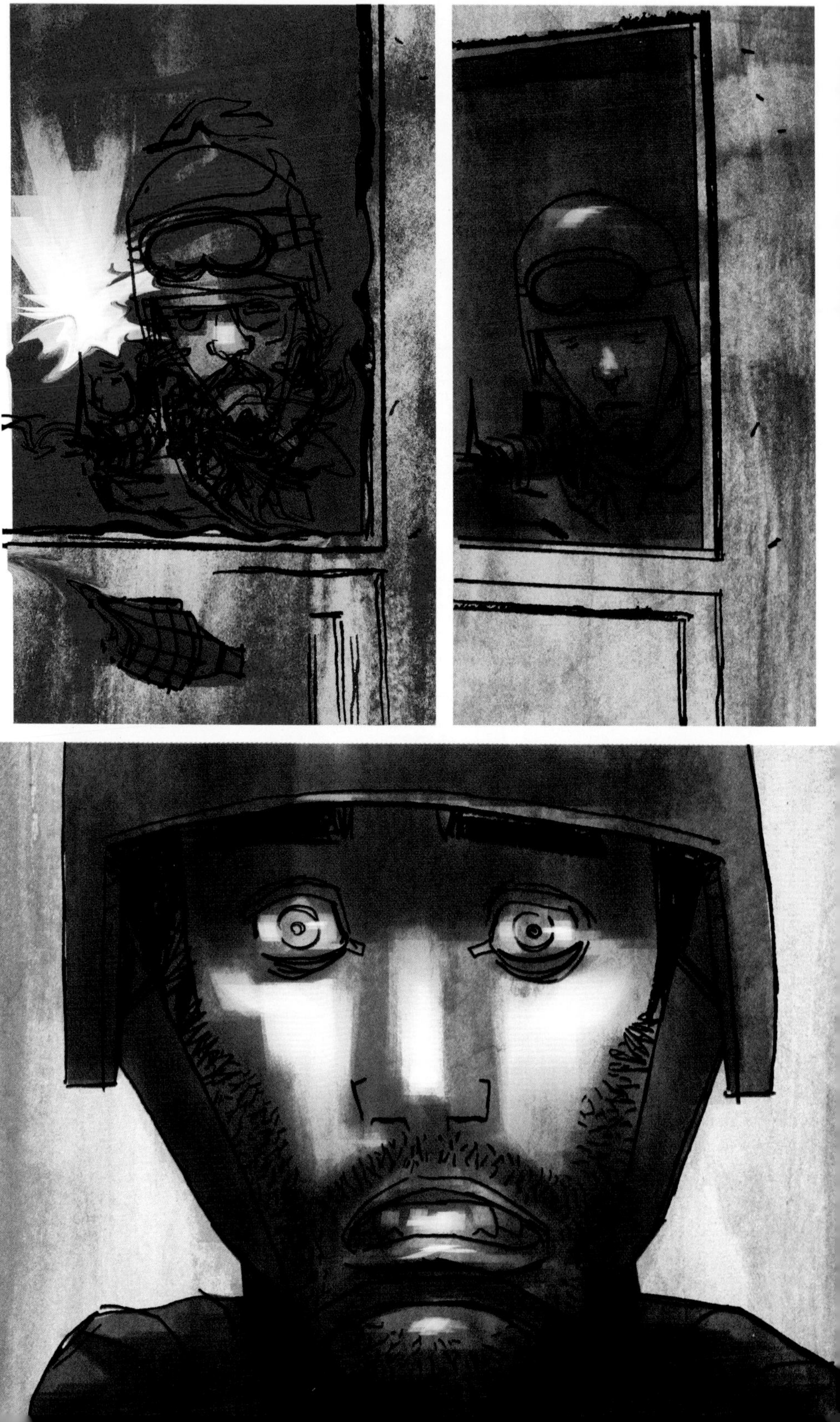

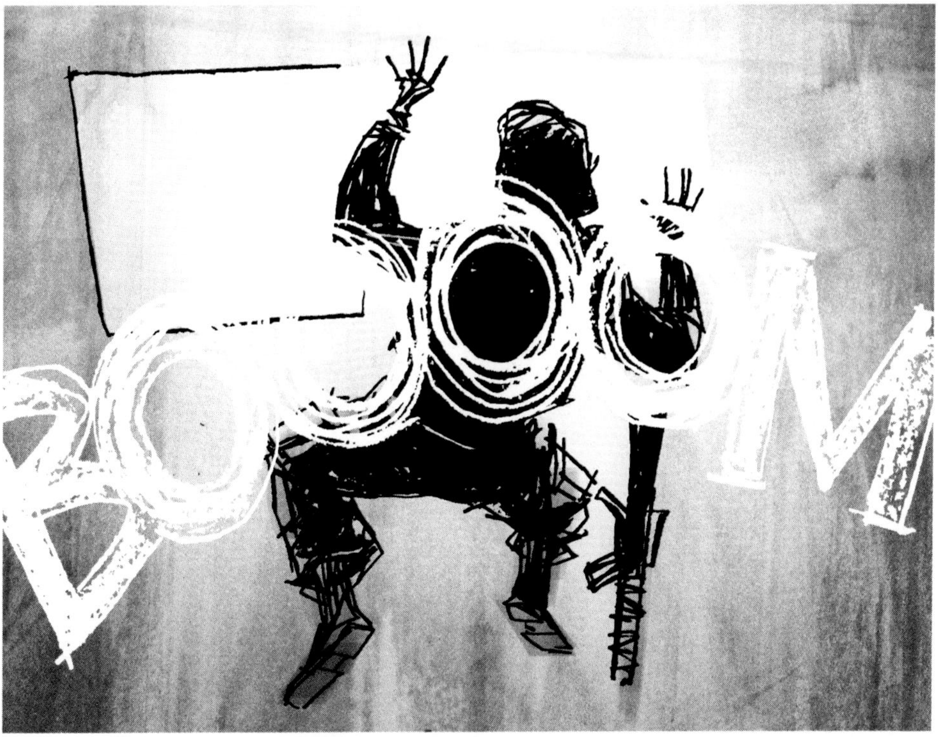
BOOOM

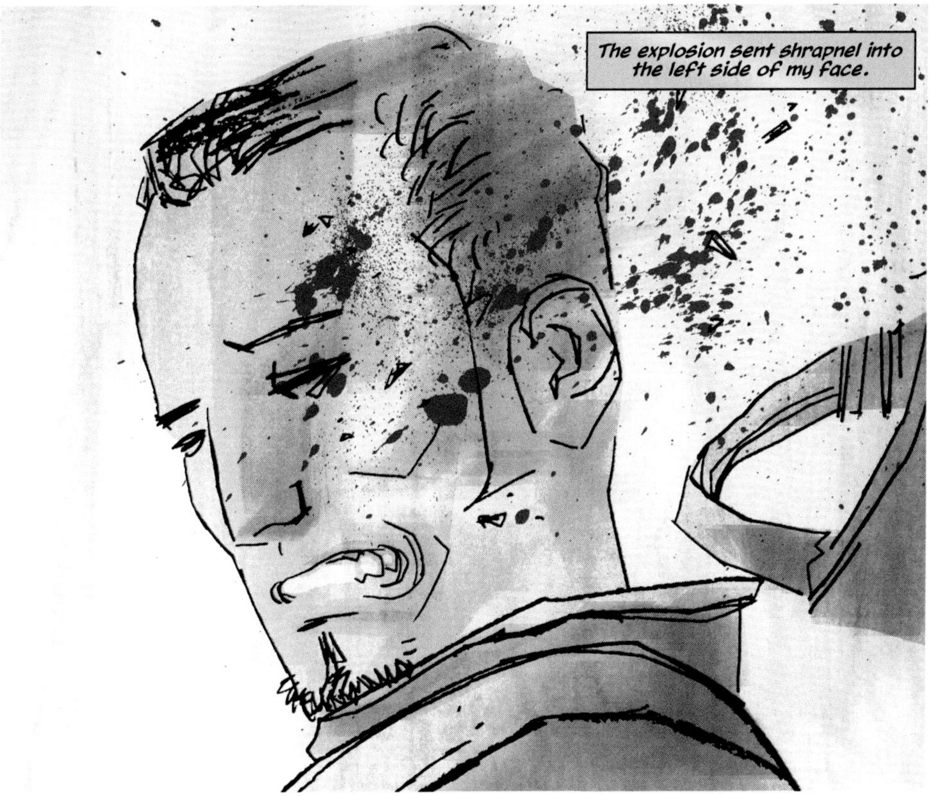
The explosion sent shrapnel into the left side of my face.

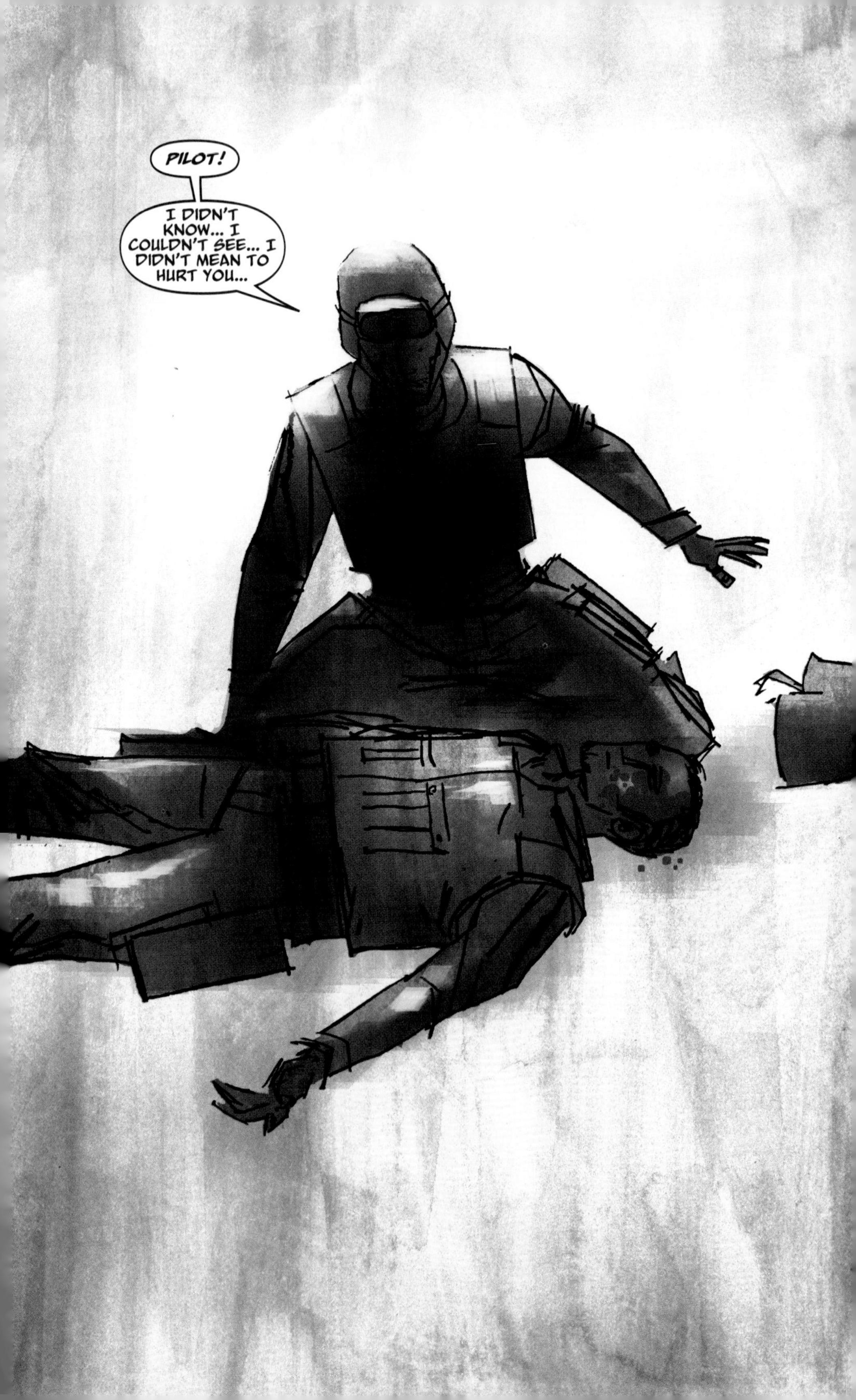
PILOT!
I DIDN'T KNOW... I COULDN'T SEE... I DIDN'T MEAN TO HURT YOU...

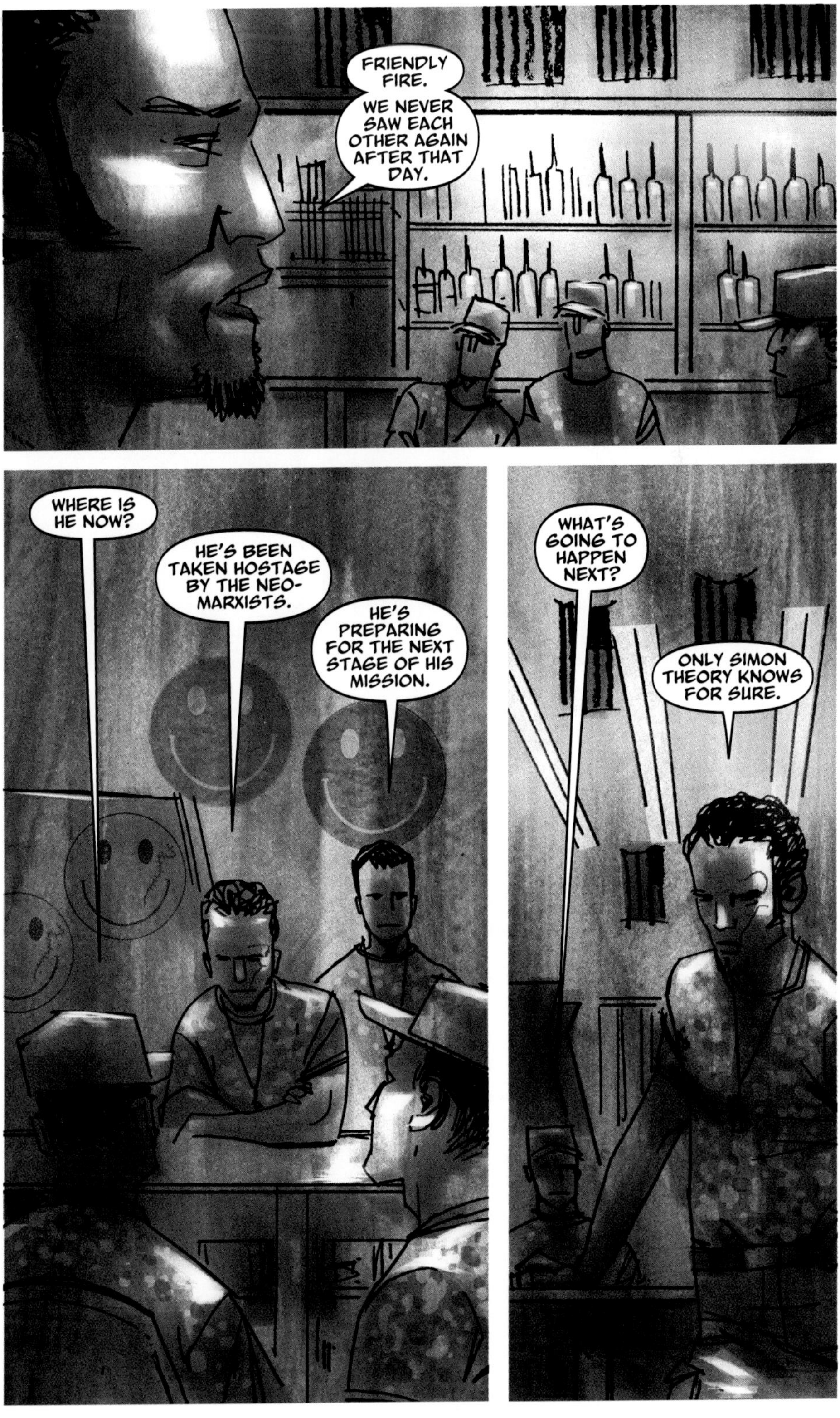
FRIENDLY FIRE.
WE NEVER SAW EACH OTHER AGAIN AFTER THAT DAY.
WHERE IS HE NOW?
HE'S BEEN TAKEN HOSTAGE BY THE NEO-MARXISTS.
HE'S PREPARING FOR THE NEXT STAGE OF HIS MISSION.
WHAT'S GOING TO HAPPEN NEXT?
ONLY SIMON THEORY KNOWS FOR SURE.

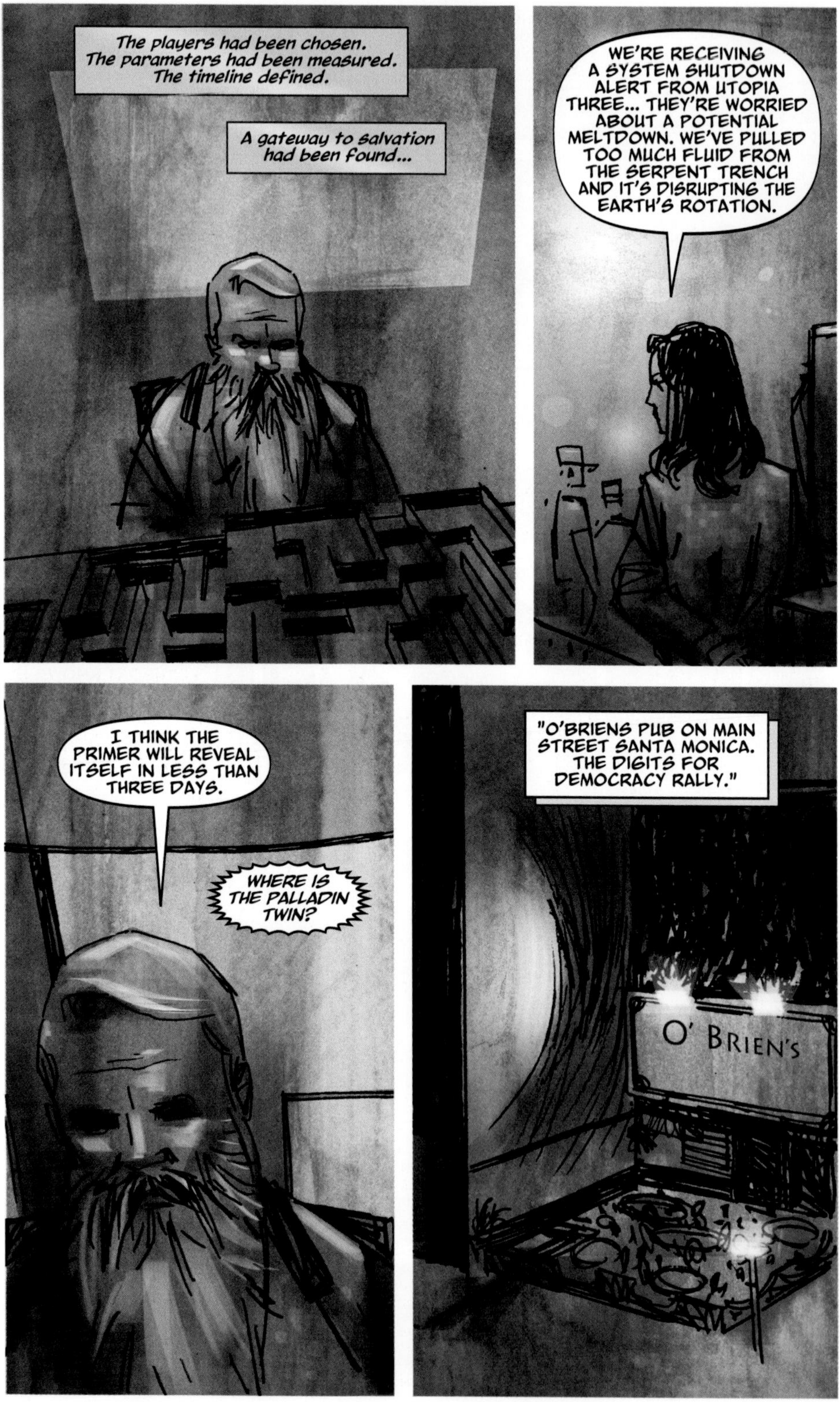
The players had been chosen. The parameters had been measured. The timeline defined.
A gateway to salvation had been found...
WE'RE RECEIVING A SYSTEM SHUTDOWN ALERT FROM UTOPIA THREE... THEY'RE WORRIED ABOUT A POTENTIAL MELTDOWN. WE'VE PULLED TOO MUCH FLUID FROM THE SERPENT TRENCH AND IT'S DISRUPTING THE EARTH'S ROTATION.
I THINK THE PRIMER WILL REVEAL ITSELF IN LESS THAN THREE DAYS.
WHERE IS THE PALLADIN TWIN?
"O'BRIENS PUB ON MAIN STREET SANTA MONICA. THE DIGITS FOR DEMOCRACY RALLY."
O' BRIEN's

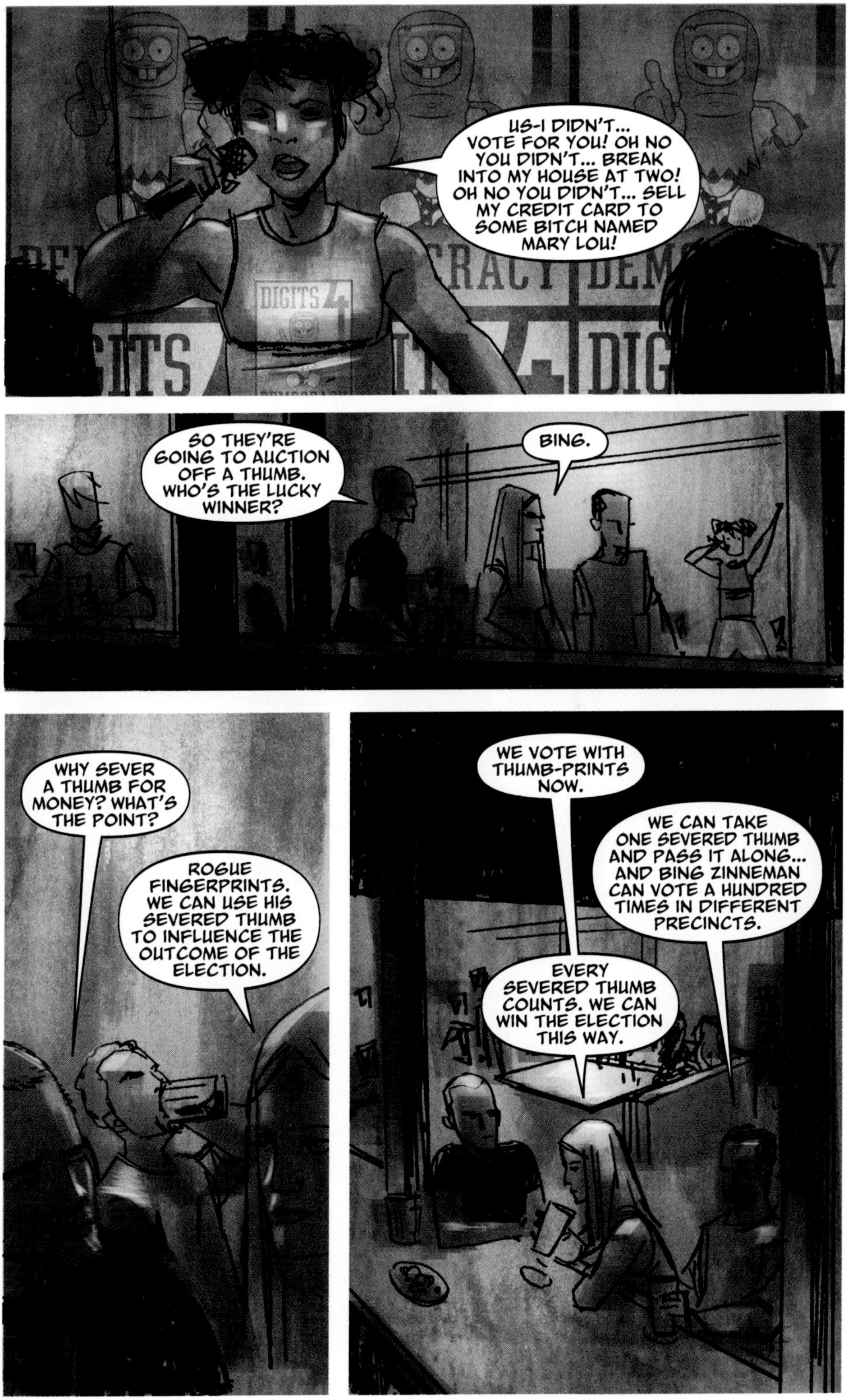
US-I DIDN'T... VOTE FOR YOU! OH NO YOU DIDN'T... BREAK INTO MY HOUSE AT TWO! OH NO YOU DIDN'T... SELL MY CREDIT CARD TO SOME BITCH NAMED MARY LOU!
SO THEY'RE GOING TO AUCTION OFF A THUMB. WHO'S THE LUCKY WINNER?
BING.
WHY SEVER A THUMB FOR MONEY? WHAT'S THE POINT?
ROGUE FINGERPRINTS. WE CAN USE HIS SEVERED THUMB TO INFLUENCE THE OUTCOME OF THE ELECTION.
WE VOTE WITH THUMB-PRINTS NOW.
WE CAN TAKE ONE SEVERED THUMB AND PASS IT ALONG... AND BING ZINNEMAN CAN VOTE A HUNDRED TIMES IN DIFFERENT PRECINCTS.
EVERY SEVERED THUMB COUNTS. WE CAN WIN THE ELECTION THIS WAY.

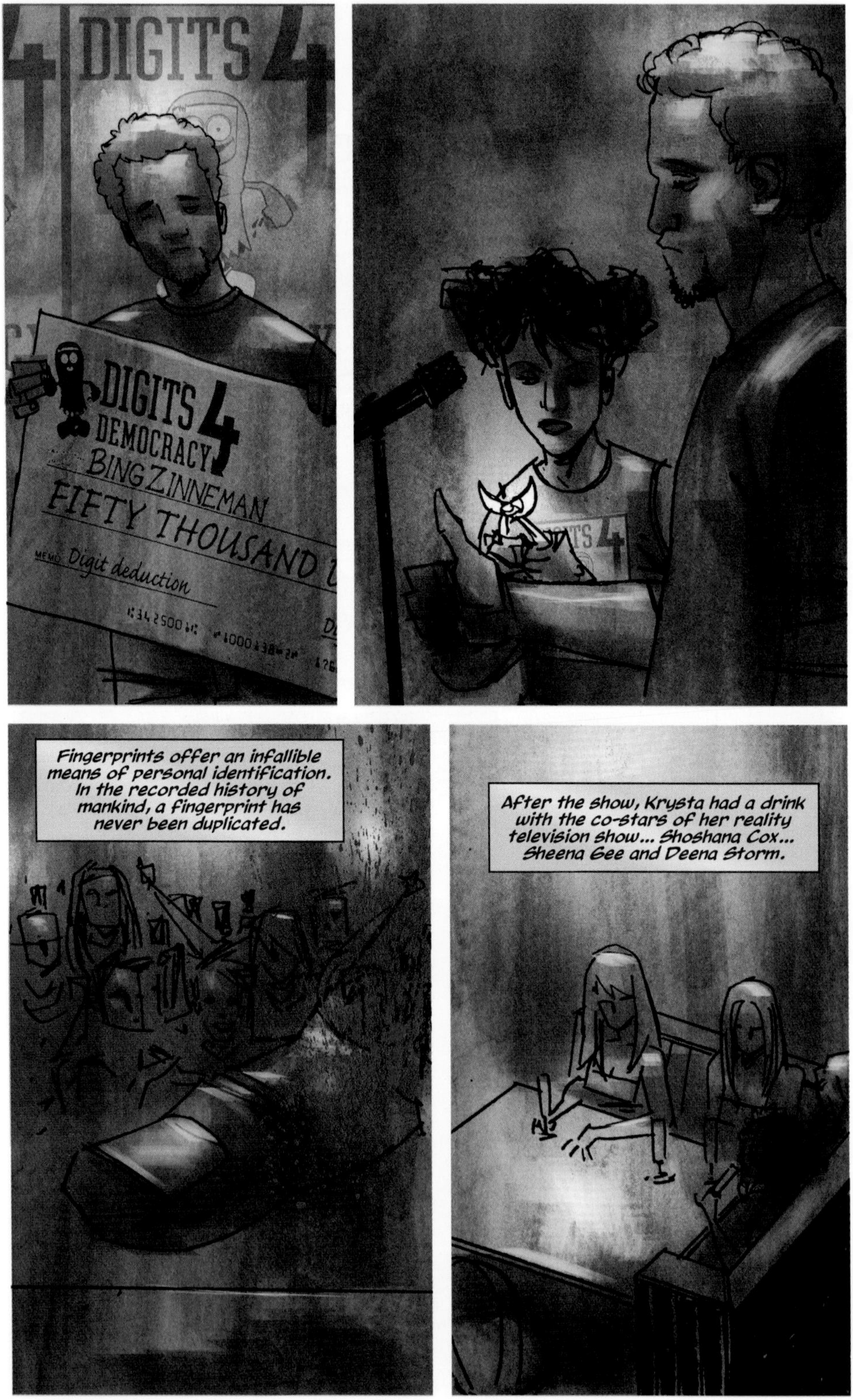
DIGITS 4
DIGITS 4 DEMOCRACY
BING ZINNEMAN
FIFTY THOUSAND
MEMO Digit deduction
Fingerprints offer an infallible means of personal identification. In the recorded history of mankind, a fingerprint has never been duplicated.
After the show, Krysta had a drink with the co-stars of her reality television show... Shoshana Cox... Sheena Gee and Deena Storm.

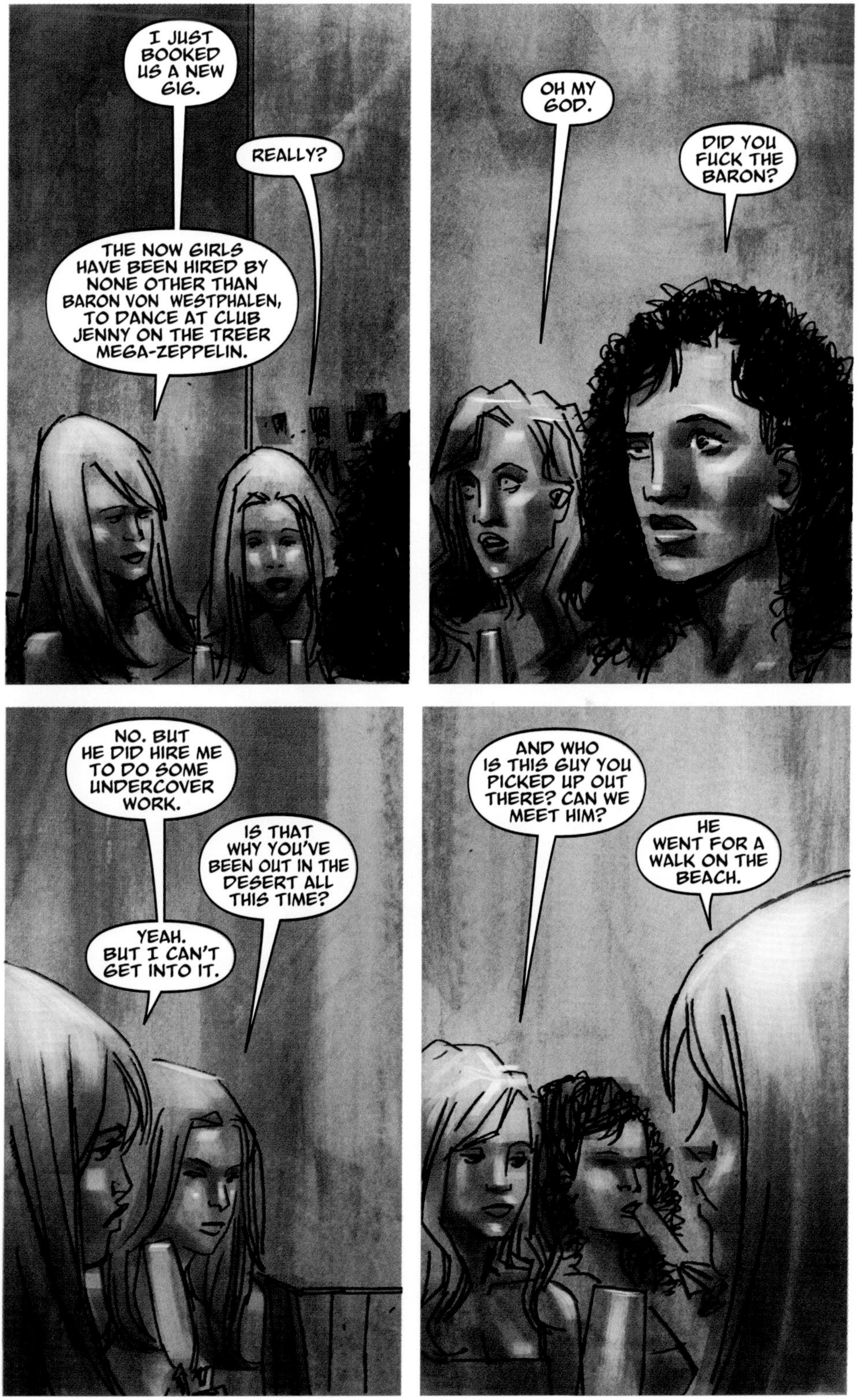
I JUST BOOKED US A NEW GIG.
REALLY?
THE NOW GIRLS HAVE BEEN HIRED BY NONE OTHER THAN BARON VON WESTPHALEN, TO DANCE AT CLUB JENNY ON THE TREER MEGA-ZEPPELIN.
OH MY GOD.
DID YOU FUCK THE BARON?
NO. BUT HE DID HIRE ME TO DO SOME UNDERCOVER WORK.
IS THAT WHY YOU'VE BEEN OUT IN THE DESERT ALL THIS TIME?
YEAH. BUT I CAN'T GET INTO IT.
AND WHO IS THIS GUY YOU PICKED UP OUT THERE? CAN WE MEET HIM?
HE WENT FOR A WALK ON THE BEACH.

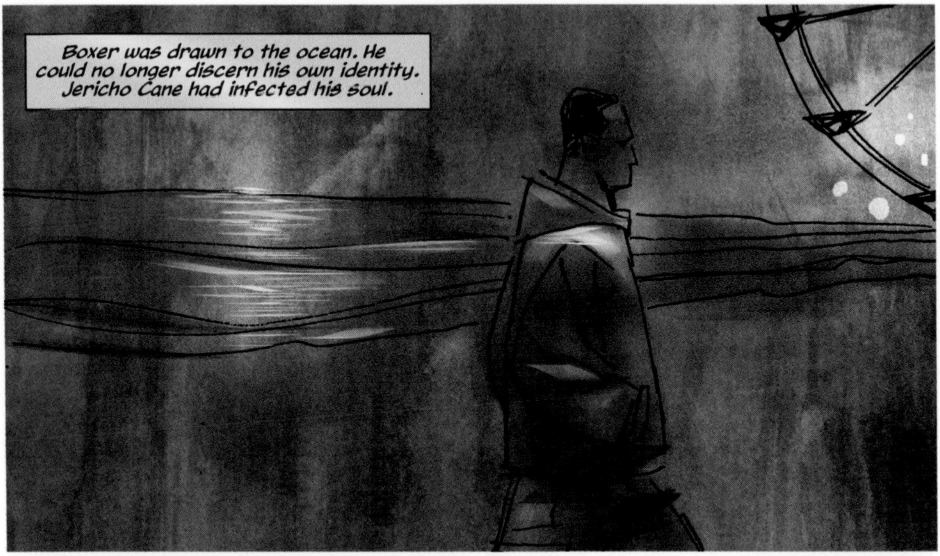
Boxer was drawn to the ocean. He could no longer discern his own identity. Jericho Cane had infected his soul.

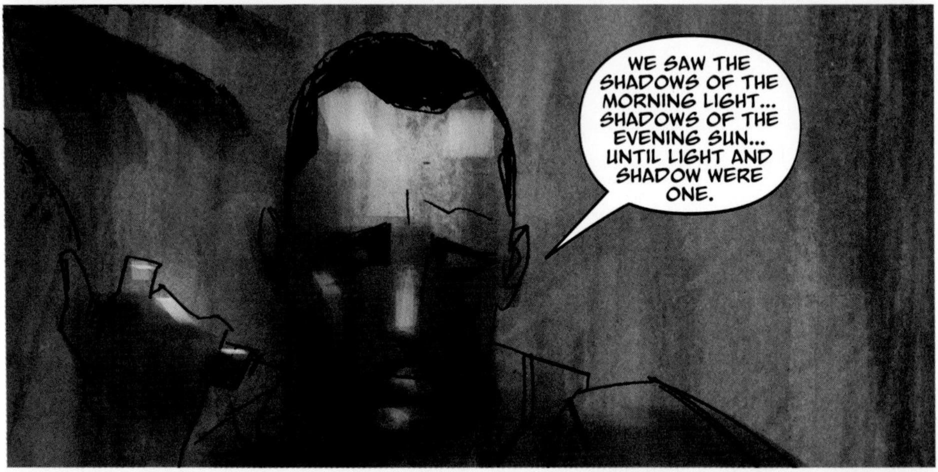
WE SAW THE SHADOWS OF THE MORNING LIGHT... SHADOWS OF THE EVENING SUN... UNTIL LIGHT AND SHADOW WERE ONE.

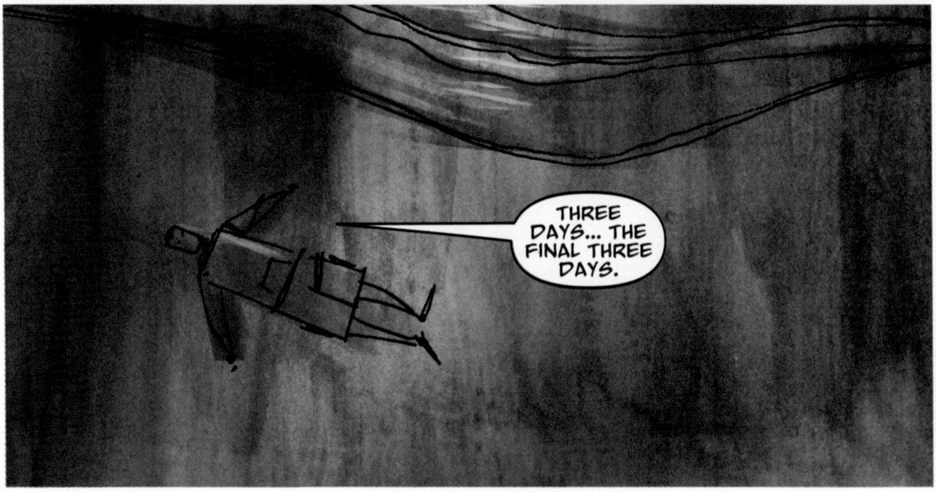
THREE DAYS... THE FINAL THREE DAYS.

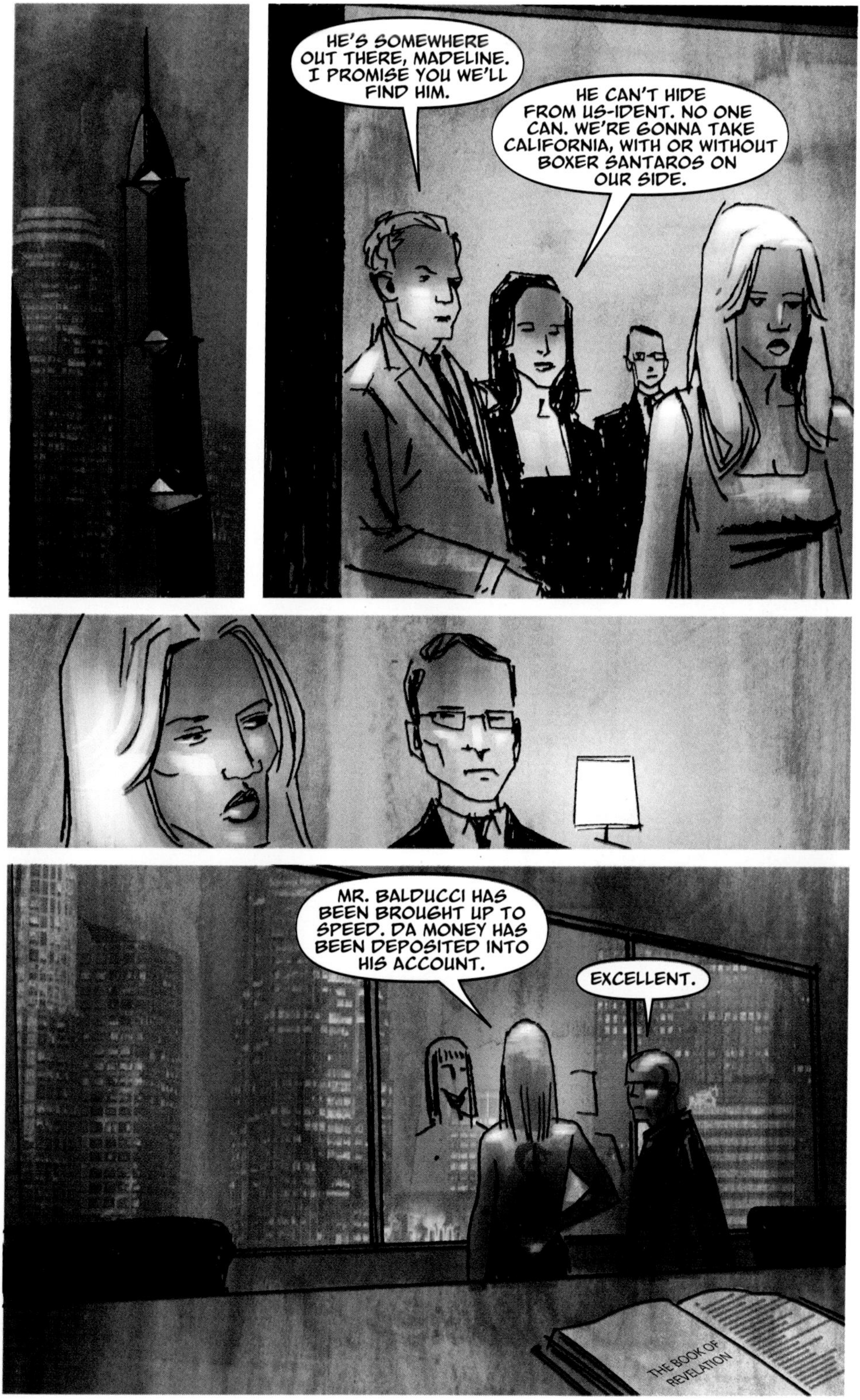
HE'S SOMEWHERE OUT THERE, MADELINE. I PROMISE YOU WE'LL FIND HIM.
HE CAN'T HIDE FROM US-IDENT. NO ONE CAN. WE'RE GONNA TAKE CALIFORNIA, WITH OR WITHOUT BOXER SANTAROS ON OUR SIDE.
MR. BALDUCCI HAS BEEN BROUGHT UP TO SPEED. DA MONEY HAS BEEN DEPOSITED INTO HIS ACCOUNT.
EXCELLENT.
THE BOOK OF REVELATION

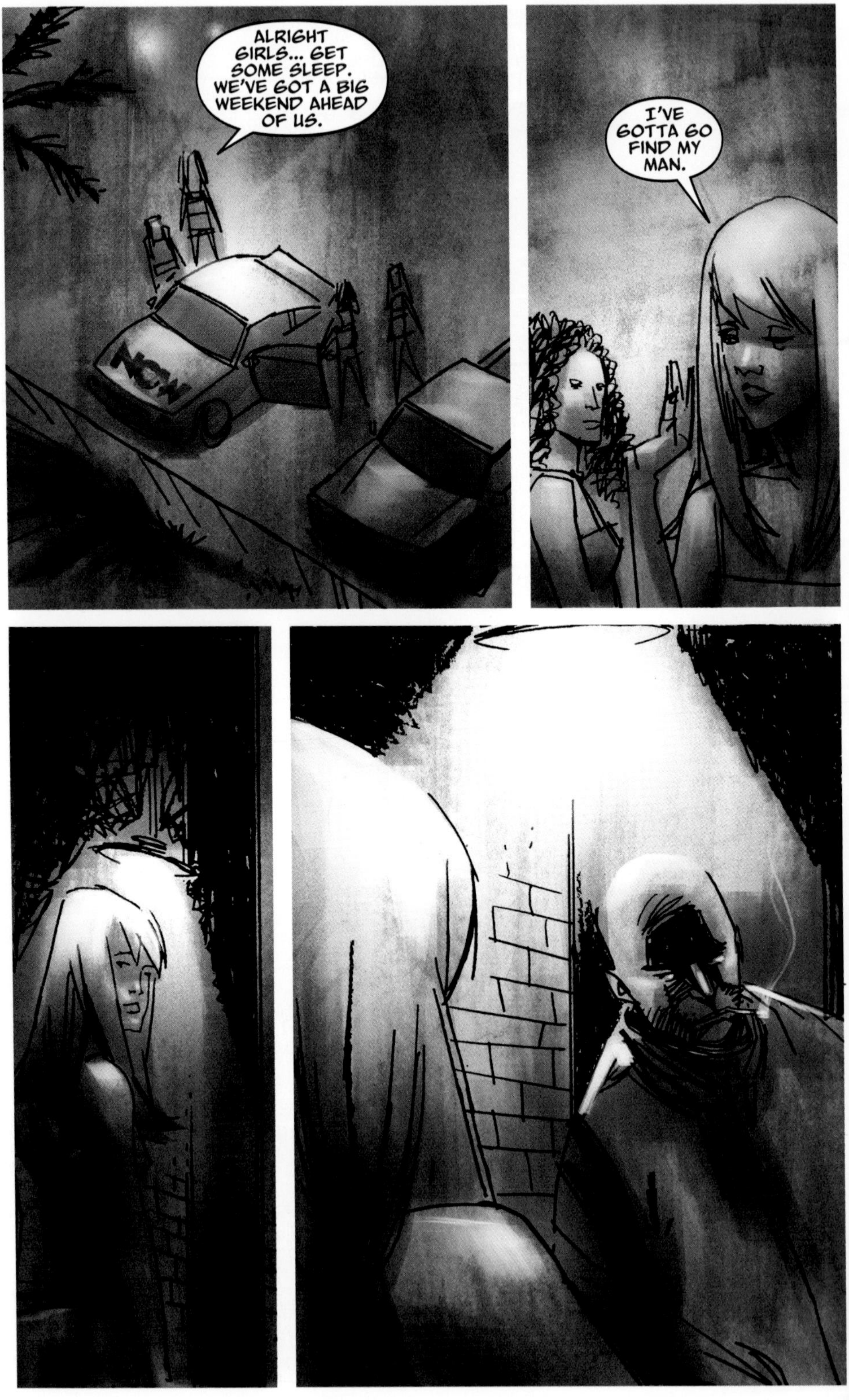
ALRIGHT GIRLS... GET SOME SLEEP. WE'VE GOT A BIG WEEKEND AHEAD OF US.
I'VE GOTTA GO FIND MY MAN.

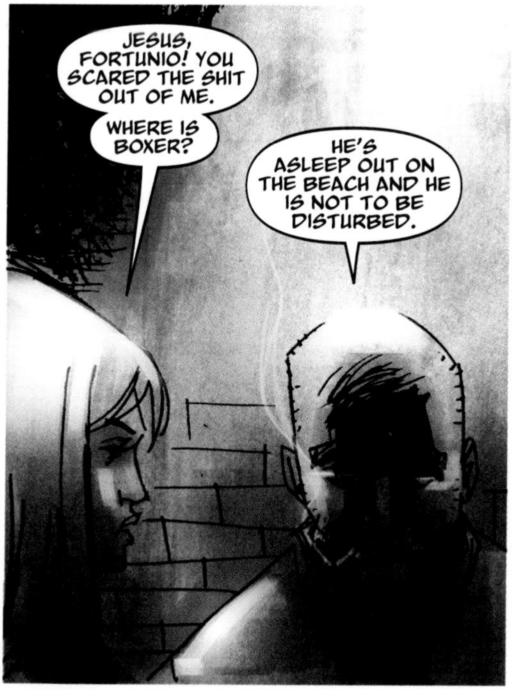
JESUS, FORTUNIO! YOU SCARED THE SHIT OUT OF ME.
WHERE IS BOXER?
HE'S ASLEEP OUT ON THE BEACH AND HE IS NOT TO BE DISTURBED.

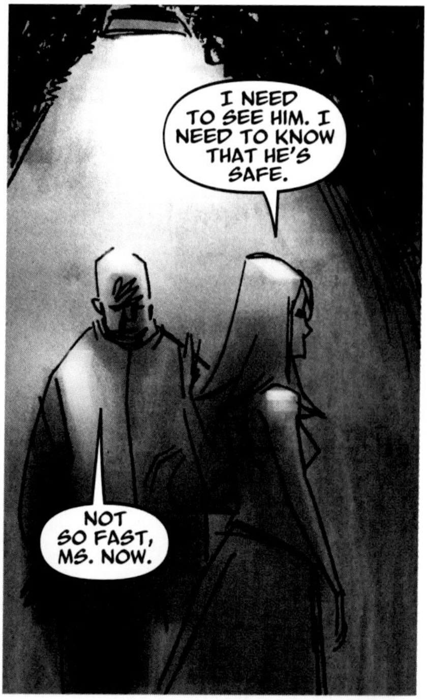
I NEED TO SEE HIM. I NEED TO KNOW THAT HE'S SAFE.
NOT SO FAST, MS. NOW.

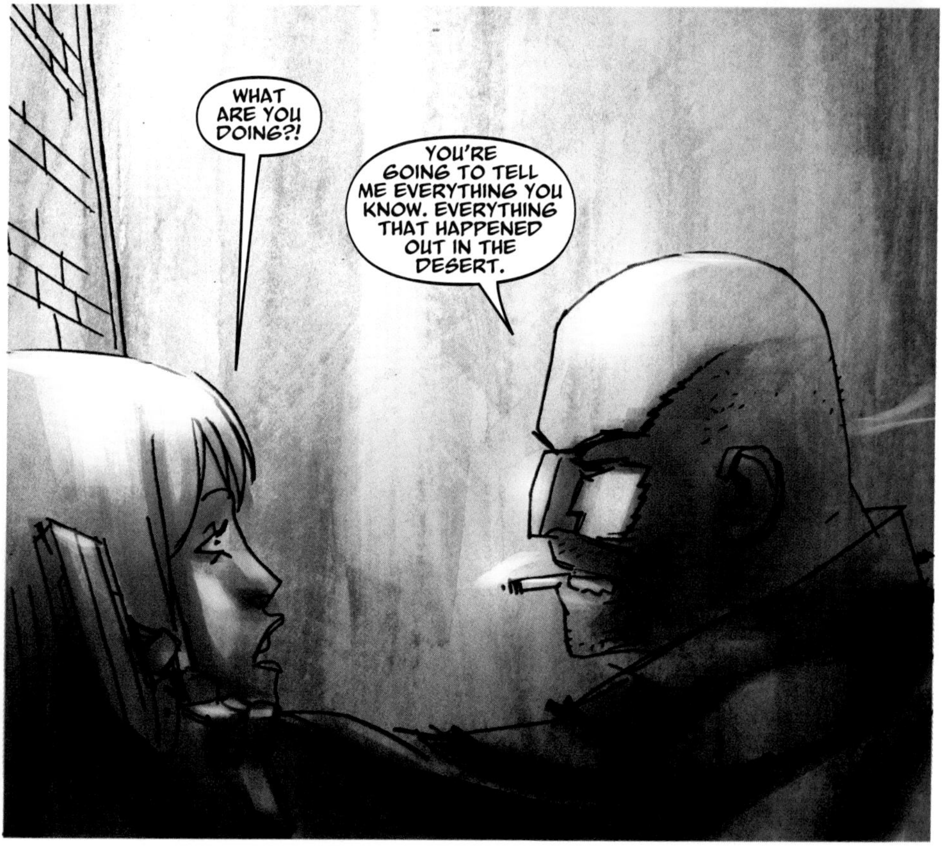
WHAT ARE YOU DOING?!
YOU'RE GOING TO TELL ME EVERYTHING YOU KNOW. EVERYTHING THAT HAPPENED OUT IN THE DESERT.

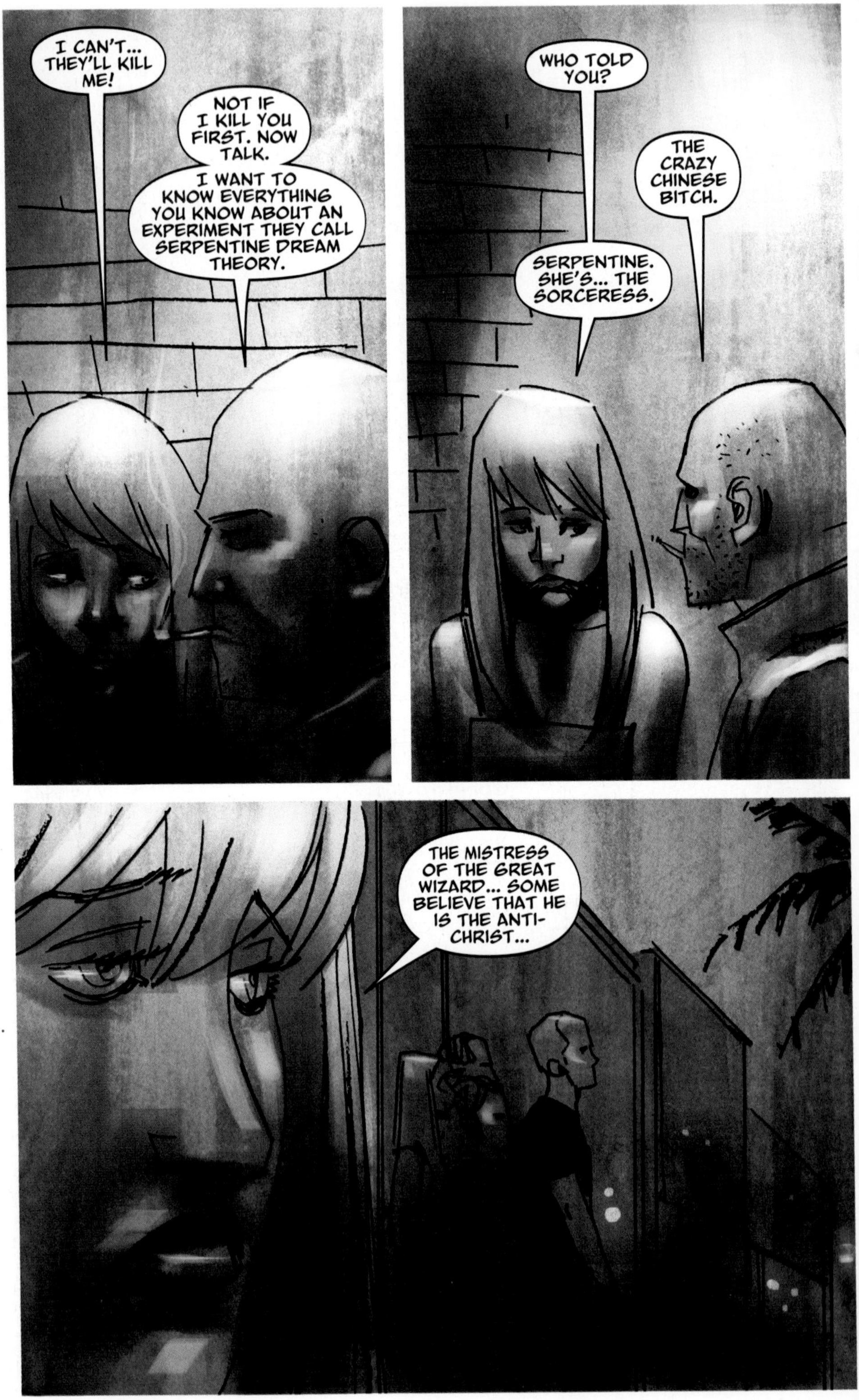
I CAN'T... THEY'LL KILL ME!
NOT IF I KILL YOU FIRST. NOW TALK.
I WANT TO KNOW EVERYTHING YOU KNOW ABOUT AN EXPERIMENT THEY CALL SERPENTINE DREAM THEORY.
WHO TOLD YOU?
THE CRAZY CHINESE BITCH.
SERPENTINE. SHE'S... THE SORCERESS.
THE MISTRESS OF THE GREAT WIZARD... SOME BELIEVE THAT HE IS THE ANTI-CHRIST...

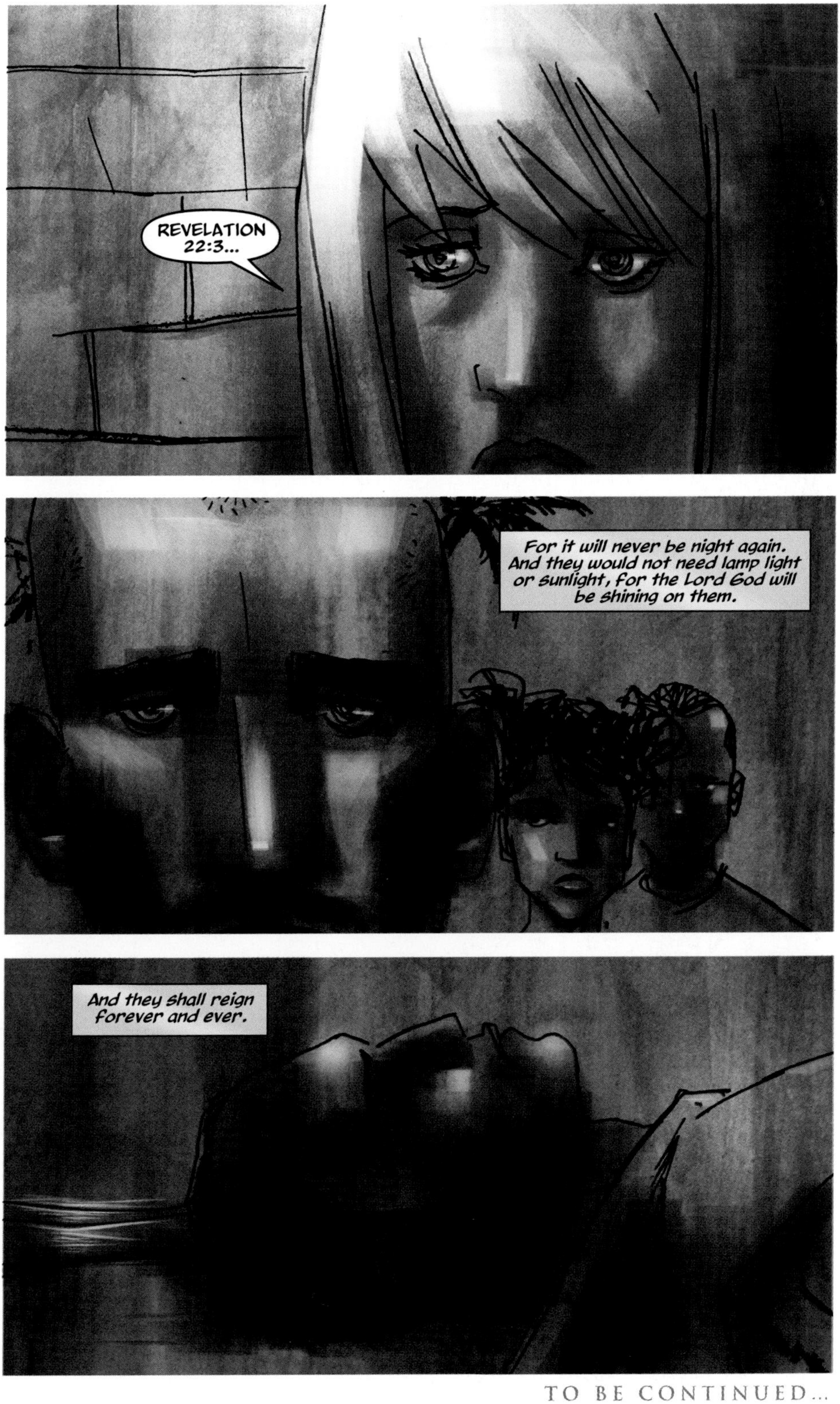
REVELATION 22:3...
For it will never be night again. And they would not need lamp light or sunlight, for the Lord God will be shining on them.
And they shall reign forever and ever.

TO BE CONTINUED...

IV V VI

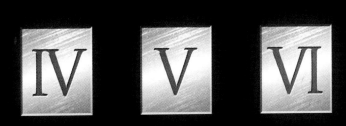

ACCESSING FILES...

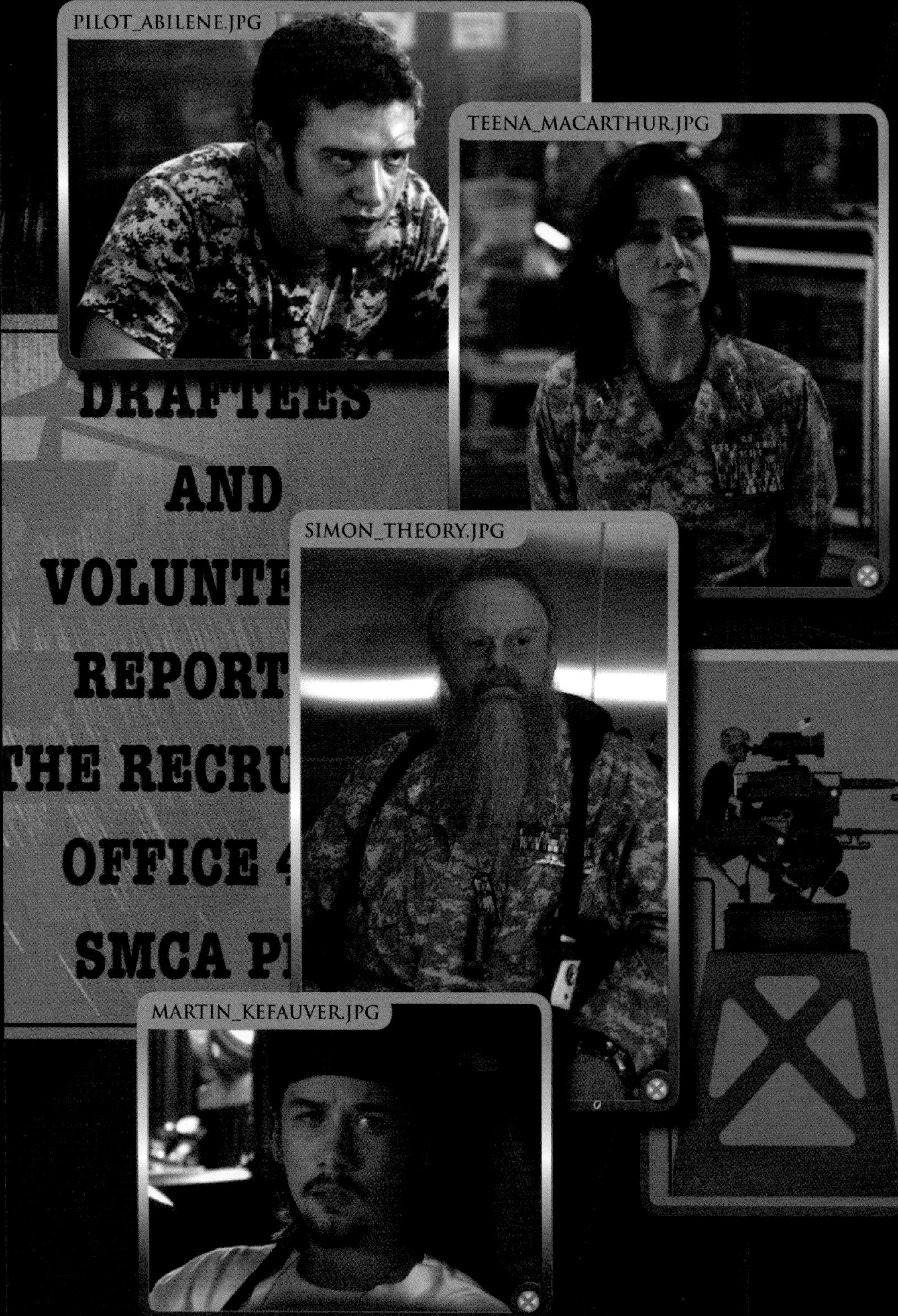
PILOT_ABILENE.JPG
TEENA_MACARTHUR.JPG
SIMON_THEORY.JPG
MARTIN_KEFAUVER.JPG
DRAFTEES
AND
VOLUNTE
REPORT
THE RECRU
OFFICE 4
SMCA P

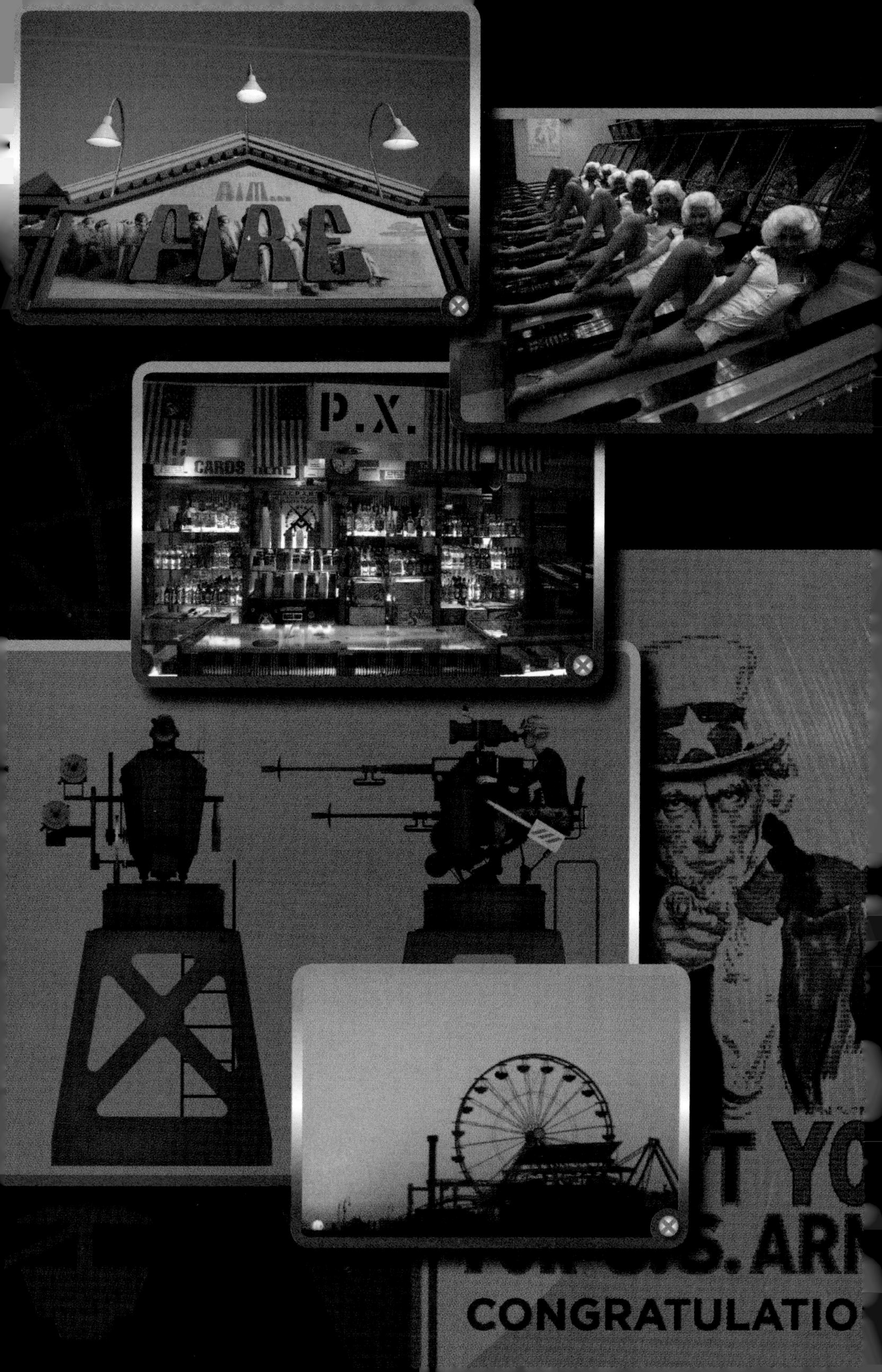

AIM...
FIRE
P.X.
CARDS
CONGRATULATIO

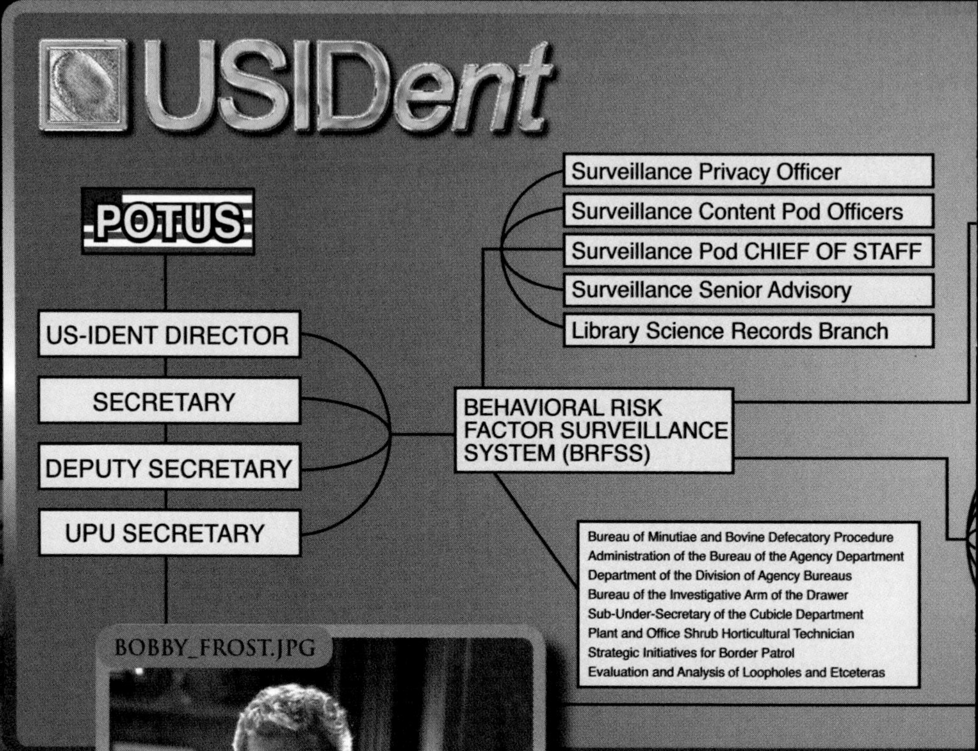
USIDent
POTUS
US-IDENT DIRECTOR
SECRETARY
DEPUTY SECRETARY
UPU SECRETARY
BEHAVIORAL RISK FACTOR SURVEILLANCE SYSTEM (BRFSS)
Surveillance Privacy Officer
Surveillance Content Pod Officers
Surveillance Pod CHIEF OF STAFF
Surveillance Senior Advisory
Library Science Records Branch
Bureau of Minutiae and Bovine Defecatory Procedure
Administration of the Bureau of the Agency Department
Department of the Division of Agency Bureaus
Bureau of the Investigative Arm of the Drawer
Sub-Under-Secretary of the Cubicle Department
Plant and Office Shrub Horticultural Technician
Strategic Initiatives for Border Patrol
Evaluation and Analysis of Loopholes and Etceteras

BOBBY_FROST.JPG

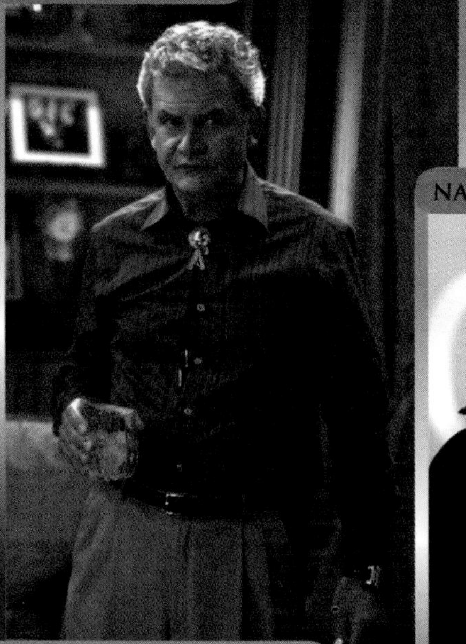

NANA_MAE_FROST.JPG

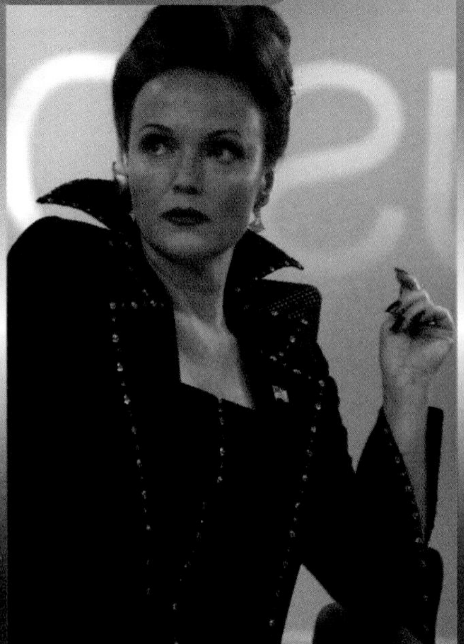

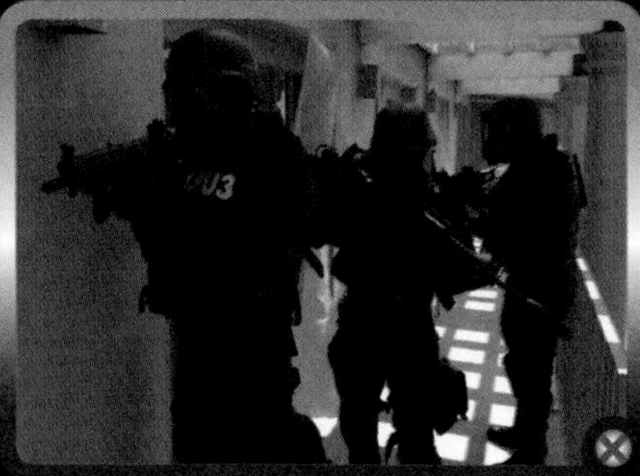

	UPU 1
Executive Secretary	Parking Enhancement Officers, Pedestrian Crosswalk & Right-of-Way Enforcement. Robotic Security Detail, Security Leasing Services, Trainable Supervision, COPS, DOT, EAR, FYSB, NIAAA, OLAW
Office of Legislative Affairs	
Office of Public Affairs	
Office for UPU Coordination	
Office for Emergency Response	**UPU 2**
Office for National Capital Coordination	Local Police, Fire, Ambulance, DWI Spotters, Minutemen AFRTS, CSAT, MARVEL, ROTC
Office of Immigration Suppression	
orate Under Secretary of the Interior	**UPU 3**
orate Under Secretary of Violent Uprisings	Elite Security Units, S.W.A.T., Sniper's Nest Guild, AHPCRC, FCC, CGMD, GILS, INS, NACIC, NCIPID, OAT
orate Under Secretary of Science & Technology	
orate Under Secretary of Infrastructure Protection skeleton Development	**UPU 4**
orate Under Secretary of Migration & Stigmatism	ANG, ATF, BARC, STB, AFROTC, BMDO,BOP, CAGE, CERCLIS, CLITORI, CHID, CIAO, DEA, DHS, DNSC, DOD, DOI, EIS, FBI, FEDRIP, GwoB, IAEA, INF, INTERPOL, NREVSS PC, PPQ, SAVE, SIC, SS, TSA, UNICOR, USUK, VGNA
orate Under Secretary of Emergency aception & Abstinence Encouragement	
orate Under Secretary of Advanced Dialysis & Cell Suppression	**UPU 5**
	CLASSIFIED - For Director's Eyes Only

MADELINE_FROST_SANTAROS.JPG

SURVEILLANCE CAM.1.VID

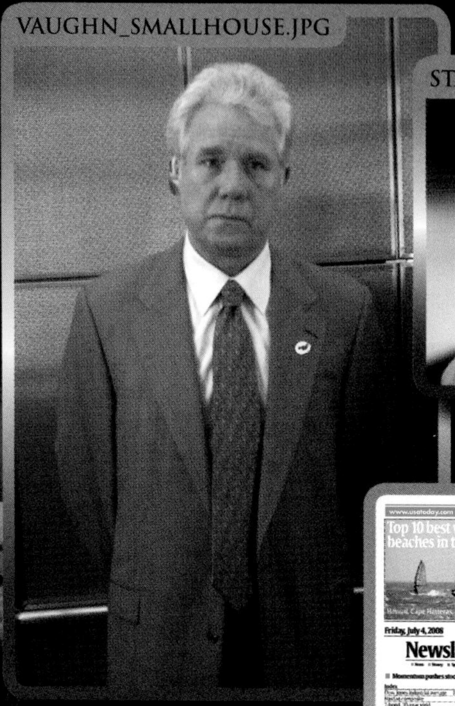
VAUGHN_SMALLHOUSE.JPG

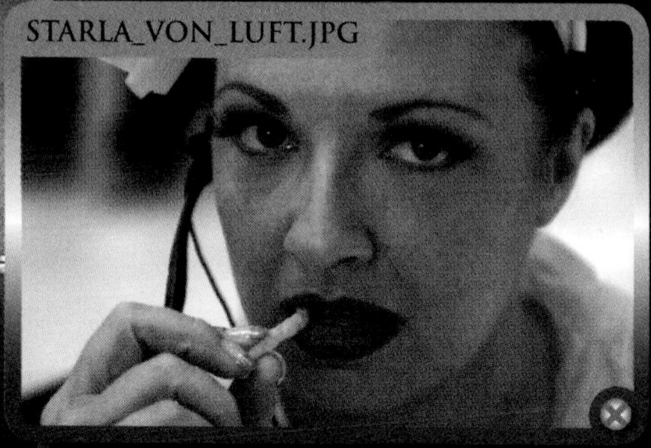
STARLA_VON_LUFT.JPG

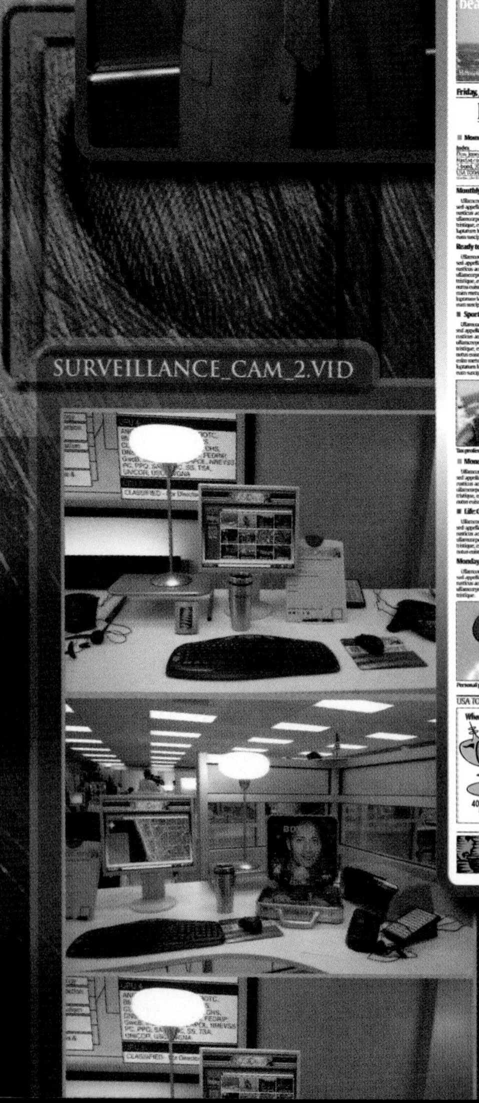
SURVEILLANCE_CAM_2.VID
CLASSIFIED

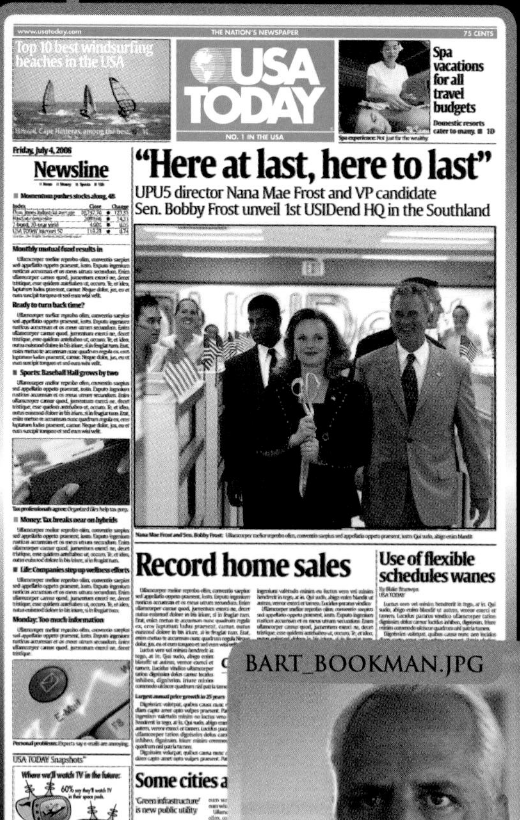

www.usatoday.com — THE NATION'S NEWSPAPER — 75 CENTS

Top 10 best windsurfing beaches in the USA

USA TODAY

NO. 1 IN THE USA

Spa vacations for all travel budgets

Domestic resorts cater to many. 1D

Spa experience: Not just for the wealthy

Friday, July 4, 2008

Newsline

Momentum pushes stocks along. 4B

Monthly mutual fund results in

Ready to turn back time?

Sports: Baseball Hall grows by two

Tax professionals agree: Organized files help tax prep.

Money: Tax breaks near on hybrids

Life: Companies step up wellness efforts

Monday: Too much information

Personal problems: Experts say e-mails are annoying.

USA TODAY Snapshots

Where we'll watch TV in the future:

60% say they'll watch TV in their space pods

40% say they'll watch TV in their space pods

"Here at last, here to last"

UPU5 director Nana Mae Frost and VP candidate Sen. Bobby Frost unveil 1st USIDend HQ in the Southland

Nana Mae Frost and Sen. Bobby Frost:

Record home sales

Use of flexible schedules wanes

Some cities a

'Green infrastructure' is new public utility

Global Delive

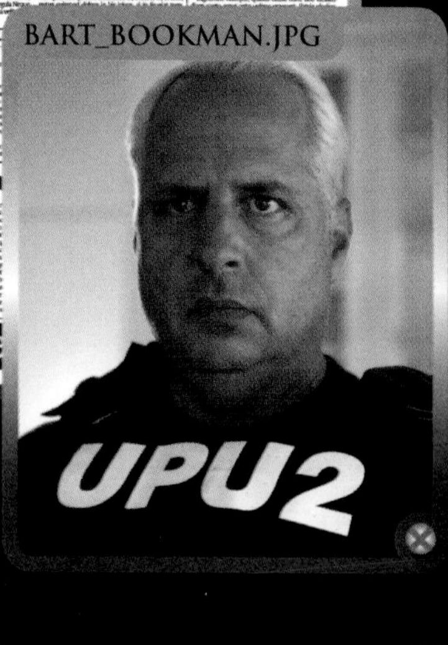
BART_BOOKMAN.JPG
UPU2

ROLAND_TAVERNER.JPG

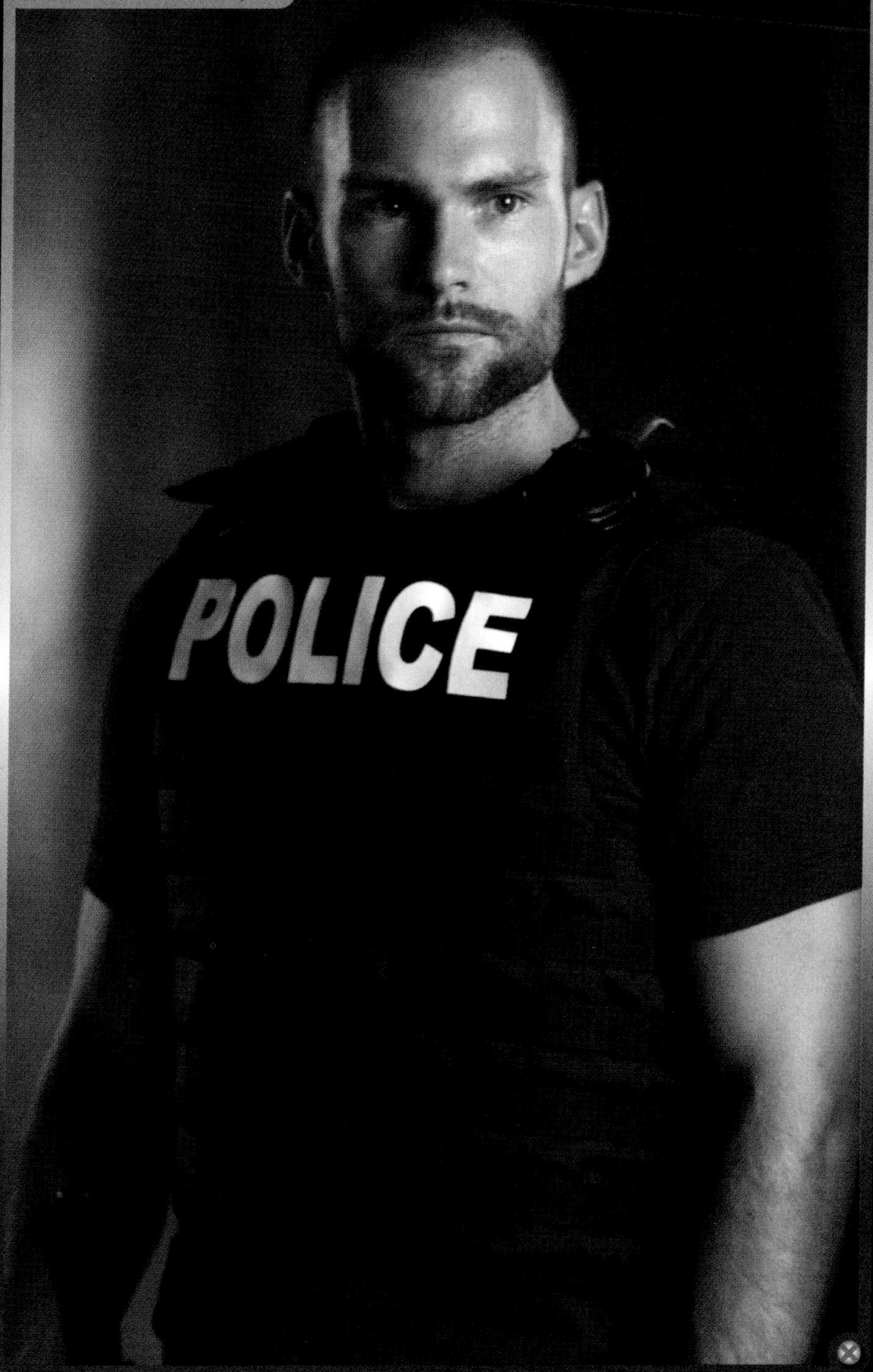
POLICE

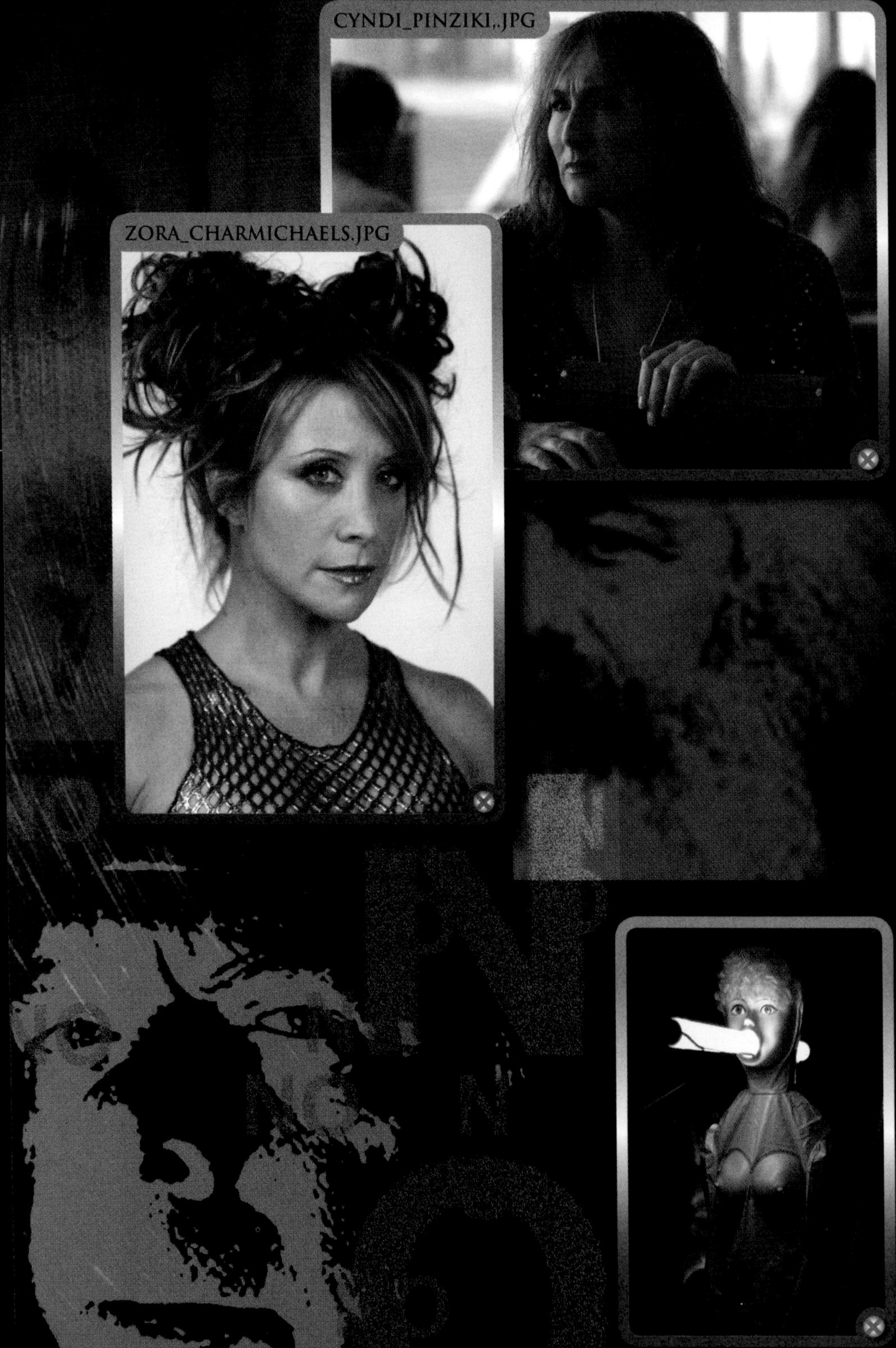
CYNDI_PINZIKI,.JPG
ZORA_CHARMICHAELS.JPG

DREAM.JPG

DION_ELEMENT.JPG

DESTROY

CAPITALISM

DETHRONE

GOD

KARL MAR

UPU2

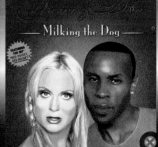

Milking the Dog

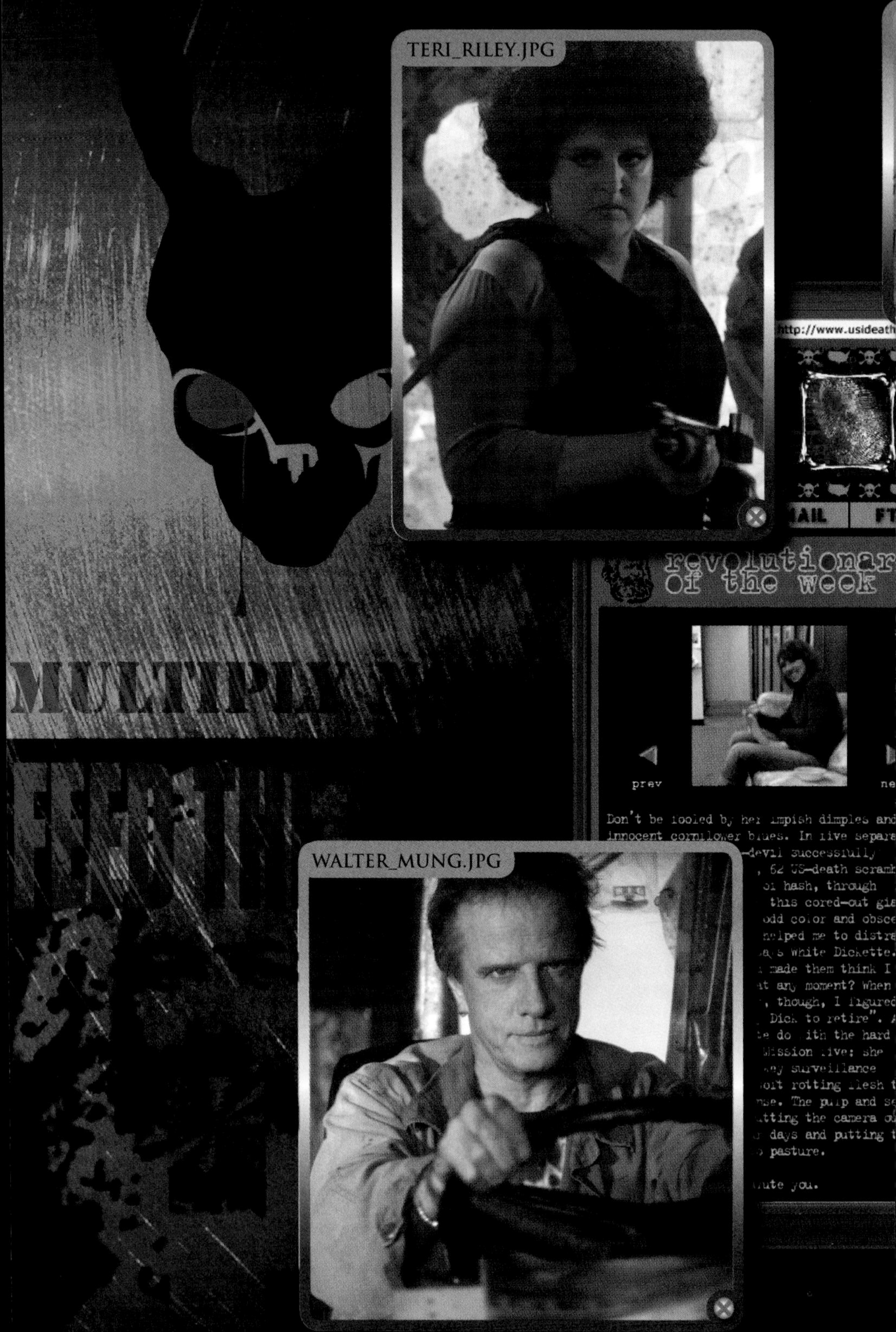
TERI_RILEY.JPG
MULTIPLE
http://www.usideath
revolutionar
of the week
prev
ne
Don't be fooled by her impish dimples and
innocent cornflower blues. In five separa
-devil successfully
, 62 US-death scramb
of hash, through
this cored-out gia
odd color and obsce
helped me to distra
's White Dickette.
made them think I
at any moment? When
, though, I figured
Dick to retire". A
be do ith the hard
Mission five: she
surveillance
soft rotting flesh t
nse. The pulp and se
utting the camera o
days and putting t
pasture.
lute you.
WALTER_MUNG.JPG

BING_ZINNEMAN.JPG

s1Death

| ING | ORDO | VOICE | D4D | PRON | SEARCH ___ → |

headlines

🔒 **id** assumed identity
encryption active

...RATION OF THE WEEK: OPERATIVE
...E DICKETTE IN THE ALBINO
...MBER OPERATION

...UAL "THUMB THE PIGS" ALL-YOU-
...EAT PORK BUFFET AND PAGAN EGG
... A CRACKING GOOD TIME

...PORT FOR 69 SPREADS THROUGHOUT
...HLAND PORN COMMUNITY

... TANGENT JOINS CRACK HACK
...eath SCRAMBLER CONSTRUCTION,
...RIBUTION AND MANAGEMENT TEAM

HJGC3XSUT7JTPN5K5P&R7U#FPYXK9LOI8$
&KSK(KLH5PDEYOIVGH8HDJHFNJHDGMSJJD
EGC3HSFT7JTPNLK5P&RGUNFPYXK9YOI8$D
EGC3HSFT7JTPNLK5P&RGUNFPYXK9YOI8$D
AFJFJ8PJLH5P&NGUNFLDJ83PYCKETOYV$D
HJGC3XSUT7JTPN5K5P&R7U#FPYXK9LOI8$
&KSK(KLH5PDEYOIVGH8HDJHFNJHDGMSJJD
AJ83H&UD74JD893DF*S9D-SJF,A83HD793
AJ83H&UD74JD893DF*S9D-SJF,A83HD793
AFJFJ8PJLH5P&NGUNFLDJ83PYCKETOYV$D
&KSK(KLH5PDEYOIVGH8HDJHFNJHDGMSJJD
&KSK(KLH5PDEYOIVGH8HDJHFNJHDGMSJJD
HJGC3XSUT7JTPN5K5P&R7U#FPYXK9LOI8$
DEYOIV&LH5PGNJHDGMKSK(KSJJDH8HDJHF
HJGC3XSUT7JTPN5K5P&R7U#FPYXK9LOI8$

**hacker tip
the week**

KENNY_CHAN.JPG

...rst hac...
...m tran...
...tory we...
...tie/arti...
...we had r...
...ally pla...
..., which...
...ccurring...
...ally be...
...want to...
...to take...
...or multi...
...t bullsh...
...g you hi...

...TENTION.

...s with Things

... do the thing with the
... move the thing over to
... thing is with the
... thing. Then you put the
...ng under the thing that
...er the thing. After that
...ant to use the thing with
...ke like a thing that has
...ing too long. Thing is,
...start to look the same
...b the thing with the
...ing that one thing has
..., hey, I'm the thing.

INTERNET.APP

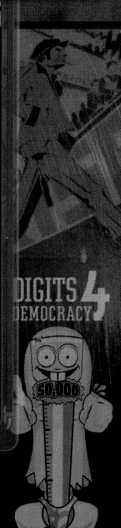

DIGITS 4
DEMOCRACY

50,000

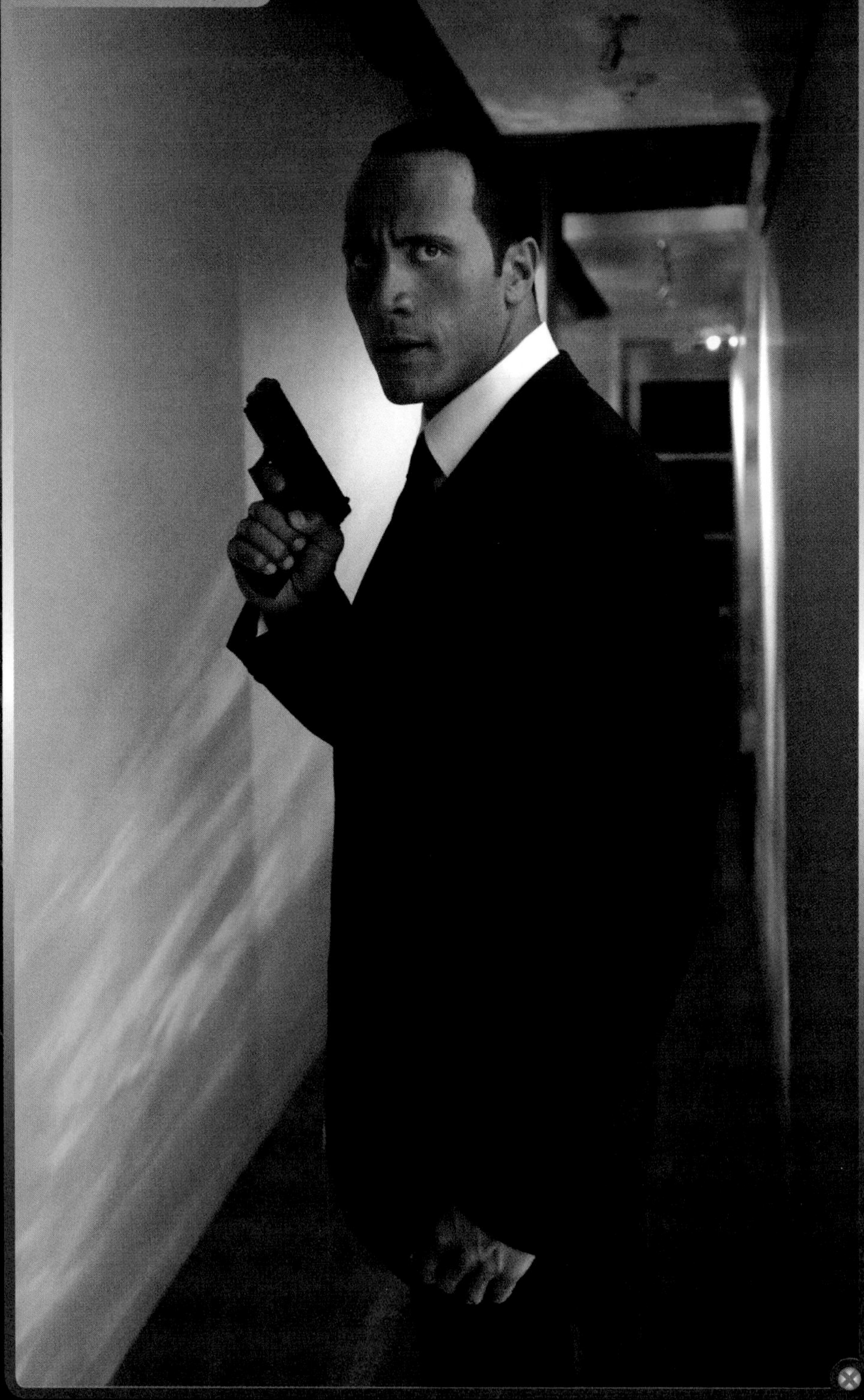

BOXER_SANTAROS.JPG

ALSO AVAILABLE:

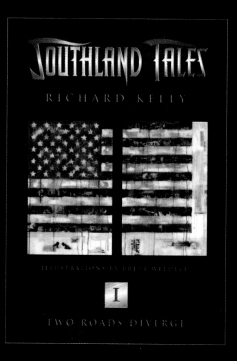

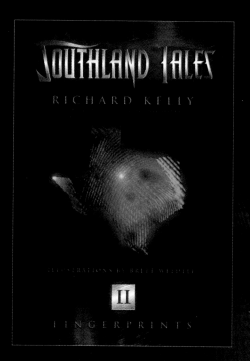

FIND THEM AT AMAZON.COM,
GRAPHITTIDESIGNS.COM OR WHEREVER
FINER BOOKS OR COMICS ARE SOLD

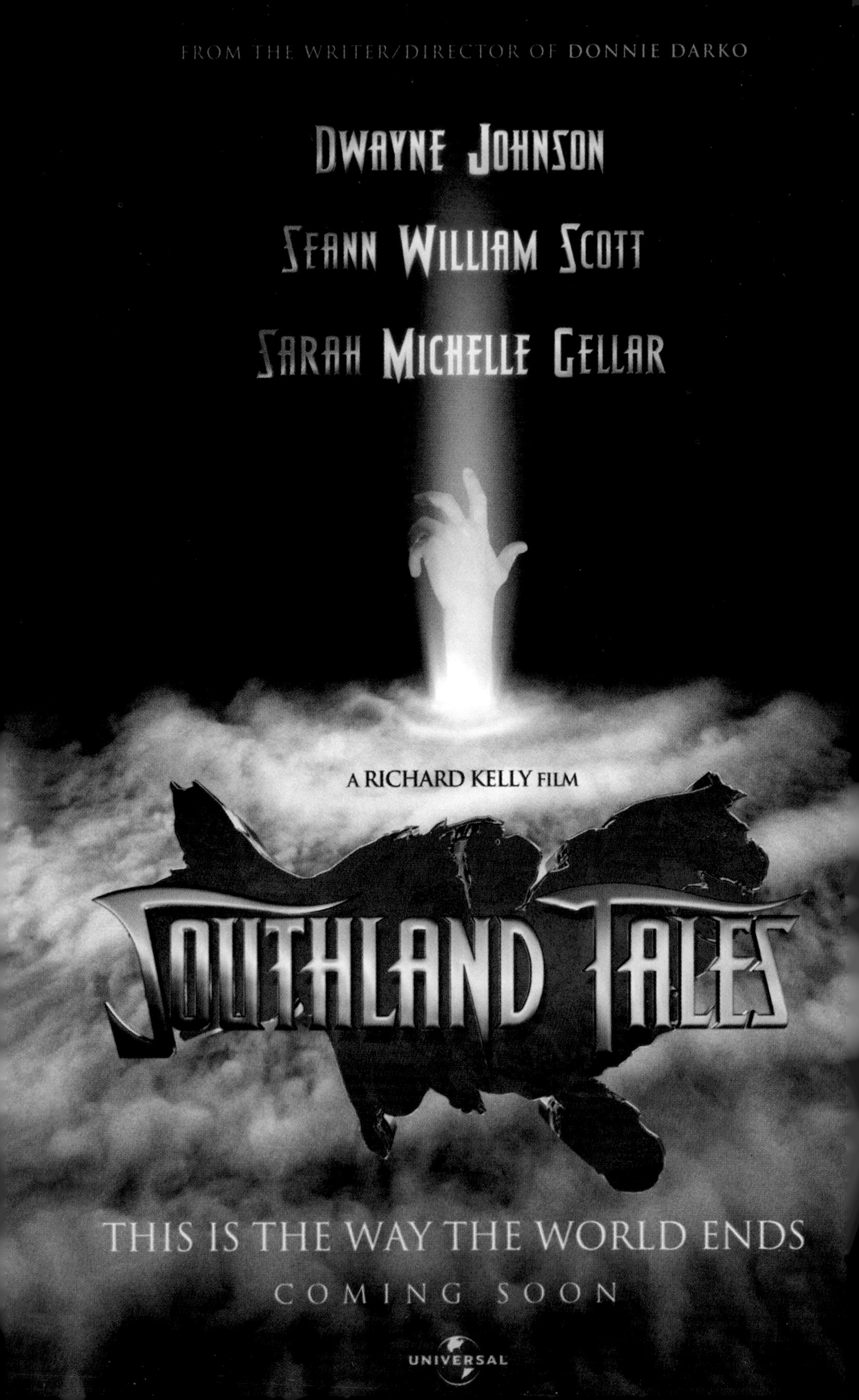
FROM THE WRITER/DIRECTOR OF DONNIE DARKO
DWAYNE JOHNSON
SEANN WILLIAM SCOTT
SARAH MICHELLE GELLAR
A RICHARD KELLY FILM
SOUTHLAND TALES
THIS IS THE WAY THE WORLD ENDS
COMING SOON
UNIVERSAL